CHESHIRE'S
EXECUTION FILES

CHESHIRE'S
EXECUTION FILES

Derek Yarwood

breedon **books**
P U B L I S H I N G

First published in Great Britain in 2007 by
The Breedon Books Publishing Company Limited
Breedon House, 3 The Parker Centre,
Derby, DE21 4SZ.

For Nick, Steve and Benjamin

ISBN 978-1-85983-590-6

Printed and bound in England by Antony Rowe Ltd, Chippenham, Wiltshire

CONTENTS

Preface

Hanging, Charles Dickens famously wrote, aroused in people 'a horrible fascination' and 'a dark and dreadful interest'. During his lifetime (1812–1870) the so-called 'Bloody Code' – the unremittingly repressive penal system that had once demanded execution for offences as trivial as stealing a handkerchief or setting fire to a haystack – was gradually dismantled, until the death penalty was effectively reserved for murder. But up to 1868 executions continued to be held in public. Staged originally on market days, public hangings were intended to send out a dire warning of the law's omnipotence to as wide an audience as possible. But, instead, they became popular entertainment, theatre of the darkest and most dreadful kind; and, horribly fascinated, thousands would turn up in carnival-like mood to watch a procession of sorry wretches – mostly poor and, sadly, often quite young men – end their short and miserable lives on the gallows.

In Cheshire equally large numbers attended executions in the county 'capital' of Chester, where the over-worked city sheriffs had more than their fair share of condemned criminals to 'launch into eternity'. Not because Chester was particularly lawless, but because of a centuries-old agreement under which the city was duty-bound to put into effect all death sentences imposed at the county assizes as well as their own local courts.

It is against the backdrop of this ancient judicial arrangement – which existed nowhere else in England – and the belated, at times acrimonious, but ultimately successful attempts by the city fathers to end it, that the cases in this book are set. The Cheshire crimes and trials featured here, all dating from the 18th and 19th centuries when the county extended well beyond its present boundaries, are based on official source material – court files, coroners' reports and other contemporary records – wherever possible; though, as a career journalist, I have inevitably looked to the newspaper reporters of the day to provide some of the livelier commentaries on the events being portrayed. From this large data-bank of information – much of it never before published – I have endeavoured to describe, in authenticated detail, the lives and characters of the people involved, both culprits and victims, and the social conditions in which they subsisted; the ritual and methodology of executions and the hangmen who carried them out; and the legal and administrative changes that finally severed the increasingly-uneasy bond between city and county that secured Cheshire's special place in the history of capital punishment.

In compiling this anthology I have received much valuable assistance, often greatly exceeding my modest inquiries. I must first acknowledge my debt to the staffs of the National Archives at Kew (formerly the Public Record Office), the Cheshire Record Office (CRO) at Chester, the Derbyshire Record Office at Matlock, the Stockport Local Heritage Library, the Tameside Local Studies and Archives Centre and the Macclesfield Reference Library, and to the Lymm and District Local History Society.

Three people to whom I turned for advice and information on a number of occasions throughout this lengthy project (and who were never less than generous in responding to

Preface

my requests) were: Vic Gatrell, whose splendid book *The Hanging Tree: Execution and the English People 1770–1868* was a constant source of inspiration; Richard Clark, who was always prepared to elaborate on topics covered by his encyclopaedic website on capital punishment, and Eve McLaughlin, author of the highly-regarded *McLaughlin Guides* for family historians, who added greatly to my understanding of the Poor Laws, parish administration and the social mores of English village life in the late 18th century.

For help with securing illustrations I am especially grateful to Cheshire County Archivist Mr Jonathan Pepler, also to Paul Newman and Peter Bamford of the CRO; to that genial and knowledgeable Northwich historian Colin Lynch and Joe Griffiths, Librarian of Lymm and District Local History Society.

I should also like to thank the following individuals, who each made important contributions: Mark Arnold, Peter Arrowsmith, Mark Beavon, Martin Bell, Mark Bevan, Ian Callister, Joanna Clark, Steve Cliffe, William Eyre, Kathryn Gill, Ian Gould, Peter Greenwood, Steve Jardine, Jeff Lee (for generously granting free use of his 'JSL Ancient' typeface in chapters one and two), George Leigh, Mike Mancey, Paulus Manders, R. Helen Phillips, David Reid, John Roberts (of the University of Manchester Archaeology Unit), Carl Rogerson, Carol Trager-Cowan, George Twigg, Eric Walker and John Whitlow.

Finally, my thanks go to my wife Chris, for allowing me the freedom to indulge my book-writing ambitions, and to Steve Caron and his colleagues at Breedon, for giving me the opportunity to fulfil them.

Derek Yarwood
Barnton, Summer 2007.

Prologue

Taking up the Hangman's Burden

'From time immemorial the city has enjoyed the unenviable distinction of strangling all the local malefactors destined to that end by Her Majesty's judges.'

Samuel Burrows was not a happy hangman. It was Saturday 29 August 1835, and he had just learned that he was to be deprived of another pay day. The one man left for execution after the recent assizes had been reprieved – the third convict to slip through his noose in a little over a year.

Midway through the decade in which Parliament finally abandoned capital punishment as its weapon of mass destruction in the war against crime – and the spectre of the gallows was banished to the darkest corner of the penal code – old Sam told friends forlornly, 'I could be out of a job.'

In failing health due to his habitual drinking, he seemed to lose the will to live…and less than two months later Cheshire's most famous 'finisher of the law' was finished himself, dead from liver disease at the age of 63.

In a career spanning 24 years, the former butcher and, latterly, rat-catcher had used his talent for killing to dispatch more than 50 criminals, who (to use the contemporary newspapers' favourite euphemism) were 'launched into eternity' with some alacrity. Although he was a freelance, a 'rope for hire' who plied his lethal trade in neighbouring counties as well, he was from 1812 to 1835 the 'Common Hangman' of Chester, where he performed most of his executions – possibly as many as 45.

And 'performed' is by no means an inappropriate description, for Sam Burrows trod the makeshift stage that was the public gallows in flamboyant style, acting out his leading role in these life-and-death dramas like a man who clearly enjoyed his work. Playing to the baser instincts of the crowd, his antics (usually fuelled by drink) weren't always applauded, however. Before one double hanging in 1820 he provoked outrage when he made a last-minute check on the length of the ropes by poking his own head through each noose in turn. Eventually, the authorities resorted to 'lodging' him with the governor of the City Gaol the night before a hanging to keep him sober.

But while Burrows appeared to revel in the notoriety of his office, to his Chester Corporation paymasters his depressingly regular official engagements were a reminder of the injustice of a civic duty that the city had been forced to discharge since mediaeval times. For by an ancient convention, unique in English judicial history, the city sheriffs were obliged to carry out death sentences handed down not just in their own local courts but at the county assizes as well.

In every other shire in England, arranging the execution of criminals capitally convicted at the assizes was the responsibility of the county's high sheriff, the officer of the Crown, who, in full-uniformed splendour, sat alongside the trial judge at the sessions and whose ceremonial sword symbolised the justice he was there to see upheld. But in Cheshire, until

8

Prologue

late in the 19th century, the rich and powerful members of the county's ruling gentry were able to wash their hands of such unpleasantness and leave the dirty work to others.

Chester's sheriffs bore the hangman's burden for more than 500 years, imposing the law's ultimate sanction almost exclusively on criminals from outside their own jurisdiction. It is not now possible to determine accurately just how many executions they arranged in that time; from chronologies published by local historians a list of 107 can be compiled for the years 1554–1866. But the total was demonstrably higher than that. In the period 1750–1866 alone, for which more reliable records exist, there were almost 100 hangings in Chester. Of that number, only eight were ordered by the city courts, four of them at one time.

What made the situation all the more incongruous was the fact that on those occasions when, following a particularly repellent case, the assize judge ordered the convict to be hung in chains after execution to act as a gruesome public warning – the disembowelled body was wrapped in pitch-soaked calico, enclosed in a hoop-iron cage and suspended from a gibbet near the scene of the crime – the county high sheriff had to arrange this second 'hanging'.

It was an unprecedented state of affairs which, according to all the surviving evidence, had its origins in the early post-Conquest period, when William I, in seeking to establish a network of military buffer zones to discourage incursions by the unruly Welsh, recognised Chester, Shrewsbury and Hereford as key defensive positions. To underline their strategic importance, he created earldoms in all three places and granted them to his most trusty lieutenants.

The first Earl of Chester was a little-known figure who rejoiced in the name of Gherbod the Fleming. But he governed only briefly before being replaced around 1077 by the redoubtable Hugh of Avranches, also known as Hugh Lupus ('The Wolf') and, rather less heroically, Hugh the Fat. He and his descendants held the title continuously until 1237.

It may have been during this dynastic tenure that apartments within the Northgate – one of the four principal entrances to the city since Roman times – were first commandeered by the Earl for use as his personal prison; certainly, the prison was well established by 1321, when the earliest documented reference to it occurs.

Ironically, it was in a concession granted by the Earl at the time of the takeover that the special relationship between county and city which established Cheshire's unique place in the history of capital punishment is said to have been fixed, shackling the city's sheriffs to the task of executing condemned criminals from throughout the earldom – and, subsequently, the administrative area of Cheshire – for the next five centuries.

For, as part of the deal, the mayor and citizens of Chester were granted the right to certain tolls payable at the Northgate in exchange for a commitment to guard the gate and the prisoners incarcerated there, to carry out various prescribed punishments and to 'hang up the condemned criminals'. It was perhaps inevitable that the exercise of these responsibilities should devolve upon the sheriffs, as they oversaw most areas of local law enforcement.

A second document, drawn up around 1400, appears to confirm the arrangements when it records that a number of prominent Chester tenants enjoyed 'certain privileges and exemptions' for watching the city and for conveying criminals safely from both the city and county courts 'as far as the gallows'.

Remarkably, the agreement survived for another 400 years virtually unchallenged…and the Northgate, which, in its last years, was Chester's official place of execution, remained a gloomy and forbidding monument to the law's dark ages until its demolition in 1808.

Cheshire's Execution Files

To Cheshire's conservative-minded administrators, it was a time-honoured tradition they were, understandably, keen to see maintained, while their city counterparts seem to have accepted the situation with a certain grudging resignation. True, there was the occasional editorial tirade in the local press and evidence of growing public concern about capital punishment in general, particularly the perception – mainly, but not exclusively, among the commonalty – of public hangings as entertainment and the inuring effect that frequent exposure to such unedifying spectacles had on the population.

But as to the city's disproportionate contribution to the carnage, it was not until the late 1820s that the good burghers of Chester began to question seriously the morality of their sheriffs continuing to act as the county's agents of death…and it would be another 40 years before they succeeded in freeing themselves from their feudal bonds.

The often acrimonious campaign began in earnest in the months leading up to the abolition of Cheshire's Palatinate Court of Great Sessions. This was another constitutional relic of the Norman earldom, which, from around the late 12th century, extended into what are now parts of North Wales, Merseyside, Greater Manchester, Lancashire and Staffordshire, and which was sufficiently powerful to be practically an independent state. It had its own 'parliament', its own tax system, institutions and legal machinery – even its own local version of the Magna Carta. It became a royal earldom in 1254 when it was granted to King Henry III's son, the Lord Edward (later King Edward I); and since 1301, when the latter's son, Edward of Caernarfon, became Prince of Wales and Earl of Chester, it has been the custom for the reigning monarch's eldest son to bear both titles.

From at least the early 14th century until the early 16th century, its 'palatine' status continued to mark Cheshire as a place that enjoyed territorial powers which, elsewhere, were usually the prerogative of the sovereign alone. But in 1830 its Court of Great Session was swept away in a tide of legal reforms that brought both Wales (which also had its own system of county courts of great session) and Cheshire into the assize circuit framework that existed in the rest of England.

Historically, these county sessions had always been referred to as 'the assizes', but when it became known that the Government intended to formalise the situation, Chester's representatives, led by the city's two MPs, saw it as an opportunity to have their execution duties reviewed, too. They claimed, not unreasonably, that as the 'contract' was with the historic Palatinate Court, it would be nullified when the court was abolished. But in this and subsequent skirmishes they were to prove no match for the county justices, the wealthy land-owning elite who governed the county through their membership of the Cheshire Quarter Sessions (forerunner of the County Council).

These country gentlemen and their MPs, members of the same aristocratic 'club', had influential friends in Parliament and skilfully out-manoeuvred their city rivals. The result was a nicely vague clause inserted at the county's insistence in the abolition act. It stated that nothing in the act 'shall be construed to abolish or affect the Obligations and Duties…imposed upon…the Mayor and Citizens of Chester'.

That these included their execution duties was successfully argued by the county's MPs when the city tried again during 1834–35. Moreover, this time they even managed to turn what had started out as a city-sponsored bill to end the existing anomaly into an Act of Parliament that not only reiterated the city's responsibilities but spelled them out in words that allowed for no further misconstruction. Thus, what before had been bound up in obscure precedent and loose phraseology, was now, for the first time, fully enshrined in the law of the land.

The catalyst for this renewed city challenge was the conviction in the summer of 1834 of two men, who, it was alleged, had been hired by trade union extremists to murder the boss of a Cheshire cotton mill during a violent and prolonged strike by spinners. In early June of that year Chester MP John Jervis, acting on the instructions of the Grand Jury of the city Quarter Sessions, had delivered a petition to the Home Office again pressing Chester's case. But the junior minister who received him made light of the issue and, possibly in an unguarded moment, suggested the city could bring matters to a head by refusing to execute the next criminal condemned at the assizes. The city took him at his word.

When, at the Cheshire Assizes in August, James Garside and Joseph Mosley were found guilty of murdering the eldest son of cotton magnate Samuel Ashton at Werneth, near Hyde, and received the death penalty, the city sheriffs made it clear they were not prepared to carry out the executions, an act of defiance given formal endorsement in a resolution passed by the Chester Grand Jury. County magistrates at the Cheshire Quarter Sessions, citing custom and practice, were equally adamant that the responsibility was not theirs. Writs were issued against both grand juries by the Attorney-General; they were ignored.

As the weeks went by and the legal wrangling dragged on, the two convicted prisoners were granted temporary respites. The deadlock was finally broken in November when the Court of King's Bench assumed jurisdiction and ruled that its marshall would execute the death warrants. The pair were duly hanged on 25 November 1834 – under the official superintendence of the high sheriff of Surrey – at London's Horsemonger Lane Gaol.

With the immediate problem solved, Chester's civic and judicial leaders could have been forgiven for feeling confident that, having beaten the county in this particular battle of wits, they could now go on to win the war. They were sadly mistaken.

In February 1835, encouraged by some informal advice from the Government's chief law officers, MP Jervis placed a bill before Parliament aimed at clarifying the 1830 Palatine Court abolition act so far as it affected executions. His intention was to see responsibility apportioned equally between the city and county sheriffs. But the move backfired spectacularly.

Amid allegations of a conspiracy over the framing of the original abolition bill – claims, subsequently denied, that the city's representatives had privately agreed to continue their execution duties in order to mollify the bill's opponents in the county – the proposed legislation was turned on its head, leaving the *Chester Chronicle*'s Parliamentary commentator to observe ruefully, 'Of the bill as introduced by Mr Jervis, nothing now remains but the title.'

The unlikely outcome was that Parliament approved 'An Act to explain an Act', which became effective on 20 March and which stated in part, 'That from and after the passing of this Act the Sheriffs...of the City of Chester for the Time being shall execute the Sentence of Death upon all Criminals condemned to die for Offences committed within the County...'

A week earlier (13 March), the *Chronicle* had described it as 'a most mortifying termination of the exertions that have been made to relieve the city from this odious burden'. For a month 'The Hanging Question' had dominated the headlines; but the paper remained unconvinced by the denials of the alleged city conspirators. In a stinging editorial, it declared, 'The citizens are indignant, and rightly indignant, at such a compromise of their interests, by whomsoever made, and while they denounce the treachery...[they] must, however, bear it with a good grace; an Act of Parliament is omnipotent; it is an effectual bar to all their complaints.'

The death of Samuel Burrows later that year closed another eventful chapter in the story of executions in Cheshire. Due partly to his roguish character and partly to the length of time he held the office, Burrows was the first of Chester's hangmen to shed the cloak of anonymity worn by his predecessors and emerge as a recognisable, if not exactly respected, public figure. He was also the last of his breed, for the Burrows years (more of which later) coincided with the last great period of executions in this country.

It has been estimated that between 1770 and 1830, around 35,000 people were sentenced to death in England and Wales, of which some 7,000 were eventually hanged. But attitudes were changing; people were becoming weary of the endless procession of petty pilferers and social misfits being led to an ignominious death at the end of a rope and increasingly critical of a system that demanded loss of life for stealing a handkerchief or setting fire to a haystack. The 1820s and 1830s saw most of the 200-plus capital offences that had formed the 'Bloody Code' wiped from the statute book, so that by the end of the period execution was effectively reserved for murder.

In Cheshire, as elsewhere, the number of hangings declined sharply. After 1834, when there were five, there was a seven-year gap to the next execution at Chester. And there were just eight more between 1842 and 1866. The latter was truly a landmark year; it not only saw the last public execution in Cheshire, but the last occasion on which the city sheriffs had to carry out their 'odious burden'.

A little over a year later, on 15 July 1867, a new Act of Parliament came into force that brought Cheshire into line with every other county in England and Wales, charging that the high sheriff 'shall carry into effect within the said County the Execution of all Persons upon whom Sentence of Death shall be passed at any Assizes or Gaol Delivery for the said County'. That meant not only the convicts of the county but the city as well – a complete reversal of the situation that had prevailed since the heyday of the Norman earldom.

Indicating just how much opinions had shifted in the intervening years, this time, while the 'Chester Courts Bill' was formally presented to Parliament by the city MPs, the pressure for change had come from the Cheshire Quarter Sessions.

The argument that convinced the county magistrates of the need for reform centred on the ceremonial transfer of condemned prisoners from the County Gaol to the City Gaol prior to execution. It was an elaborate rigmarole that involved the city sheriffs, accompanied by the town clerk on horseback, leading an entourage of bailiffs and constables in formal procession through the city to Chester Castle – Cheshire's military and administrative centre since William the Conqueror fortified the site in 1070, 'home' to the assizes and location of the County Gaol.

On the eastern edge of the castle precincts, and also extra-territorial to the city, was the tiny parish of Gloverstone, now long-since disappeared; there, as the cavalcade halted, one of the bailiffs went ahead to greet the constable of the castle and demand the convict. Flanked by a military guard, the constable emerged from the castle's main gate and marched his prisoner the 60 or 70 yards to Gloverstone for the handover. The condemned man or woman was then placed in an open cart and, with the hangman leading the horse, paraded through the streets to the place of execution, originally Boughton on Chester's eastern outskirts and latterly the City Gaol.

The ritual – a part of the whole carefully stage-managed process of execution that was designed to put the fear of the law into the hearts of the public – had remained essentially the same for hundreds of years, made no less objectionable by the one logistical change introduced unannounced in 1822. Up until then the transfer had taken place about an hour or so before the appointed time of the execution (usually about 1pm); but, beginning with the double execution of rapist William Tongue and highway robber George Groom in May of that year, it was brought forward to 5am. It was further decided that the prisoners were to be conveyed to the City Gaol in a less obtrusive manner by covered cart.

It was envisaged that this would reduce the number of spectators and curb the unseemly public behaviour often exhibited on these occasions. But, as was demonstrated at this and all subsequent hangings in the city, such was the degree of morbid curiosity they aroused that large numbers of people were still prepared to turn out even at that early hour to watch the departing malefactor's traditional 'last journey'. All the revised arrangements served to do, as the Quarter Sessions pointed out in its petition to the Home Department, was to 'add greatly to the sufferings, and tend to disturb the peace of mind, of the wretched criminals'.

With only one dissenting voice among the county magistrates, the case for new legislation was well nigh incontestable and, with all-party support, the Chester Courts Bill passed through both Houses of Parliament without division.

Compared to the extensive coverage generated by 'The Hanging Question' in earlier times, local press reaction to the successful conclusion of the city's campaign was fairly muted. The *Chester Chronicle* – which, as long ago as 1801, had pressed for the removal of the gallows to the castle, to end what it described as the 'barbarous custom' of dragging convicted felons through the streets to the place of execution – conveyed the news in an editorial in its edition of 8 June. Anticipating the formality of the bill's third reading in the Lords nine days later, the paper rejoiced in a victory that was 'at length virtually gained'.

The move, stated the *Chronicle*, would bring a welcome end to 'those distressing scenes which have occurred on the removal of the culprit from the County to the City Gaol', adding, 'Sheriff, prison-keepers, and all who have been of necessity concerned in them, draw such a harrowing picture of the trial to which the unfortunate prisoner is subjected as at once to furnish a substantial reason for desiring an alteration in the law.'

And it concluded, 'For centuries now – we think we are right in saying from time immemorial – the city has enjoyed the unenviable distinction of strangling all the local malefactors destined to that end by Her Majesty's judges...but the judiciousness of parting with the privilege will not be questioned when it is known that the sheriff is of all persons the most anxious to yield up the bowstring.'

It may have been coincidence that the city finally lost its 'distinction of strangling' at a time when, mercifully, such an end was the destiny of few malefactors. But the fact is that the county grandees were prepared to accept their responsibilities and allow the city sheriffs to 'yield up the bowstring', only when it had become apparent that their high sheriff would, in future, be called upon to loose off the arrow of ultimate retribution only rarely.

Incidentally, in speaking of 'strangling', the editor of the *Chronicle* was not indulging in hyperbole. Despite the 'refinements' of the raised platform and the collapsing trapdoor – the so-called 'new drop' type of scaffold had been in use at Chester since 1809 – hanging was still an inexact science. And until the introduction in 1872 of the 'long drop' method, designed to cause instantaneous death through dislocation of the vertebrae, victims of hanging still routinely suffered death by strangulation just as they had in the bad old days when they were 'turned off' a ladder or sent tumbling off the back of a cart.

In that summer of 1867 the county Quarter Sessions would also have been aware of another legal move that was expected to make the high sheriff's newly-imposed execution role an arguably less disagreeable task, one that would no longer have to be carried out in the gaze of a usually large, often unruly and sometimes hostile audience.

After two failed attempts in 1865 and 1866, the 'Capital Punishment Within Prisons Bill' – its purpose to put an end to executions in public and to confine them instead to the privacy of the county gaols – was before Parliament for the third time. Its proponents, catching the prevailing mood not only of MPs but of the country at large, were confident of success. But in the face of competition from the momentous Reform Bill, with its far-reaching proposals to redistribute Parliamentary seats and extend voting rights, it had to be withdrawn once again due to lack of parliamentary time.

However, the bill was reintroduced in November 1867, had its first reading in the Commons on 5 March 1868 and received the royal assent on 29 May. With its history of failed execution reforms, the act's passing was no more warmly welcomed than in Chester.

Over the next 16 years four men – all murderers – were hanged privately at Chester Castle. Then in 1884 the prison was taken over by the military and, as the City Gaol had been demolished five years earlier, the remaining inmates were transferred to the recently-enlarged Knutsford Gaol. From then until 1912, when the death of a Birkenhead printer named John Williams stamped him as the last person to be hanged in Cheshire, it was Knutsford's turn to assume the title of 'the town where executions take place'…the 'unenviable distinction' Chester had 'enjoyed' for more than half a millennium.

* * *

Chester lays claim to being the first English town to have a sheriff; from 1244 until 1835 two were appointed each year by the city assembly. Next in the pecking order to the mayor, they performed the same routine legal duties as the county high sheriffs, such as executing writs; they were also responsible for the City Gaol and its prisoners, collected fines and customs dues payable at the port of Chester, took oaths and recognisances and scrutinised civic elections. It was the 'Hangman's Burden', however, that rested heaviest on the sheriffs' shoulders. Onerous enough at the best of times, at one particular execution in 1763 it became an even more harrowing experience for the officers concerned, one that would sear itself into their memories for ever…

Chapter One

Consumed by the Flames of Passion

The note is brief, the tone businesslike: 11 lines of fading copperplate script acknowledging receipt of a bill for services rendered and authorising due payment. Only its subject matter marks it out as something more than just a book-keeping exercise.

Sandwiched between a land grant and a schedule of work to secure a dangerous well, it is one of a countless number of transactions inscribed in similarly-formal style in the yellowing pages of Chester Corporation's Assembly Books, half-a-dozen painstakingly preserved volumes logging the meetings and decisions of the city's council from 1539–1835.

In this particular tome, covering the years 1725–1785 – five inches thick and aptly ledger-like – are also to be found particulars of rent settlements and tenancy agreements, of property leases, building repairs, estimates for road maintenance and all the other minutiae of income and expenditure associated with the day-to-day functions of local government.

But item number eight in the report of the Assembly meeting of 14 September 1763 is no ordinary financial statement. Behind the unvarnished words and clerkly phrases lies a disturbing tale of hidden passions and domestic secrets, of mystifying murder and awful retribution…and of how a woman brought to account for poisoning her husband paid the most terrible price for her treachery.

It's not surprising, perhaps, that in the official records of the City Corporation it is little more than an oblique reference buried among the voluminous pages of a council minute book, a mere bureaucratic footnote. But in the annals of Cheshire crime the case of Mary

Like Mary Heald, the last woman to be burned at the stake in Cheshire, Catherine Hayes, suffered the same barbaric fate at Tyburn in 1726, also for murdering her husband. As this engraving shows, however, Hayes was burned alive after the executioner scorched his fingers and was unable to administer the *coup de grâce*. (From the author's collection.)

Heald stands alone, her barbaric punishment – enforced with the full panoply of the law – one of the most shameful excerpts from the mournful litany of executions at Chester.

On Saturday 23 April 1763, after being dragged through the streets of Chester lashed to a horse-drawn wooden sledge, the 43-year-old Quaker and mother of five from Mere, near Knutsford, was burned at the stake. It was market day and hundreds lined the roads to watch the city officials, mounted marshals and liveried attendants conduct her in ceremonial procession to the place of execution, close to the site of the public gallows at Boughton, a mile from the city centre. There, many more stood and gawped in awe as, on a specially-prepared bonfire, her body was reduced to ashes.

She had been found guilty at the Cheshire Spring Assizes less than two weeks earlier of murdering her husband Samuel – for reasons that are not fully discernible from the surviving records – by spiking his lunch with arsenic. At that time, whereas men who killed their wives were hanged for murder, the law ruled that women who did away with their husbands had committed the more serious crime of petty treason. And while a man convicted of petty treason – for killing his master, for example – could be hung, drawn and quartered, incineration was deemed a more fitting sentence for a woman. The distinction was made, apparently, on the grounds of decency, burning being considered a lesser indignity for a woman than having her naked body disembowelled and displayed on a gibbet.

As the Assembly Book records show, however, it was to the more practical aspects of Mary Heald's sentence that the city's elder statesmen were asked to apply their minds when they gathered at their September council meeting. As a tacit acknowledgement of the authority's part in her destruction, the resulting minute was understandably terse. It revealed that, compared with hanging, burning someone at the stake was a much costlier business…and that the two serving sheriffs tasked with arranging the execution had been obliged to make an official claim for extra money to cover their unbudgeted expenses.

Their appeal was heard by the mayor (the Right Worshipful Henry Hesketh), the aldermen and members of the common council at what was their first assembly after the execution, five months later. The full text of the minute reads:

'Also at this same Assembly, upon reading the Petition of the Worshipfull [sic] John Drake and William Dicas, Sheriffs of this City, setting forth that they had unavoidably expended the sum of twelve pounds sixteen shillings and eight pence on account of the Execution of Mary Heald, who on Saturday the twenty third day of April last had been burnt at Spittal Boughton for the Murder of her Husband, which expences [sic] far exceeded those normally disbursed by the Sheriffs in respect of their offices on the Common Execution of Felons and malefactors, it is ordered that Mr Treasurer shall pay to the petitioners…the sum of seven pounds, sixteen shillings and eight pence in aid of their Extraordinary Expences relative to the Execution of the said Mary Heald.'

In keeping with the principles of government accountability and sound fiscal practice, the sheriffs had prepared a detailed breakdown of costs to substantiate their claim. The bizarre bill, handwritten on a single folio, came to light during a search of the assembly files held at the Cheshire Record Office (CRO) in Chester, buried among reams of otherwise dry and dusty supporting papers. It must rank as one of the most extraordinary documents in the Chester Corporation archives.

Consumed by the Flames of Passion

Headed 'Expences attend'g the Execution of Mary Heald burnt for poisoning her Husband', it lists 15 separate items of expenditure, beginning with the kindling for the execution pyre and the other combustibles required to ensure the body was consumed with decent haste. Thus:

1763

Ap'l 22d	To 2 Cart Loads of Faggots	0	14s 0d
	To a Load of Coals	0	10s 6d
	To 6 Tar Barrells	0	7s 0d
	To Mr Rathborn the Carpenter's Bill	3	10s 0d
	To a Bill for the Workmen to Drink when fix'g up the Place of Ex'on	0	11s 4d
	p^d for a Horse to draw the Hurdle	0	10s 6d
	p^d for Ale to treat the owner of the Horse	0	1s 8d
23d	To 6 Glasses of Brandy at Evans's	0	1s 8d
	To paid a Bill at Lysten's House	0	7s 0d
	To p^d Mr. Totty for a Chain	0	5s 0d
	To p^d Mr. Roughley for 2 Pikells	0	2s 0d
	To p^d Mrs. Battrick her Bill	2	1s 0d
	To p^d Mr. Morris of the Bulls Head a Bill	2	4s 6d
	To the Hire of Horses for 17 Constables attend'g the Ex'on at 1/6	1	5s 6d
	To p^d Men for watch'g the Faggots &c	0	5s 0d
		£12	16s 8d

That 'Mr Rathborn the Carpenter's Bill' was the single largest payment reflected the work involved in constructing the special execution stake. Contrary to popular belief, women condemned to die in this manner were not burned alive, at least not deliberately. Nothing so uncivilised. The stake was fitted with a noose and pulley attachment, or a halter chain, by which the executioner was supposed to strangle the victim to death before the flames took hold.

The 'bill' for burning Mary Heald at the stake in 1763, as prepared by the Chester sheriffs in support of their claim for extra expenses. This remarkable document, never before published, was discovered by the author in the city archives.
(By permission of Cheshire and Chester Archives and Local Studies – CCALS.)

This was considered a much more humane procedure, though it was not unheard of for the fire to flare up prematurely, scorching the executioner's fingers and preventing him from administering the *coup de grâce*. The most famous instance of this happening was at Tyburn in 1726, when Catherine Hayes was accidentally burned alive for murdering her husband. Mary Heald's execution was marred by no such mishap, and the reference to 'Mr Totty's chain' may indicate the method of strangulation adopted by the executioner on this occasion.

And what are we to make of the second-largest amount itemised, the £2 4s 6d paid to Mr Morris of the Bull's Head? Could it have been for post-execution drinks to take away the unpleasant taste of the day's business? The hire of horses for 17 constables was a prudent crowd control measure in view of the large number of people expected to attend the execution, while the final item on the bill showed the officials were taking every precaution to prevent any embarrassing last-minute hitches.

In their formal petition to the council (also to be found among the Assembly papers), sheriffs Drake and Dicas argued that the execution had been the most expensive ever known – 'no instance of the like having ever happened within memory here'. They also asked the councilmen to take into consideration 'the disagreeableness of doing their duty at that time'.

The petitioners pointed out that, ordinarily, an execution (i.e. a hanging) cost them 'about £4'. They could reasonably have supposed, therefore, that they would be reimbursed the full amount of their additional expenditure; but, as can be calculated from the aforementioned Assembly Book extract, the council's decision fell a little short of their expectations.

What makes the case of Mary Heald unique is the fact that she is the only woman so far identified as having been burned at the stake in Cheshire. She was also the last to suffer the punishment, which was outlawed in 1790.

The murder of Samuel Heald had scandalised the tiny township of Mere, a close-knit farming community straddling the old main road from Northwich to Manchester (now the A556). It was an event of doubly-tragic proportions for the Healds' orphaned children and a shocking affront to the strict religious principles of the extended Quaker 'family' of which they were a part. The facts are scanty, but from the much-depleted court file in the National Archives in Kew (formerly the Public Record Office), and from newspaper reports and other contemporary sources, a picture emerges of a middle-aged woman who, after years trapped in an unhappy marriage, decides there is only one way out of her personal prison. In desperation, she embarks on a course of action that is destined to end with her losing not just her husband, but her children, her home... and her life.

Mary Heald was born Mary Barlow in the township of Over Alderley, in the parish of Alderley, midway between Knutsford and Macclesfield, and she was baptised in the 14th-century parish church of St Mary's (it is actually situated in the adjoining township of Nether Alderley) on 16 September 1719. The daughter of John and Mary Barlow, she appears to have been one of at least nine children. An elder brother died at the age of 14, when she was 12, and one of her younger brothers, a twin, lived only a few months.

Mary does not seem to have had much in the way of an education, and she never learned to read or write. In her early years her parents left the Church of England and

Consumed by the Flames of Passion

Alderley Parish Church, pictured about 1905, where Mary Heald was baptised and where she and her family worshipped before converting to Quakerism. (From the author's collection.)

joined the Religious Society of Friends – the Quakers. Consequently, the Barlow children were all brought up to follow the sect's almost Puritanical code of behaviour and encouraged to lead moral, disciplined and virtuous lives.

It was through her attendance at Quaker meetings that Mary met Samuel Heald, a yeoman farmer with modest land holdings who lived in 'Mere Town' and who was nine years her senior. They were married, according to Quaker custom, in the old Friends' Meeting House in Mill Street, Macclesfield, on 14 November 1739. A copy of the official marriage registration, which reveals a little about the form the ceremony took and the vows the couple made, can be seen in the records of the Cheshire and Staffordshire Society of Friends at the CRO. It also indicates that, at the time of her wedding, Mary Barlow had moved from Over Alderley and was living in the nearby township of Chorley, in the parish of Wilmslow.

The registration's preamble recalls that the couple had 'declared their Intentions of Marriage With Each other before several Publick meetings of the People Called Quakers in Cheshire' and received the 'concent [sic] of Parents and friends' to move to the next stage of the formalities. The document goes on:

'Now these are to Certifie [to] all whom it may Concern that for the full accomplishing of their said Intentions…the said Samuel Heald and Mary Barlow appeared in a Solemn and Public Assembly of the aforesaid people and Others met together for that End and Purpose in their Publick Meeting house in Macclesfield in Cheshire aforesaid and In a Solemn Manner according to the Exampel of Holy men recorded in the Scriptures of truth, he the said Samuel Heald taking the said Mary Barlow by the Hand did openly declare as followeth or to this effect, to wit, friends in the Fear of the Lord and before you my witnesses, I Samuel Heald take this my friend Mary Barlow to be my wife

Promising through devine assistance to be unto her a Loving & faithful Husband till it Pleas the Lord by death to separate us, and then and there in the said Assembly the said Mary Barlow did Likewise declare as followeth or to this Effect, to wit, Friends in the fear of the Lord and before you my witnesses, I Mary Barlow take this my friend Samuel Heald to be my Husband promising through devine assistance to be unto him a faithfull and Loving wife till it Please the Lord by Death to Separate us...'

It concludes with the names of the couple and no fewer than 41 witnesses. The list, copied out in the same handwriting as the rest of the marriage entry, suggests that only one of those present was unable to sign the register personally, whereas the original version would have borne the bride's mark, too.

The wedding over, the 20-year-old Mary settled down to her new life in Mere, first as a wife and then, three years later, as a mother. How well she adjusted to the routine of a small farm, and her elevation to the rural middle class, we have no way of knowing. We learn from the Quaker registers that between 1742 and 1754 she and Samuel produced seven children (two of whom died at a young age). But despite that (or, possibly, because of it) her relationship with her husband became increasingly strained.

In pursuance of the Quaker belief that encouraging good behaviour is a collective responsibility, friends of the couple regularly exhorted them to seek a reconciliation. But matters went from bad to worse; Mary's simmering resentment turned to hatred and, ultimately, to thoughts of murder. Faced with the prospect of spending the rest of her life in a joyless marriage (divorce, then possible only by private Act of Parliament, would not have been an option), she made her fateful move.

Around midday on Tuesday 19 October 1762, after preparing 'a mess of fleetings' (soft cheesy curds produced by adding buttermilk to boiling whey), she set a generous portion of this nutritious old country dish before her husband when he came in for his 'dinner' (lunch). Into it she had sprinkled a sizeable quantity of arsenic.

It was not long before the poison started to take effect. Samuel became violently ill and continued 'Sick and Greatly distempered in his body' (as the court papers would later term it) until 22 October, when, at about 7 o'clock in the morning, he died. He was 52. His body was buried two days later in the old Quaker cemetery in Mobberley. Now disused, the tiny walled burial ground lies down a winding track known as Graveyard Lane.

And that's about as much as we know for certain about Samuel Heald's death and Mary Heald's motive for murdering him. Officially, at least, there is nothing to explain the personal conflicts and the domestic turmoil that led to the crime and, crucially, Mary's state of mind at the time. To find the only available clues to these key aspects of the case, we have to look elsewhere – specifically, to an article written 120 years after the event. Since it was based on a source of information that has proved notoriously unreliable, it has to be treated with some caution – though the author's credentials are impeccable enough.

The article in question, by respected Chester historian Thomas Hughes (1826–1890), first appeared in the 8 August 1883 edition of the *Chester Courant* in a regular feature called 'The Cheshire Sheaf'. Sub-titled 'Being Local Gleanings, Historical and Antiquarian, from many scattered fields', the columns, containing notes, queries and comments relating to old Cheshire manuscripts and other original source documents,

Consumed by the Flames of Passion

were also reprinted in bound volumes. This quarterly publication, also titled *The Cheshire Sheaf*, was launched in 1880 and Thomas Hughes, a Fellow of the Society of Antiquarians, was its first editor. He was also a former sheriff of Chester (in 1873–4) and an expert in shrieval history, so he wrote with authority.

In his article he reproduced the text of a contemporary handbill, a copy of which he had in his private collection, which included Heald's 'authentick written Confession'. Ignoring for a moment that the murderess was illiterate and could not, therefore, have written the confession herself (as, indeed, was confirmed by a representation of her mark at the foot of the page), the handbill was typical of the 'gallows literature' that was a popular by-product of public executions in the late 18th and early 19th centuries.

Usually composed by an enterprising journalist, prison official or cleric – with or without the benefit of an interview with the condemned person – and published at the local newspaper printing office, the handbills, broadsides and pamphlets invariably set down 'the last dying words' of the culprit, together with a résumé of the crime(s) and an eye-witness account of the execution. Often costing less than a penny, they were snapped up by a voracious public at a time when the newspaper was not the inexpensive medium of mass communication it is today.

The Heald 'confession' began, 'I was born in the parish of Alderley in Cheshire. My Parents at the Time of my Birth (and for some years afterwards) were Members of the Church of England. In my childhood my Parents went amongst the People called Quakers, and educated me and their other children in that way.'

Of the breakdown of her marriage and the events leading up to the murder, she was quoted as saying, 'Amongst the People I was married to my late Husband Samuel Heald; but, unhappily, in a short time after our Marriage, uneasiness grew between us, and, for

The old Quaker graveyard at Mobberley, now abandoned, where Samuel Heald was laid to rest in 1762. (Photograph by Geoff Statham.)

Want of Watchfulness, it increased to a very great degree. Several of the Society from time to time visited, and advised us to a better conduct. I am now very sensible of their care and kindness therein, and happy it had been for me [*sic*] if I had duly regarded their good Advice and Council [counsel], and the Convictions of Divine Grace in my own Heart. But alas! I disregarded them, and having given myself up to Rage and Passion against my Husband, was tempted to take away his Life; into which dreadful Temptation I was suffered to fall, after this manner.

'One day, going into his Desk to take a little sugar, I found some Poison in a little paper, which I took, and intended to burn it, but did not, but kept it in my Custody some weeks; when one Day, having a strong Temptation to give it my Husband, I put it into a Mess of Fleetings, which, he eating of, caused his Death, for which horrible Cruelty and Wickedness I am now justly to suffer death.'

Seemingly at pains to dispel any notion of a 'love triangle' or that a third party was in any way involved in the tragedy (though one cannot resist the thought that, perhaps, 'the lady doth protest too much'), she insisted, 'I am deeply sensible of the Heinousness of the crime I have been guilty of, [in] which no one was concerned or knew of, but myself; and I desire no Reflections may be cast on any Persons after I am dead, as it was my own Act!'

The broadside concluded – another common feature of the genre – with an appeal by the condemned woman urging others to learn from her mistakes: 'I have grievously sinned against God and Man: May my dreadful Example be a Caution and a Warning to all (especially married people), that they guard against the first Entrance of Anger and Passion into their Minds one against another!'

A little of the foregoing can be corroborated by reference to the case papers in the National Archives. However, the all-important witness statements, and the vital pieces of evidence they would have contained, are missing; all that remain to testify to the crime and Mary Heald's subsequent court appearance are the formal indictment, a handful of witnesses' recognisances and a statement recording the findings of the coroner's inquest into Samuel Heald's death. Though bare-bones in content, the latter is the most revealing.

The inquest was held at Mere on 23 October 1762 – the day after Samuel Heald died – before coroner John Hollins of Knutsford and a jury of 16 'Good and lawful Men of the village of Mere and of three other [adjoining] villages'. In the solemn, stylised legal language of the day, the written verdict recorded:

'[The jurors] say that Mary Heald, wife of Samuel Heald, not having the fear of God before her eyes, but being seduced by the instigation of the devil, on Tuesday the nineteenth day of October instant about 12 o'clock at noon in her dwelling house in Mere...feloniously voluntarily and of her malice aforethought took some grains of arsenic into her hands and put or mixed the said arsenic amongst some Fleetings or Whey Butter which she the said Mary Heald had there provided for her said husband Samuel Heald's dinner, which said Fleetings or Whey Butter he the said Samuel Heald then and there took and did eat...he the said Samuel Heald languished and languishing lived until Friday the twenty second day of October instant [when] about 7 o'clock in the morning [he] Dyed...

Consumed by the Flames of Passion

And the said jurors further also say that the said Mary Heald did then and there feloniously, wilfully and of her malice aforethought poison and kill the said Samuel Heald, her husband, against the peace of our said Lord the King his Crown and dignity and that she the said Mary Heald is guilty of Murder in the manner and form aforesaid.'

Couched in the same convoluted style, though in slightly more censorious terms, the indictment charged that she administered the poison 'feloniously, *traitoriously* and wilfully and of her malice aforethought' and that she 'did mix and mingle *a great quantity*' of the arsenic into her husband's meal '*well knowing the said Arsenick to be a deadly poison*' (author's italics).

An attached sheaf of recognisances shows that the witnesses bound over to appear at Mary Heald's trial included Samuel Partington and John Kinder, constables of the township of Mere, whose inquiries led to her arrest, and Daniel Howard and Roger Allen, surgeons of Nether Knutsford, who examined Samuel Heald's body and determined the cause of death. Two further witnesses, their roles in the affair unknown, were named as Peter Wood, yeoman, and Catharine Broady, single woman, both of Mere.

The evidence of the two medical experts would have been crucial in helping the inquest jury arrive at their murder verdict. Their postmortem report, had it survived, would almost certainly have revealed the distinctive signs of arsenic poisoning they observed on the deceased's body – blueness of the skin is the most marked external characteristic while, internally, the lining membrane of the stomach appears much inflamed and often badly ulcerated – and the telltale symptoms that eventually brought about the victim's death.

Typically, assuming a single large dose was administered, Samuel Heald would have begun to feel ill within an hour of eating his lunch. Soon the irritation and burning in his throat would have been accompanied by faintness and nausea, followed by uncontrollable vomiting and diarrhoea, pains in the abdomen – which have been likened to having red-hot coals placed on the stomach – leg cramps, a weakening pulse and complete collapse leading rapidly to death. Some victims of arsenic poisoning succumb within hours; Samuel Heald continued in this excruciating and malodorous state for more than two-and-a-half days.

Arsenic is not for nothing the poison that has been most favoured by murderers down the ages; one of its biggest 'attractions' is that, even in large doses, its sweet, slightly metallic taste is virtually unnoticeable when ingested in food. Furthermore, until the advances in medical knowledge in the 19th century, there was a good chance that the killer's handiwork would be mistaken for cholera or dysentery (bowel diseases common in England at this time), gastric fever or plain old food poisoning, all of whose symptoms are, to a large extent, similar to those of arsenic poisoning.

What led to the correct diagnosis of Samuel Heald's death – and the murder charge against his wife – we can now only guess at; the missing depositions also make it impossible to determine exactly the part played in the investigation by the two local constables. However, the fact that the coroner's jury was able to reach such an unequivocal verdict just a day after Samuel Heald died, indicates this was very much an open-and-shut case...and that the most obvious suspect was unable to hide her guilt for long.

Mary Heald was taken into custody on the day of the inquest and lodged in Chester Castle on a warrant signed by local magistrate George Heron. As a result of the inquest jury's verdict, she was automatically committed for trial at the next county sessions. As the Winter Assizes had recently ended, she was forced to spend the next six months – a total of 166 days – in the dank and noisome confines of the old county gaol, awaiting the start of the 1763 Spring Assizes.

Penal reformer John Howard famously likened the felons' dungeons at the castle to the 'Black Hole at Calcutta', after visiting the gaol during his prisons survey of the 1770s and 1780s. There is no evidence that the female prisoners were treated more humanely than the male inmates, or that conditions at the gaol were less unwholesome in the 1760s, so the widow Heald's lengthy incarceration would not have been a pleasant experience.

To add to her discomfort, she seems to have become the object of much curiosity, exploited by prison officials like some circus freak. In his *Cheshire Sheaf* article, Thomas Hughes recounted, 'The affair created intense interest and excitement at Chester, and hundreds of persons, through the winter of 1762, sought and obtained permission to visit the dungeon in our old Castle in which the unhappy woman was confined, the gaoler, &c, taking large amounts of largesse for permitting the wretched exhibition. And this sort of thing (and worse still, I fear) went on and was winked at by the authorities, until the Easter of 1763, when the County Assizes came on at Chester Castle.'

Among her more welcome visitors during those arduous winter months in the castle gaol – though their meetings would no doubt have been distressing enough – was her eldest son John, aged 20 and soon to become the head of the household, and the family solicitor. Samuel Heald had not left a will, so between them they had to sort out his estate.

The legal papers drawn up to resolve the matter are in the Cheshire Record Office files. Because of her uncertain situation – and the fact that her five surviving children were all minors – Mary agreed to allow letters of administration to be granted to one 'Joseph Hayes of Tatton, husbandman'. She duly put her mark to the document, dated 17 November 1762, authorising him to dispose of Samuel Heald's 'Goods, Chattels and Credits'.

A second document, undated, contains John Heald's consent to the appointment, which he signed on behalf of himself and his four brothers: Samuel, (18), Joshua (12), James (8) and William (5). The agreement would have been binding for only a short time, however, as John reached the legal age of majority (then 21) the following February.

Quaker friends also visited Mary in gaol. At the Cheshire Women's Quarterly Meeting, held on 19 April 1763, a 'Testimony of denial' against their errant sister was rather belatedly read out. This was the formal process of 'disownment' by which she was effectively expelled from the Society. It was also reported that several Friends had 'manifested their Christian concern for the Immortal spirit of the unhappy party in Visiting her in prison and endeavouring to settle her under a sence [*sic*] of the Heinousness of her Offence and where help was'.

Where Mary was, at this moment, was back in the castle dungeons. Amid nationwide preparations to celebrate the end of the Seven Years War (the peace had been formally concluded by the signing of the Treaty of Paris a month earlier), she had been tried and convicted at the Assizes on 12 April. From annotations later added to the indictment by

Consumed by the Flames of Passion

the clerk of the court, we learn that she pleaded not guilty but that 'the jury say guilty'.

The first brief reports of the trial appeared on Tuesday 19 April in the *Chester Courant*, then the city's only newspaper, and the *Manchester Mercury*. The *Courant* stated, 'Last week ended the assize here, when Mary Heald, widow of Samuel Heald, late of Mere, near Knutsford, in this county, yeoman (both of the people called Quakers) was convicted of PETIT TREASON, in killing her said husband, after twenty years cohabitation, by giving him a certain quantity of arsenick in a mess of fleetings on the nineteenth day of October last, of which poison he died in about four days after taking the same.'

The *Mercury*'s otherwise identical piece added, 'For which horrid crime, she was condemned to be burned on the third day after sentence, but upon application to the judges, they were pleased to respite her execution until Saturday the 23rd of this instant.'

Her stay of execution had obviously been granted to give Mary's lawyers an opportunity to mount an appeal for clemency and, consequently, a full reprieve. Whatever their arguments, however, they failed. The execution went ahead on the 23rd. Unlike other convicted murderers, who were hauled off to the gallows in a cart, husband-killer Mary Heald, whose crime was ranked as treason, was first chained to a wooden hurdle or sledge and then pulled through the streets behind a horse – the traditional means of conveyance for traitors.

The *Courant* (employing the peculiar period typeface that displayed the lower-case 's' almost like an 'f', except where it ended a word) reported on 26 April:

> 'Accordingly, foon after ten of the clock in the forenoon of that day, the Sheriffs of Chefter, with their attendants, came to Gloverftone, where the gaoler of the Caftle deliver'd to them the faid Mary Heald, who, perfuant to fentence, was drawn from thence in a fledge through the city to Spital-Boughton, where, after due time having been allowed for her private devotion, fhe was affixed to a ftake on the north fide of the great road, almoft oppofite to the gallows; and, having been firft ftrangled, faggots, pitch-barrels and other combuftibles were properly placed all around her, and the fire being lighted up, her body was confumed to afhes.'

Confirming that at least some sort of confession was in circulation at this time (a reference, perhaps, to the same handbill from which historian Thomas Hughes quoted in his *Cheshire Sheaf* article of 1883), the report added, 'The unhappy woman behaved with much decency, and left an authentick written declaration, confessing her crime, and expressing much penitence and contrition.'

The vast crowd of people who gathered to witness Mary Heald's fiery exit also seems to have behaved with uncommon dignity. As if wonder-struck by the occasion and the dreadful scene about to be enacted before them, the spectators exhibited none of the rowdiness and callous disregard so often in evidence at public executions. For which sheriffs Drake and Dicas, reluctant participants though they were, received due credit.

It came in a letter to the editor of the *Courant*, penned by a prominent local businessman, Mr Peter Leadbeater, and printed directly below the paper's execution report. Addressed to the mayor, the recorder and justices of the peace, as well as the sheriffs (who alone were responsible for the arrangements, of course), the letter stated effusively 'Your tender regard relating to the execution of the unfortunate Mary Heald…justly merits an acknowledgement in a public manner; be pleased to accept it in such. The concern of many of you at the poor criminal's unhappy fate, and the care you took in preserving the peace, is highly commendable in the eye of every impartial spectator. The stillness and decency wherewith the execution was conducted by the Sheriffs will continue on many minds, an instance of their candour and great humanity.'

*   *   *

Boughton, or Spital Boughton as it was previously known (after the leper hospital of St Giles, founded there in the 12th century), was Chester's place of execution, Cheshire's 'Tyburn', from ancient times. On this spot in April 1555, Protestant martyr George Marsh was burned at the stake for his religious beliefs, an event commemorated on the obelisk that identifies the site beside what is now the main eastern (A51) approach to the city. Like the monument, the old gallows was on the south side of the road near the top of Barrel Well Hill ('Gallows Hill'), overlooking the River Dee. And it was there, 21 years after the burning of Mary Heald, that another name was added to the roll of poisonous women executed for murder at Chester in the second half of the 18th century…

Chapter Two

The Mystery of the Poisoned Pie

With death staring her in the face, convicted murderess Elizabeth Wood contrived to put on a bold front – in more ways than one. Standing in the dock, after being found guilty of poisoning her best friend's 'sweetheart', she announced defiantly that she was pregnant.

Under 18th-century law, a condemned woman who successfully pleaded pregnancy – or claimed 'Benefit of the Belly', as it was charmingly known – automatically had her sentence postponed until one month after giving birth. Some more liberal judges were prepared to set a woman free once her child was born.

In Elizabeth Wood's case, it was all a desperate ruse, but, despite being at least 42 years old, she managed to bluff her way through the examination subsequently ordered by the court and so convinced the trial judge that she was indeed expecting. Granted the usual stay of execution, she was returned to prison where she maintained the outward signs of her 'condition' by stuffing pieces of leather inside her clothing.

The charade was doomed to fail, of course. Although she added more and more padding as the weeks went by, her leather 'underwear' could only hide the naked truth for so long. When the time came to prove her claim, she simply could not deliver. Finally exposed as a fraud, she was brought back to court and once again sentenced to death. She was hanged at Boughton on Monday 26 April 1784. Her phantom pregnancy had prolonged her worldly existence by just seven months.

An early 20th-century view of Bredbury, from where Betty Wood set out on a summer's evening in 1783 to deliver a poisoned veal pie to her lodger's 'sweetheart' James Simister.
(By permission of Stockport Heritage Library.)

Weaving with a handloom. This was how convicted murderer Betty Wood and her friend and lodger Fanny Tomlinson spent their working days, employed by local cloth merchants under the old 'putting out' system of domestic employment.
(By permission of Tameside Local Studies and Archives.)

Unlike the Heald case, here there is an abundance of official documentation available, yet the answer to that most fundamental question – 'Why did she do it?' – is even more elusive; the crime, ultimately, that much more baffling.

Elizabeth (Betty) Wood lived with her farmer husband William and her friend and lodger Fanny Tomlinson at Bredbury, near Stockport. As was the tradition in many farming families at the time, the Woods also earned their living from weaving, which, along with spinning, was one of the area's two main cottage industries then. Both Betty and Fanny were handloom weavers who seem to have worked together under the old 'putting-out' system, which involved spinners and weavers working at home for one or more of the local cloth merchants. The spinners would get the raw cotton from the merchant, clean it and spin it into yarn or thread, then the spun yarn was passed on to the weavers to be turned into cloth. Only when the merchant had sold the finished product would his outworkers be paid.

By this time, due to the advances in mechanisation, spinning had already begun to move into the factory era, which in the course of the next few decades – as the Industrial Revolution rolled relentlessly on – would transform this part of Cheshire and the adjoining towns of south Lancashire into the foremost cotton manufacturing region in the world. But domestic handloom weavers continued working with spun cotton supplied by the mills until well into the 19th century.

On the morning of Sunday 15 June 1783 Fanny's boyfriend James Simister was found dead at his home in nearby Werneth – a scattered community spread across the rolling landscape of the Cheshire 'panhandle', the county's former north-eastern arm amputated by Boundary Commission 'surgery' in the local government reforms of the early 1970s. He died after eating a veal pie, which had been dosed with arsenic.

A week earlier Betty Wood was said to have told a neighbour that she was thinking of baking James Simister a veal pie…a rather special veal pie. She wanted to play a trick on him, she said – though without explaining why, seemingly – and intended putting some 'jallop' (laxative) in it 'to make him loose'. Later she insisted she had not gone ahead with her plan and had burned the offending pie.

The evening before James Simister's body was discovered, another neighbour saw Wood approach him carrying a basket containing a round 'parcel' wrapped in cloth. She claimed she had been asked to deliver the parcel to him by a stranger she had met on the road. She said she did not know what was in it.

The Mystery of the Poisoned Pie

These and other incriminating conversations were reported to Cheshire coroner John Hollins when he opened the inquest into James Simister's death at Werneth on Wednesday 18 June. At a time when there was no recognisable police force, coroners had a much wider remit than today, and in cases of suspected murder the purpose of an inquest was not merely to determine the cause of death. It was effectively the preliminary investigation into the crime, and, in gathering together the evidence, examining witnesses and committing suspects to gaol, the coroner prepared much of the ground for the eventual trial.

The depositions of nine of the witnesses who appeared at the inquest – which would have constituted the core of the evidence coroner Hollins later forwarded to the Crown prosecutors – are filed among the Chester Assize records on the case in the National Archives in London. They provide some interesting insights into the events before and after the murder, and the relationships between the three principal characters in the drama…but precious little in the way of motive.

James Simister was the brother of Thomas Simister, a Werneth cotton spinner who seems to have remained part of the putting-out system, employing several people – operating spinning jennies, presumably – in what appears to have been some kind of workshop attached to his home, a sort of halfway house between domestic and factory production. Though there is no mention of his occupation anywhere in the surviving records, it may have been that James was also involved in the business. The two men lived in a pair of adjoining cottages.

In his deposition, Thomas Simister stated that on the morning of 15 June he was talking to one of his cousins, also called James Simister, in the road outside his house. He had not seen his brother so far that day and surmised that 'he might be gone to see his sweetheart, Fanny Tomlinson'. After trying the front door and finding it locked, he peered in through the window. He became concerned when he saw that his brother (who lived alone) had 'puked upon the house floor in several places'.

Returning to his own house, he went upstairs to his bedroom, where only a single wall separated the two properties, and called out his brother's name several times. There was no reply. Thomas returned to James's front door and tried to peek through the keyhole, but the key was in the lock on the inside of the door.

Alarmed now that 'something was amiss', he put a ladder up to his brother's bedroom window and his cousin climbed up. James Simister was lying in his bed, apparently dead – an impression confirmed a few minutes later when Thomas took a mattock and smashed open the front door.

That evening Thomas Simister made another discovery: in the drawer of his brother's kitchen table he found the remains of a veal pie 'in a poke' (a small cloth bag). Suspecting nothing, he left it there, but on the following Tuesday, when he was again in his brother's house, one of his two young daughters, who were cleaning up the place, brought him the part-eaten pie.

His deposition (taken down in the customary third-person style) went on: 'He broke a piece off the pye and put it into his mouth and…swallowed down several small pieces thereof, and in about two hours time afterwards was strangely disordered in his bowells and puked very much and he then thought that something was wrong in the pye or cake he had before tasted.'

Thomas consulted his friend, schoolmaster Joel Chetham, who, after examining the pie, 'told this deponent that it was full of poison and advised him to send for the coroner for he was afraid his brother was poisoned'.

The fear became fact when Stockport surgeon James Briscall carried out a postmortem examination of James Simister's body. He found 'a considerable quantity of a rough white powder' in the stomach and livid spots on the stomach lining 'where the powder seemed to have exercised its most virulent effects'. He noticed further traces in the duodenum and the abdominal cavity. His report went on: '[The] whole contents of the thorax and abdomen seemed to have suffered a considerable degree of inflammation, but the liver, diaphragm and other viscera that lay in contact with the stomach appeared evidently to have suffered the most.'

Dr Briscall, who founded the first dispensary in Stockport and was one of the pioneering figures in the provision of health care in the town, collected some of the white powder for analysis. He explained, '[It] was put upon a heated iron, which emitted a thick white smoak [*sic*], and afforded a smell not unlike that of garlick. I held a piece of iron over this smoak, which was immediately covered with a white powder.'

At that time – and until more scientifically-accurate testing procedures were developed in the first half of the 19th century – the hot-iron experiment seems to have been the standard method for detecting the presence of arsenic.

The surgeon concluded, '[From] the above experiments, and other appearances, I am of opinion that his death was owing to a quantity of arsenic, or some other poison, which he had swallowed.'

James Simister was last seen alive on the evening of Saturday 14 June, at his brother's house. Nancy Swindells, a young woman from Bredbury, who was one of Thomas

Old cottages at Werneth. It was in one of a pair of similar dwellings, and next door to his brother Thomas's spinning workshop, that James Simister was found poisoned in 1783. (By permission of Tameside Local Studies and Archives.)

The Mystery of the Poisoned Pie

Simister's employees, was working that evening and, for some untold reason, Betty Wood was also there (perhaps she was collecting yarn for weaving). Nancy overheard a conversation between the two, which had begun with a polite, if cool, exchange of greetings. She said the woman asked James how he was, 'to which he said he was middling'. When he reciprocated, she said Wood 'answered him much the same'.

Nancy's deposition continued: 'She heard the woman say to James Simister she had brought him a parcel, which was put into her basket upon the road by a man, and she said to James he must take it out of the basket with his own hands for she had not touched it, nor would she. James Simister said he did not know what it should be or where it should come from and the woman said she did not know.'

Whether it showed that she knew more than she was admitting or she was simply judging by the parcel's shape and size, Betty then added that the stranger who had put the 'cake' into her basket had told her that he and his mother would be calling to see James in a few weeks time. Despite his uncertainty, James accepted the mystery gift.

Betty Wood was seen 'upon the road' to Werneth between 7 and 8 o'clock that summer's evening by another young Bredbury woman, Kitty Taylor. She was also a domestic weaver and one of her regular employers was Benjamin Ashton of Werneth. She testified that she was on her way from Butterworth Green to Mr Ashton's house to drop off 'some work she had been weaving for him' when, just before she got there, she became aware of Betty Wood walking about 100 yards behind her. She had a basket on her arm.

Kitty Taylor said that, 'in her presence', Wood also handed over some weaving she had completed. It had been in the basket, presumably, and as the witness did not mention seeing anything unusual in it, we must assume that Wood had not yet been approached by the mystery man with the parcel.

There was time for one further deposition before the coroner adjourned the inquest. As the girlfriend of the deceased, Fanny Tomlinson was an important witness; what was not so obvious from the evidence thus far presented – and she herself may not have been aware of it as the day's proceedings drew to a close – was that she was also suspected of being involved in the murder. The content of her statement gave little warning of the bombshell to come.

She said she had lived with William and Betty Wood for seven years, during which time James Simister had 'visited [her] as his sweetheart by times'. On his last visit, on Sunday 8 June, while the Woods were having supper, he had proposed to her. Her deposition stated, 'She went out of doors with James Simister and…before he went home he said he would marry her by lycence [sic] the day following if she would, but she told him she did not then choose it. After some time they parted good friends and, as she was then poorly, he promised to come to see her again.' He never returned; a week later he was dead.

Fanny was then led into more controversial territory. Asked if anyone in the Wood household had bought any veal lately, she said that 'last Saturday was a fortnight [31 May], to the best of her remembrance, Betty Wood went with this deponent's work to Mr Gee in Stockport [another cotton merchant, presumably] and brought home a piece of a neck of veal, part of which was boiled on the Sabbath Day following [1 June] and the remainder, she believes, was used the same week'.

So Fanny's friend and landlady had had the means to make a pie similar to the one that had apparently killed James Simister – hardly the most damning evidence. However, things really started to look bad for Betty Wood three days later when the inquest was resumed, this time at Stockport. Two witnesses now alleged that she had also recently acquired a supply of that other 'ingredient' contained in the half-eaten pie found in James Simister's kitchen-table drawer.

Mary Smith, also of Bredbury, recalled that on Sunday 25 May she had accompanied Betty Wood, a neighbour of hers, to Ashton-under-Lyne to visit Betty's uncle. That evening, on their way home, they called off in Hyde at a shop owned by John Smith (no relation), where, she said, 'Betty Wood bought some arsenic...in order to kill rats and fleas, as she said.'

John Smith, who described himself as a weaver and dealer in 'phisical [*sic*] drugs', also remembered the Sunday evening transaction in his shop. He said he sold the woman Wood three or four pence worth of arsenic, at the same time cautioning her to take care when using the poison.

While there was now some measure of circumstantial evidence against Wood, there was still nothing to implicate Fanny Tomlinson. Yet at the end of the second day of the inquest, both women would stand accused of murder. Now, while it is obvious that the case papers have not survived intact – after more than 200 years it would be surprising if they had – and do not, therefore, tell the whole story, the two remaining statements taken that day, 21 June, must have contributed in some part to the jury's startling conclusion.

First, weaver's wife Phoebe Harrison of Bredbury told of a visit James Simister had paid her on the evening of Saturday 7 June, a week before he was murdered. He was a regular caller at her house, she said; her husband was out at the time (she did not say whether this was a prerequisite for James's visits) and they began chatting about his friendship with Fanny Tomlinson. Almost immediately, she said, James told her that a few days earlier, completely out of the blue, Betty Wood had called at his house and begged a drink of water. She left her basket with him while she went to Benjamin Ashton's to see if he wanted any work doing, returning shortly afterwards with some cotton caps she was taking home to finish off. Before leaving she thanked him for the water.

James was 'gloppened' (astonished) by Wood's pleasant manner because, as he put it, 'he thought [she] had some policy in her heart against him'. For reasons that are not now apparent, there was obviously some history of animosity between the two of them; maybe Wood's unexpected visit was intended to establish more friendly contact with James so that when she next called on him (with her deadly package) it would not arouse suspicion and he would be off his guard.

James Simister had been at Phoebe Harrison's the previous week, too. On that occasion he told her about a quarrel he had had with Fanny and asked Phoebe to help him make up with his lady friend. Phoebe later spoke to Fanny, who said James could call on her the following day (Sunday 8 June) – their last meeting at the Woods' house and the 'date' on which a remorseful James had proposed marriage.

Mrs Harrison was also a friend of Fanny Tomlinson. She said Fanny had visited her on the Tuesday after James's death (17 June) and appeared much concerned about him. Then the conversation took a curious turn when Fanny mentioned some money that had apparently gone missing from Simister's house. The deposition explained, 'Fanny told Phoebe that James Simister's money he formerly had, could not be met with. Phoebe replied "Fanny, folk will judge that you have it." Fanny said, "I have it not, neither have I seen any silver or brass of his, except once when I was with him at Cornelius Bridge's in Stockport [a public house, presumably] where he pulled out some money to pay his shot."'

If the interlude was intended to reflect badly on Fanny Tomlinson's character, the single most damaging piece of evidence against her from within the surviving batch of inquest depositions is, however, to be found in a viewpoint expressed rather forcibly by Betty Wood's husband William. His statement was short…but clearly persuasive.

Without preamble, it asserted bluntly, 'William Wood…is of an opinion that if his wife Betty Wood was guilty of poisoning James Simister, Fanny Tomlinson must be privy to the transaction because nothing was done in the house but what the one knew of as well as the other.' He also seemed to be suggesting that they might have been conspiring together, when he related that, on the night of 11–12 June (three days before the murder), he 'saw them in bed together betwixt the hours of 12 and 1 o'clock' and that 'both were then awake'.

Betty Wood and Fanny Tomlinson were obviously close friends, but to infer from their sleeping arrangements that the relationship was any more intimate than that may be putting too modern an interpretation on it. In small households, with few rooms, same-sex bed sharing was often a practical necessity. In the case of the Woods, while we know they had at least two bedrooms and that they do not appear to have had children at home, William Wood's early-to-bed-early-to-rise farming routine may have made it expedient for him to sleep alone.

However, whether it was simply the protective instinct of an older woman or the product of a deeper affection, Betty Wood's concern for her young lodger may well have been sufficiently strong for her to want to pay James Simister back for some perceived hurt he had inflicted on Fanny (the cause of their recent quarrel, perhaps) or, at the other extreme, to put an end to the relationship altogether. We know from James's own words that she seemed to harbour some ill will towards him.

As to committing murder, however, the various bits of the jigsaw that were slowly being laid on the table were still some way short of producing a convincing picture of Betty Wood's guilt. And with his next statement, William Wood dropped another stray piece on to the puzzle board. He continued, 'In about three hours time after [seeing Betty and Fanny in bed together], Fanny Tomlinson came into his room and said "William, Betty is gone." He got out of bed and went in search of his wife but could not find her.'

Though there is nothing in the case papers to account for Betty Wood's absence in the middle of the night (or to explain her husband's apparent unconcern about it), it was plainly thought to be of some significance. Why else would it rate a mention in William Wood's all-too-brief memoir? But how was it relevant to the crime? Had she gone to some secret hideaway to prepare the poisoned pie? While the questions piled up, answers came there none.

As the parting shot in his potentially wounding salvo, William Wood took a pot at Fanny Tomlinson's recollection about his wife purchasing veal. He insisted he had not seen any in the house 'since the first day of May last'. If Fanny was right, and Betty had used up part of a joint of veal during the first week in June, why had the master of the house not received his share? What had Betty done with it? The 16 'good and lawful men' of the inquest jury believed they knew the answer to that one, at least.

Possibly swayed by William Wood's testimony as by anything else they had heard over the two days of the hearing, the jurors delivered their dramatic verdict. Their written pronouncement first alleged that Betty Wood had killed James Simister by administering to him 'a quantity of white arsenic, being a deadly poison, in a certain Pye made up of flour and veal'. It then went on, 'The jurors say that Fanny Tomlinson of Bredbury, single woman...before the felony and murder did incite move instigate councel [sic] and advise Betty Wood to do and commit the felony and murder and that both Betty Wood and Fanny Tomlinson did commit the murder in the manner and form aforesaid.'

The two women were committed for trial at Chester Castle. At that stage, the case against Tomlinson looked especially weak, and does not seem to have improved over the course of the next three months. What new evidence came to light only cast its shadow over the hapless Mrs Wood. The two remaining witness depositions in the official files are once again full of intriguing possibilities.

A month later, on 19 July, Nancy Bennett of Smithy Green, Bredbury, another of Fanny Tomlinson's friends, made a statement to local magistrate Henry Wright, in which she referred to a visit she had made to the Woods' house on 9 June, the Monday before James Simister was killed. She had called to see Fanny but was told by Betty Wood that she was 'very bad in bed'. The two women were talking in 'the slop' (rear scullery or washroom) when, to her surprise, Wood suddenly confided, 'Nancy, I am for having a mank with James Simister.'

The *Dictionary of Archaic and Provincial Words* defines 'mank' as a Yorkshire word for a trick or prank (though it seems likely that there is a common link with the old Cheshire expression 'to mank about', meaning lark around).

Nancy Bennett's statement went on: 'This examinant asked what sort of a mank and Betty Wood said she was for making him a veal pye and putting jallop into it and for baking it...and that this examinant must invite James Simister to her house and [invite] him to eat it. This examinant said, "Betty, I will not, for it will make him very badly." She said, "Nay, but it will not. Yes, it will make him very loose and that will make him badly", whereupon Betty Wood turned herself from her and said, "If you'll not let [help] me do it, I will do it."'

It's interesting that Nancy Bennett, even if she was aware of some bad feeling between Wood and James Simister, does not seem to have quizzed her as to why she would want to do such a thing in the first place; it's equally odd that the examining magistrate did not ask the witness whether she knew the reason. That, said Nancy, was the extent of their conversation at that time.

However, on the Monday after the murder she was again at Betty Wood's house, and she raised the subject of the 'veal-and-jallop' pie and the proposed 'mank' with James Simister. Wood, it seems, had changed her mind; she told Nancy that the previous evening she had lingered downstairs after her husband had gone to bed and burned the pie in the kitchen grate.

The Mystery of the Poisoned Pie

So Betty Wood *had* made a veal pie and 'doctored' it in the way she said she planned to do – but then decided not to go ahead with her playful scheme? By now most of the evidence was suggesting a different diagnosis: that the 'sick joke' had turned deadly serious and that she had given James Simister a pie containing something rather more potent than laxative.

Two days later, Betty Wood gave a slightly more detailed version of the story of her encounter with the mysterious 'pieman' to Elizabeth Clayton, the second new witness to come forward. Examined on 20 August by JP Samuel Finney, Miss Clayton said that on the morning of the inquest she and Wood met by chance at the home of Benjamin Bennett (another cloth merchant?) at Barrack Hill, Bredbury. In the presence of Bennett, his wife and another woman, the witness said the conversation went as follows: 'Betty Wood turned to this examinant and said, "They say I have poisoned James Simister." This examinant said she had heard something of it. Betty Wood said she had met a man on [the] side of Mr Murray's orchard, whose dress she described, and he had given her a parcel to take to James Simister and leave it there. This examinant asked her what sort of a parcel. She said it was something hard and lapped [wrapped] in a cloth and it trundled [rolled about] in her basket.'

Berating the stranger, Betty allegedly said that 'when she comes to lay her hand on him, he will skreeve [cry out] for me carrying of it, if it was the cake' – meaning she would make him suffer if it was proved that the pie in the parcel had been responsible for James Simister's death.

Elizabeth Clayton assured Betty she would be in the clear provided she had had no hand in making the pie. Betty did not reply, even when the point was put to her a second time. Instead, she reflected, 'If I can get out of this hobble [tricky situation], I will never take any thing from a strange man again. But I think I never shall.' Finally, almost desperately – as if seeking to absolve herself on a technicality – she insisted, 'I did not give it to him, for he took it out of my basket.'

From the names listed on the reverse of the handwritten indictment preserved within the case file, it appears that, in addition to the witnesses already mentioned, at least four other people were due to give evidence when, jointly charged with murder, Wood and Tomlinson appeared before the county's Summer Assizes beginning on Monday 8 September 1783. It quickly became clear that, as far as Fanny Tomlinson was concerned, there was no case to answer. Accordingly, the Grand Jury (the body of prominent citizens which, under the judicial system then in place, carried out a preliminary review of the evidence to decide whether it should go to trial) returned a 'No True Bill' verdict against her and she was discharged.

After spending three months in gaol with her co-defendant, Betty Wood found herself in the dock alone. She pleaded not guilty to the charge of murder but the jury found her guilty and the judge, the Honourable Richard Pepper Arden, the newly-appointed Chief Justice of Chester, pronounced the inevitable sentence. It was then that she played the pregnancy card.

As the law stood, the judge had no choice but to empanel a 'Jury of Matrons' (experienced married women) to investigate Wood's claim. How thoroughly they examined her is not known, but, according to the Chester Crown Book – in which the business of the assizes was minuted – the clerk of the court was subsequently informed that '[the] Jury of Matrons say she is Quick with child'.

The clerk communicated the news to the judge, who revised the terms of Wood's sentence as follows: 'That she be taken to a place of execution upon the first Saturday next after one month from her delivery between the hours of 10 and 4 o'clock of the same day and then and there hanged by the neck until she be dead and that her body be delivered to a surgeon to be anatomised and that, in case some surgeon [does] not accept of her body, it shall be hung in chains within the county of Chester.'

As we have seen, Betty Wood's outrageous gamble – with which she was probably hoping to win the time to assemble a more convincing case for clemency – failed to pay off. Like her false front once the padding had been removed, her futile stunt fell flat, and, on Monday 19 April 1784, seven months after her original conviction, she again stood at the bar of the assize court. This time she remained silent.

The Crown Book noted, '[She] being now called up and asked whether she be now pregnant or hath any thing to say why execution shall not be ordered, according to the sentence pronounced, saith nothing.' Her execution was rescheduled for the following Monday (26 April) and, as a surgeon had been found who was prepared to accept it, the judge ordered that her body should afterwards be delivered to Chester Infirmary for dissection.

This latter option had been available, as an alternative to hanging in chains, since the passing of 'An Act for better preventing the horrid Crime of Murder' (more commonly known as the Murder Act) in 1752. As it provided the anatomists with subjects on which to practise their surgical skills, thereby increasing their understanding of human biology and disease, it became the preferred choice of most judges when dealing with convicted murderers until it was rendered obsolete by the provisions of the 1832 Anatomy Act.

Make no mistake, however: the added 'punishment' was very much about retribution first and medical knowledge second. Like the execution itself, the opening up and examination of the corpse also had to be carried out in public. It was intended as a 'further terror and peculiar Mark of Infamy' designed to deny the deceased a grave, for, as the act stated, 'In no case whatsoever shall the body of any murderer be suffered to be buried.'

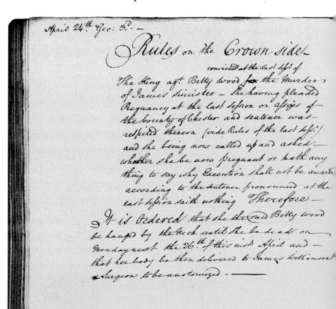

The Crown Book entry of 24 April 1784, which formally confirmed the death sentence passed on Elizabeth (Betty) Wood for murder, following her bogus pregnancy. (By permission of the National Archives.)

The Mystery of the Poisoned Pie

The *Chester Courant* had first revealed the sensational news of Betty Wood's attempts to cheat the law on 13 April. Listing the prisoners due to appear at the forthcoming Spring Assizes, the paper reported:

> 'Elizabeth Wood, condemned the laſt Aſſizes for Murder, but afterwards ſentence reſpited, from the Opinion of a Jury of Matrons, who pronounced her then pregnant, has been ſince found (from the natural Impulſe of protracting even the Miſeries of Life), to have been guilty of Deceit, by having Recourſe to artificial Methods, in gradually increaſing her Prominence by placing a Quantity of Leather under her Stays.'

As to how she acquired the pieces of leather, the *Courant* offered no explanation, though it would probably not have been difficult for someone, possibly her friend Fanny or husband William, to smuggle such small and seemingly innocuous items into the gaol. The newspaper report ended, approvingly:

> 'The Artifice, however, being diſcovered, it is ſuppoſed that her Execution will ſpeedily take place.'

The *Courant*'s coverage of that event was comparatively brief, though the report in its issue of Tuesday 27 April was still more detailed than the version carried by the *Chester Chronicle*. As the execution had taken place close to its weekly deadline, the *Courant* had the added kudos of bringing its readers the news the day after it happened and three days ahead of its local rival.

After recalling how Betty Wood's 'pretended Pregnancy' had delayed her sentence by more than six months, the paper observed piously, 'It is, therefore, to be hoped that she cultivated the Length of Time allotted her in such a Manner as to secure to her that Remission in *another* State which the Enormity of her Crime rendered impossible in *this*.' Wood, added the *Courant*, 'met her melancholy End with the utmost Resignation'.

In neither newspaper, however, was there the slightest hint as to what had provoked Betty Wood into cooking up her poisoned-pie plot – an unforgivable omission by today's standards, though at that time both papers, with their minimal pagination and emphasis on national and international news, reported local court cases in only the barest detail. With the official records also silent on this vital issue, we are left to reflect that while the farmer's wife may have found killing James Simister as easy as pie, understanding her motive for murder is now no longer so.

Unlike the old nursery recitation she brings to mind with her account of how she 'met a pieman', the crime seems to have been without rhyme or reason.

✳ ✳ ✳

There was nothing bogus about Sarah Malone's pregnancy. The middle-aged mother of three, whose husband had abandoned her some years earlier, was eight months gone and her condition was all too apparent. When the woman was found murdered in the old mill pool in the picturesque little village of Lymm in 1798, it was no secret, either, who the father was. Immediately, this man became the number-one suspect. The problem was that several credible witnesses could swear to having been in his company for most of the time on the night of the killing...

Chapter Three

The Butler and the Washerwoman

It promised to be a busy night up at the parsonage, not least for John Thornhill. As head servant to the Rector of Lymm, he was employed primarily as the butler; but, as the only man among an indoor staff of five, he also doubled up as his master's valet and, in between, was expected to lend a hand with the heavier day-to-day chores as well. That Friday there was the added complication of overnight guests. The rector's wife had friends staying; that meant rooms to prepare, fires to tend, luggage to haul – and two extra for supper.

Though he was used to juggling several jobs at once, John Thornhill, general factotum, gentleman's gentleman and, first and foremost, waiter at table, plainly had a lot on his plate. There was also the small matter of a murder to fit in.

Sarah Malone had only one thing on her mind that evening. The 44-year-old mother of three, who had been left to bring up her children alone when her husband walked out on her some years before, was off to see the man whose baby she was carrying to discuss her plans for the future. Marriage was out of the question, of course, but she felt sure he could be persuaded to come to some private arrangement over maintenance rather than have her expose him publicly as the father of her unborn child.

His identity, naturally, had been the subject of much debate in the village, and though his name had been mentioned to her more than once she had never openly admitted it. Best for now, therefore, that no one else should know about their assignation, so she told her son she was going to visit her brother. It was just after 8 o'clock on 5 January 1798 when, wrapped in a warm dressing gown (she did not expect to be gone long), she gathered up her petticoats and set out for her date with destiny.

Earlier in the day the weather had turned stormy and now rain clouds lowered ominously in a moonless sky as Sarah made her way through the unlit streets towards the little hollow in which they had arranged to meet. The Dingle after dark was no place for a woman alone, and it was a measure of her desperation that she had agreed to go there on a night like this. Nevertheless, as she joined the path that led up through the wooded valley, it may just have occurred to her that this might not be such a good idea after all. With the bare oaks rattling

and moaning in the wind like restless skeletons, their branches reaching out with bony fingers as if to grasp her into their cold embrace, she entered the dell and was swallowed up in the blackness.

The former parsonage in Lymm (*c*.1890, by which time it had been restyled 'The Rectory'), where John Thornhill laid his murder plans.
(Photograph courtesy of Mr Joe Griffiths.)

The Butler and the Washerwoman

Some little time later, by the old mill stream that twisted and tumbled beside the woodland path, the eight-months-pregnant Sarah and the beleaguered butler (for it was he) had their secret rendezvous. The Dingle, which lay just below the walled garden of the parson's house, was a romantic spot, popular then as now with courting couples. But this was no moonlit tryst between starry-eyed lovers: the meeting was as ugly and chilling as the weather.

To her pay-up-or-else ultimatum his response was short and brutish, and Sarah, who had started out pleading for money, ended up begging for mercy as the stockily-built Thornhill laid into her with a claw hammer. She was a big, robust woman and she fought fiercely for her life, but after surviving several blows to the back of the head her resistance finally ended when Thornhill drove the sharp end of the heavy implement into her right temple. She slumped to the ground with blood coursing through her long, flowing hair and staining the white cotton bonnet that had slipped down around her neck in the struggle.

Soon the crystal stream ran red as Thornhill bundled the unconscious Sarah into the freezing water. The current, which powered the flour mill in the middle of the village, carried the body down into the mill pool, where it would eventually come to rest against the head of the dam and sink to the bottom (though, as we shall see, it may not have been such a straightforward process as that). A spell of severe frost would later entomb the body in ice, hiding it from view and delaying its discovery.

With Sarah consigned to a watery grave, Thornhill's immediate concern was to return to the big house before anyone noticed he was missing. From The Dingle it was a steep and slippery climb up to the parsonage grounds and another 100 yards to the house. However, in pitch darkness, he made it back without mishap. And, once inside, he quickly changed out of his blood-stained clothes and within minutes of the murder he had resumed his place as the faithful young retainer (he was only 29) as if nothing had happened.

His fellow servants would later be unable to recall anything unusual about his demeanour that evening, Thornhill evidently managing to maintain the same impassive expression in their presence as he had learned to assume 'above stairs' as the unobtrusively attentive butler. It was an act, therefore, that owed as much to his professional training as his strength of character (the mask would slip noticeably in the days ahead), but it was an impressive performance nonetheless.

Thornhill also displayed a remarkable sense of timing. Either that or he was incredibly lucky. For, having picked his moment to leave the house, he had to make sure that his absence was not too long to arouse suspicion, that when he returned – wet, bloody and dishevelled – he was not observed and that his extramural activities did not disturb the strict routine of his domestic duties. All of which he seems to have accomplished in his normally efficient manner.

It wasn't until three days later, after searchers had broken through the mill pool's covering of ice to retrieve Sarah Malone's battered and bedraggled body, that the first cracks began to appear in John Thornhill's composure. Having finally admitted that it was he who had made Sarah pregnant, he was twice taken into custody for questioning. After being released for the second time, he panicked and fled the village. He didn't get far.

He was spotted scurrying through the fields in the direction of High Legh and was captured and brought back to Lymm, just in time for the conclusion of the inquest into Sarah's death. And it was there, as witnesses told how the hunt for the missing woman

The idyllic setting in which butler John Thornhill carried out his bloody hammer attack on Sarah
Malone, as depicted in the early 19th century by Peter de Wint in George Ormerod's authoritative
history of Cheshire. (Print courtesy of Mr Colin Lynch.)

had ended when her corpse was fished from the icy dam with an iron hook, that the truth about her furtive affair with the dapper young butler – and the events of that frantic Friday when the conflicting demands of the two women in Thornhill's life drove him to murder – also surfaced for the first time.

It was an unlikely liaison: he the respected head of staff in the household of an eminent churchman, a snappily-dressed, rather dandyish figure if a little on the stout side, and she a middle-aged single mother, 15 years his senior, a simple woman of ample proportions who may already have had one illegitimate child before her ill-fated dalliance with Thornhill.

They had met during the winter of 1795–96, when he was appointed butler to the Reverend Egerton Leigh, Rector of Lymm and Archdeacon of Salop. Born in 1769 in Stow-on-the-Wold, Gloucestershire, he had previously worked for several respectable families in the Cotswolds, latterly in Moreton-in-Marsh. Though he was young to be a butler, he came with excellent references and had been personally recommended by Revd Leigh's sister-in-law, who lived in Broadwell.

Sarah, the former Miss Sarah Statham, had married Irishman Patrick Malone at Lymm Parish Church on 23 May 1784. By then she was already six months pregnant – a situation, it seems, that was fairly common at the time. For while pre-marital sex was discountenanced, betrothal seems to have been regarded as a licence to indulge and conception a consequence that merely hastened the wedding arrangements. The Malones' first child, a boy named John, was born on 28 August. Three years later, on 7 July 1787, a second son, James, arrived and – after some indeterminate interval of time – Patrick Malone left.

It is not clear what caused the marital break up, or what befell Malone or young James, who also disappears from the narrative around this time. All we know is that by the beginning of 1798 only one of the brothers, John, was still living at home with his mother. And by now, Sarah, husbandless but obviously not lacking for male company, also had a daughter. Aged about five, the girl was born almost certainly after Patrick Malone's departure and well before Thornhill appeared on the scene. But (not altogether surprisingly perhaps) there is no record of her baptism in the local church registers to indicate who the father was.

Sarah and her family lived in a cottage that had been divided into two separate tenements (the only clue to its location is that it was about a quarter-of-a-mile from the parsonage). She seems to have worked for the rector from time to time and that was probably how she first made the acquaintance of John Thornhill, though their relationship blossomed after she left the rector's service and began doing the butler's washing. It was a means of supplementing the meagre wage she received for winding cotton for son John, who, though only 13, was already earning his living as a hand-loom weaver in the village.

Some time in May 1797, the couple eventually consummated their friendship and Sarah fell pregnant. According to Thornhill, it was the only time they were intimate, for by then there was another woman occupying the attentions of the philandering flunkey.

Rebecca Clarke was maid to Mrs Theodosia Leigh, the rector's wife. As they both 'lived in', she and Thornhill saw a lot of each other and, gradually, a closer bond developed. In October 1797 (five months after his seduction of Sarah), they became engaged. Before promising to marry him, however, Rebecca pressed her fiancé-to-be to make an additional vow.

Like the other servants at the parsonage, she had heard the village gossip about Sarah Malone's baby. But now she wanted to know once and for all whether Thornhill was the father. Rather than simply denying it yet again, this time he took Rebecca to see Sarah to confront her with the question. There seems little doubt that, at five months pregnant, Sarah would already have been pressurising Thornhill into facing up to his responsibilities, yet she went along with his shameless charade and responded to Rebecca's inquiry with an insistent 'No'.

What Rebecca did not know, however, was that Thornhill had called at Sarah's house earlier in the day and forewarned her of the visit. Misguidedly, she was persuaded not to betray him. However, as he would soon discover, there was a limit to her loyalty.

When 1797 gave way to 1798, and there was still no sign that John Thornhill was going to do the honourable thing, she decided she would 'father' her baby – that is, name the father so that, in accordance with the Poor Law regulations then in force, the local overseer could begin the formal process of encouraging the man to admit paternity and undertake to support the child. When, on Friday 5 January, Thornhill visited her to collect his clean laundry, she let it be known that she was going to make him pay for her confinement and the child's upbringing one way or another.

We can only guess at the mood and nature of the conversation, but the news must have rattled Thornhill. Though working 'in service' would not have earned him a particularly handsome wage, it wasn't just the money – his whole future was at stake. If the truth came out he would surely lose his job: the rector could not be seen to condone such immoral behaviour by continuing to employ him. And the life he planned with Rebecca would be forfeit, too, for she had made it abundantly clear that if she ever found out that he had fathered Sarah's child then she would have nothing more to do with him.

One can imagine him blustering that he needed more time to consider the matter, and suggesting that they meet again that Friday evening to talk about it some more. He knew he was going to be busy but, faced with this imminent threat to his well-ordered lifestyle, for once the obedient servant could not stand and wait. He had to do something about it. And quickly.

Once again Sarah was taken in by Thornhill's persuasive charm and she agreed to meet him later in The Dingle, where, in glorious seclusion, water from Lymm's spectacular Upper Dam cascades down a rock-strewn course before disgorging into the much smaller mill pool (also known as the Lower or Mill Dam) 60 feet below. Twenty years later the distinguished Cheshire historian George Ormerod would immortalise this delightful local beauty spot in his epic, three-volume *History of Cheshire*. The scene is captured in all its silvan splendour in Peter de Wint's illustration in Volume One of Ormerod's masterwork, first published in 1819.

After describing Lymm's 14th-century Parish Church of St Mary the Virgin, perched imposingly on the sandstone hillside and the Upper Dam spread out below, the author wrote, 'From this the waters descend by a deep and rapid fall, into a vale below, of most exquisite beauty, the sides of which consist of rocks hung with oaks, the middle of the vale forming the bed of the stream, which dashes through a variety of successive waterfalls. At the head of the stream, where the vale is the widest, the first and great fall exhibits itself through the trees, under an alpine bridge, over which the tower of the church is seen in the distance.'

In 1824 the alpine bridge was replaced by the new Church Road (A56) crossing and the level of the Upper Dam was raised, but the essential character of The Dingle – part of a ragged fissure that cuts through the southern slope of the Mersey Valley and bisects the village – has changed little in over two centuries.

Wander on a summer's day down the shady, sun-dappled path that meanders beside the now more tranquil waters and it is easy to see why this idyllic, enchanting place so enraptured Ormerod – and hard to imagine it being the setting for so horrific a crime.

Almost as difficult to comprehend, more than 200 years later, is how on such a night as this, when he was so busily occupied indoors and there were at least eight people at the parsonage to witness his comings and goings, Thornhill was able to execute what was a hastily prepared, and very messy, murder without anyone suspecting a thing. Both upstairs and downstairs – and in his master's chamber – whether waiting at table, attending to his employer's personal needs or supervising the staff, he was seen busying himself about the house throughout the evening, his appearance and behaviour at all times open to the closest scrutiny. So where, in the midst of all this activity, did he find the opportunity to sneak out of the house, kill Sarah and dispose of her body, then return in no time at all, change his clothes and carry on working as unruffled as if he had just popped down to the wine cellar for a fresh bottle of the rector's favourite claret?

Careful study of all the available evidence points inescapably to the conclusion that, while the desperate butler may not have committed murder in between courses exactly, his wretched scheme was almost as audacious.

It is possible to recreate a fairly accurate picture of Thornhill's movements that evening thanks to the existence of two separate (and extensive) sources of information, chief of which is the sizeable assize court file in the National Archives. The other is an interesting old notebook containing what is said to be a copy of a report of Thornhill's trial that appeared in a contemporary broadside. It was written out, more than 100 years later, by the Reverend Granville Thurston, who was Rector of Lymm between 1898–1917. The text was kindly made available to me by the Lymm and District Local History Society.

Ordinarily, one would not place too much reliance on this type of original source document – even when, as with this one, the broadside insisted that the evidence was 'written in court' and had been 'compared and corrected with the Judge's notes' (and threatened prosecution of anyone 'pirating' the material, for which the publishers had paid 'a considerable sum'). It is a fact, however, that in all the major aspects of the case the Thurston transcript conforms closely with the official version.

After the months in which he must have agonised over what he should do about Sarah Malone's inconvenient pregnancy, it seems likely that John Thornhill only settled on murder as the solution to his problems after his Friday afternoon visit to Sarah's home. The meeting was first revealed by Mrs Phoebe Hough in a statement to the coroner (Mr John Hollins) on Thursday 11 January, the second and final day of the inquest, which was held at the Spread Eagle pub in Lymm. The widow Hough, better known in the village by her maiden name of Daniel, would also be a key witness at Thornhill's trial.

Phoebe and her butcher son William occupied the other half of Sarah's cottage. The two families each had apartments on the ground floor and separate bedrooms above. Phoebe had known Sarah (or Sally Statham, as she referred to her) for 20 years.

She recalled that Thornhill had turned up some time after 1pm. He and Sarah were together for about half an hour, but she said she did not know what they had discussed. After Thornhill left, Sarah gave no hint of any animosity between them, mentioning only that Thornhill had seemed pleased with her for obtaining a yard of cloth with which to mend one of his shirts. Over their customary afternoon cup of tea, however, Sarah told Phoebe that Thornhill had been 'four times that week with his linen to be washed'. His visits may have reflected a growing obsession with personal hygiene, of course…or they just might have indicated that his on-going dialogue with Sarah over her pregnancy was reaching a critical stage and that he was taking every opportunity to dissuade her from 'going public'.

Sarah, too, seems to have contrived to see more of her former lover that week, for, according to Phoebe Daniel, she went to see him at the parsonage on the Wednesday evening (3 January). Before leaving, she told Phoebe she was going to collect some money Thornhill owed her. Sarah, she said, was away a good hour and a half – a time lapse that suggests it was more than just an unpaid laundry bill she wanted to see settled.

In her inquest deposition, Phoebe confirmed that on the night Sarah disappeared she had seen her pass by her living-room door on her way to put her daughter to bed, and shortly afterwards she heard Sarah giving her son instructions for getting his own supper ready. She said the time was 'either immediately before or after the church clock at Lymm struck eight'. Phoebe assumed her housemate was going out, but she did not see her leave.

It must have been around 8.15pm, therefore, when Sarah set out for her last meeting with Thornhill. In view of the distance she would have had to walk to reach The Dingle, they had probably fixed 8.30pm as the rendezvous time. It is safe to assume, too, that Sarah would not have been keen to tarry too long alone in such unnerving surroundings on such a wild night. If Thornhill had been delayed for any length of time, the chances are she would have beaten a hasty retreat – and lived to see another day. As it was, all the evidence indicates that the methodical manservant was on time…and that Sarah Malone was dead well before 9 o'clock.

Rebecca Clarke's lengthy testimony was particularly instructive. In all she made three formal statements, one to the coroner at the inquest and two to a local JP later. In these and her subsequent evidence at the trial (as recorded in the Thurston transcript), she provided the most detailed timetable for that Friday evening at the parsonage. From this it becomes clear just how well judged – or, alternatively, how utterly reckless – John Thornhill's murder plan really was.

She said that Thornhill 'went out several times between 7 and 9 o'clock', but she did not think he was out for more than 10 minutes at any one time. Between seven and eight he 'complained several times of being unwell' (this, apparently, necessitated periodic visits

The Butler and the Washerwoman

to the outside privy and looks to have been a pretence by which he would be able to cover up any absence from the house, should he be challenged about it later). From 9pm–10pm, said Rebecca, Thornhill was definitely in the house. She knew this because the butler always took up the Revd Leigh's supper 'at 9 o'clock or thereabouts' and the rector retired to bed at 10. He was not in the best of health and Thornhill, switching to the role of valet, accompanied him to help him undress and to attend to his medical needs. 'John Thornhill always dressed his master's legs between 10 and 11 o'clock,' Rebecca explained.

It was customary for the staff to dine in the servants' hall between 8 and 9 o'clock, and (in the Thurston account) the Leighs' coachman, George Harrison, said he remembered Thornhill being there on that particular night.

In that same critical period cook Elizabeth Hand also remembered the butler leaving the house. In her inquest deposition she told of making Thornhill some 'drink meat' (gruel) between 8 and 9 o'clock after he had asked her for something to treat 'a complaint in his bowels'. During this time, she said, Thornhill 'went out for more than a few minutes together'. If the butler did have an upset stomach, it was only natural that he would have gone outside – the servants' privy was in the back yard – and Mrs Hand may have been inferring no more than that.

But her statement was further confirmation that John Thornhill was not as omnipresent in the Leighs' household that evening as he had seemed; that, despite his hectic toing and froing, he did have the opportunity to slip out and kill Sarah Malone. The cook's evidence, along with that of Rebecca Clarke and George Harrison, helped pinpoint the time window in which he committed the crime. It almost certainly happened like this (all times approximate):

8.15pm: Sarah leaves home for the last time.
8.00–8.20pm: Up at the parsonage, Thornhill has supper with coachman Harrison. Having complained of tummy trouble, he raises no suspicions when he opts for a light repast – that bowl of the cook's gruel, perhaps – and leaves the table early.
8.30pm: Having armed himself with a claw hammer, Thornhill meets Sarah in the wooded hollow behind the parsonage. It's a moonless night and the weather wet and blustery.
8.30pm–8.40pm: With Sarah continuing to insist he must support her and his baby, the butler batters her senseless and casts her into the mill stream.
8.50pm: Thornhill dashes back to the parsonage; a quick change of clothes later and he is ready to resume his duties.
9.00pm: He serves supper to his master at the usual time and continues to work normally until going to bed shortly after 11pm.

He no doubt blessed his luck that his high-risk plan had gone so smoothly, but if Thornhill spent an uncomfortable night, kept awake by that still small voice whispering insistently inside his head that he could not possibly hope to get away with it, the picture does not square with the remarkable self-control he was able to exercise in the immediate aftermath of his murderous foray. Again, the most revealing evidence was supplied by Rebecca Clarke.

Some time around 10.30pm she left Thornhill in the kitchen while she went upstairs to attend to Mrs Leigh and her guests. But she had to come downstairs on several occasions and, she said, 'each time John Thornhill was doing nothing but sat by the fire'. And during the whole of Friday night and throughout the weekend she said she 'did not see any difference in him'.

On the Friday Rebecca and Thornhill, who were the last to retire, had gone upstairs together just after 11 o'clock. She, the housemaid and the cook all slept in the bedroom next to Thornhill's, and she said none of them had heard him leave his room during the night. The statement is a significant pointer in another puzzling feature of the case: the mystery of the butler's bloodied hand.

The following morning Thornhill was seen to have injured his right hand. He himself, in the (surprisingly short) statement he made to the coroner, claimed it was the result of a fall he had had at about 11 o'clock the night before. His deposition read, 'He took a candle and went outside [to go to the privy] and fell upon a heap of cinders at the back door in consequence of his candle going out; that, in falling, he cut his hand and his [fore]finger and dirtied his breeches. He got up and went to the necessary and came in again and went into the pantry and wiped the blood off his hand upon an old waistcoat and then went to the boiler and took a bowl with which he took a quantity of warm water out of it and washed his hands and the parts that had been injured by the fall. The injury to his finger produced a blister but no blood and the injury to the ball of his hand produced a good deal of blood. In about five minutes after washing…the wound on the ball of his hand ceased bleeding.'

He said he put some 'diaculum plaister' (lead-plaster) on the latter and 'tied his finger up with a rag and string'. All this, he insisted, was after he had put his master to bed and before he and Rebecca retired. However, the more likely explanation is that he did not, in fact, sustain the injuries at the time – or in the manner – he described. It hardly seems possible that, during the five minutes he and the maid were together in the kitchen, or as they made their way upstairs to bed, Rebecca could have failed to notice that her fiancé's right hand was patched up with a plaster and a rag bandage tied up with string.

It was only after breakfast the following morning, when Thornhill asked her to make a poultice for his finger, that Rebecca and the other servants first learned of his fall.

The case file tends to give the impression that Thornhill injured himself when wielding the heavy hammer against the battling Sarah. But this simply could not have been so. If, as logic dictates, Sarah was killed around 8.30pm and Thornhill was serving supper half-an-hour later, he would surely have been unable to conceal his injuries as he handled plates and carried food to the table? He would have been equally handicapped when he came to dress his master's legs.

His explanation *was* a smoke screen, but the more likely truth it was intended to obscure was that Thornhill hurt his hand the following morning when he returned to the scene of the crime to cover up his tracks from the night before. Sarah Malone's missing underskirts – and the early morning observations of a local farm worker – may provide the answer to the mystery.

The two petticoats that Thornhill presumably stripped from Sarah's body to make it less buoyant before putting her into the mill stream were uncovered on 11 February, more than five weeks after the murder, by a young man fishing for eels. According to the Revd Thurston's notebook, Thomas Roberts stated at Thornhill's trial, 'The water was very low and in turning over the stones to look for eels I found the petticoats. They were under a big stone and two or three little ones, and there was a clod or two on them.' He added, 'The place where I found them is about 14 strides from Mr [Revd] Leigh's garden wall.'

At about 7.30am on Saturday 6 January, according to the same trial account, farmer's son Hugh Holt was working with his father's team of horses when he saw Thornhill walking down what is now Rectory Lane in the direction of the mill pool. 'It was then just getting daylight,' he stated. 'I said to him it was very dirty [weather]. He answered it was and proceeded on. He was walking very slow by the wall side with his hand on the wall and he had a long white apron before him.'

We know that the butler had not left the house on an errand for his master, so what was the reason for his Saturday morning excursion? Was the murderer revisiting the place where he had disposed of the troublesome Sarah to check, in the dawn's revealing light, that he had left no obvious clues to his presence there? And that the woman's body was, in fact, safely out of sight somewhere in the murky depths of the dam?

Given the strictly limited amount of time available to him the previous night – and the fact that he would have been working in total darkness – it is possible that he was only able to hide the petticoats properly the following morning, and that he took the skin off his hand and blistered his finger as he worked quickly to lift the rocks and clods of earth that he piled on top of the garments. It would have been a mucky job, too, and his 'long white apron' would have been useful in protecting his working clothes.

It is even conceivable that what the butler saw when he arrived at the spot was Sarah's body still floating in the water, and that it was only then that he took off her bulky underclothes and sent her to the bottom.

It was probably at this time, rather than the frenzied night before, that he also removed two other potentially-revealing items of evidence from the crime scene: one of Sarah's shoes, which had come off in the struggle, and her 'neck handkerchief' (this was a square of material more akin to the modern head scarf than a neckerchief and usually worn by women of the period around the shoulders like a shawl). They were found three weeks later by the Leighs' gardener, John Pass, dumped in a pond in the parsonage grounds. There were spots of blood on the handkerchief.

In her evidence to the inquest, Phoebe Daniel had earlier explained how she had become concerned when Sarah had not returned by 10pm on that Friday night. She spoke to John Malone and he repeated what his mother had told him: that she had gone to visit his uncle. Somehow sensing that something was wrong, Phoebe dispatched the boy to his uncle's house to check that she was there. She was not. Nor was she there when he went a second time, again at Phoebe's insistence, around midnight.

Phoebe thought Sarah might have stayed out because she was 'keeping company' with Thornhill, but she 'did not suspect at all that she was dead'. She told the coroner she had 'no reason to suppose that anyone kept company with her [Sarah] besides John Thornhill'.

Her fears for the missing Sarah may have stemmed from a telling remark her friend had made to her some days earlier. Phoebe had mentioned that she had heard that some of the other servants at the parsonage had accused Thornhill of being the father of Sarah's baby and that he had ridiculed the idea. Phoebe's deposition went on: 'The deceased told this witness that his denying that the child was his only made the sin the greater.' After her previous evasiveness, that she was now virtually admitting to her best friend that the child she was expecting was indeed Thornhill's indicated that her patience with him was fast running out.

Witnesses' recollections about the clothes he wore on the night Sarah Malone was murdered – and the unfolding events at the parsonage over the course of the next four days – heaped further suspicion on to John Thornhill's well-tailored shoulders. The coachman, Harrison, testified that, when they dined together some time after 8 o'clock, Thornhill was wearing his morning jacket, a snazzy item in light grey cotton with a red cape, whereas when the butler served supper to Revd Leigh less than an hour later, he was dressed in a more sober striped jacket (presumably the purple and black one that Rebecca Clarke also remembered him wearing when he went upstairs to wait on his master).

At about 11am on the following Monday (8 January), the grey and red morning jacket was seen drying in front of the kitchen fire after Thornhill had seemingly attempted (unsuccessfully) to wash off what must have been a considerable quantity of blood from the front of the garment and both the sleeves. Later, a shirt and a waistcoat, both bloodstained, and a pair of wet breeches, all belonging to Thornhill, were found hidden in a vent in the passageway outside the door to the butler's pantry (the vent drew heat from the kitchen chimney on the other side of the wall and was being used that morning for drying hams); also, a pair of stockings, muddied and spotted with blood, were seen lying on a table in the butler's pantry.

In his inquest deposition, John Pass, the gardener, said that at lunch that day he challenged Thornhill about the discarded clothing and the butler confirmed that it was his. Of the wet breeches, Thornhill claimed that he had been taken short the night before and soiled them due to 'the looseness that was upon him'. He had washed them and put them in the smoke-hole so that the other servants would not see them drying. If they found out what had happened, they would laugh at him, he said.

Throughout the anxious weekend, and for most of Monday, Thornhill maintained his air of determined indifference. Whereas, for the rest of the parsonage staff – and the whole village – there was but one topic of conversation, he alone of the servants refused to join in the discussions. Then, during lunch in the servants' hall on the Monday, when Pass broke the news that Sarah's body had been found, Thornhill immediately left the table and sat in the kitchen by himself. Later that day Pass went to view Sarah's body, and when he reported what he had seen of her injuries Thornhill, he said, just 'sat stupid and said nothing'.

By then, however, the increasingly-suspicious gardener had managed to dig up one highly-relevant fact about the tight-lipped butler. A few hours before Sarah's body was found, he finally got him to admit that he had made her pregnant. With a bad grace, and clearly irritated by the gardener's probing, Thornhill told Pass dismissively that he had been 'concerned with her in May last'.

The next day, Tuesday, when Thornhill complained to Pass that local people were saying he had murdered Sarah, Pass challenged him to come clean. But Thornhill insisted he had 'not been anywise accessory to her death'. Nevertheless, he said he was thinking of catching the stage coach to Liverpool and then a boat to London, to get away from his accusers. The next day he bundled up some clothes and made his first unsuccessful escape attempt.

The rest of the surviving inquest depositions concern themselves with medical evidence and speculation about the possible cause of Sarah Malone's death. The initial examination of the body was carried out in the late afternoon of Tuesday 9 January, by surgeons Thomas Grundy, of Lymm, and Peter Holland, from Nether Knutsford. In their separate postmortem reports they agreed that there were three significant head wounds: one three-inches long by half-an-inch wide on the right temple, and two more, of five inches and three to four inches in length respectively, on the back of the head – all of 'a ragged appearance'.

Given the length of time that had elapsed since death (and the extent of medical knowledge at the end of the 18th century), the surgeons were unable to determine the precise cause of death. Holland said it was impossible to say whether she had died from the head injuries, while Grundy's report conceded that the major injury to the forehead, coupled with the resulting loss of blood, 'might possibly' have killed her.

After examining the lungs, heart and bladder for the usual signs, the surgeons concluded, however, that drowning was 'not the sole cause of death'.

It was labourer John Knight who eventually recovered Sarah's body after searchers had smashed the mill dam's covering of ice. He had a length of wood with some kind of iron attachment at one end (possibly an old cart shaft) and he poked it into the water. His deposition went on: 'He put the pole gently down by the side of the pool and after it had once been put down about seven foot he felt something at the end of it give way and for a few seconds he placed the pole upright upon it, and then he drew up the pole and brought up…the body of the deceased.'

Asked by the coroner whether Sarah's injuries could have been caused accidentally when her body was being dragged from the water, Knight said he believed that 'the pole could not do the body any external injury from the gentle manner in which it touched her'.

The body, he added, was dressed in a dark cotton bedgown, stays, a shift and stockings, but neither petticoats nor shoes.

Mr Hollins closed the inquest in the late afternoon of Thursday 11 January. The official cause of Sarah Malone's death was recorded as 'one mortal bruise of the

The Lower Dam in Lymm, photographed early in the 20th century when the old mill (left) was still standing, though no longer in use. It was from here that the body of the murdered Sarah Malone was recovered in January 1798. (Photograph courtesy of Mr Joe Griffiths.)

length of three inches and of the breadth of half-an-inch' (the blow to the right temple). But, to the surprise of most of the people who had sat through the two days of testimony, the jury's verdict was 'murder by some person unknown'.

Although Thornhill was heavily implicated, the jurors felt unable to charge him with the crime and he was set at liberty once again. Within days, however, he was back in custody after his employers had come forward with some sensational new evidence.

It centred on conversations Rector Leigh and his wife Theodosia had had with their increasingly-troubled butler in the days following the discovery of Sarah's body. To both his master and mistress, it appeared, he had all but admitted his guilt and had even sought their connivance in a pathetic attempt to escape justice.

His self-incriminating outbursts were occurring even as John Hollins was making his preliminary inquiries into Sarah Malone's death, but the information did not become a matter of public record until Saturday 3 January. Had the members of the jury been aware of it, they could not have failed to name their suspect.

It was provided by the Revd and Mrs Leigh in separate statements to a local magistrate. What they had to tell was to provide the most poignant, and decisive, moment of Thornhill's trial, as the Leighs, obviously torn between their Christian duty and gratitude for a man who had served them admirably – and, in the case of the ailing rector, with great kindness – gave the evidence that sent him to the scaffold.

Following his obstinately unresponsive reaction to the developments in the search for Sarah, by the late afternoon of Monday 8 January Thornhill had found his tongue and was in the mood to talk. He first of all sought out the rector. The butler, leaning wearily against the wainscotting of the rector's study, admitted he had 'been concerned with her once and once only' and had made her pregnant, but, said Revd Leigh, he denied murdering her.

Then, suddenly, Thornhill's attitude changed. He became aggressive and blustered, 'Nobody saw me do it. Nobody can prove it. How can they hurt me?' Revd Leigh's deposition added, 'This he often repeated, and seemed ever agitated and distressed.'

Early the next morning, Thornhill had an equally emotionally-charged conversation with Mrs Leigh in the tearoom adjoining her private quarters on the first floor of the parsonage. According to Mrs Leigh, he looked dreadful and she said to him, 'Oh God John, you terrify me to death. I see you are guilty.'

She slumped into a chair and Thornhill immediately knelt in front of her, clasping her knees and laying his head in her lap. Mrs Leigh's statement went on: 'This examinant, apprehending he was going to make some confession, said, "John, make no confession to me. I cannot bear it."' Thornhill said, 'What shall I do? Do advise me. Shall I make off?'

After breakfast she returned to the tearoom and Thornhill followed her inside. Again he asked her whether he should run away. Then, as had happened when he was speaking to the rector, he regained his composure and snapped, 'Why should I? How can they touch me? Nobody saw me.'

Mrs Leigh replied, 'There is an eye above who doth see and there are numberless little circumstances that will lead to a discovery, if you are guilty, which you cannot guard against. I believe you are guilty and, if so, you have nothing to do but confess and repent,' – to which, she alleged, Thornhill replied, 'But if I do so, I shall be hanged.'

The Butler and the Washerwoman

Later Thornhill begged her to hide him in the cellar if the parish constables came to arrest him. Mrs Leigh said she told him, 'I would not do it on any consideration…You would certainly be found.'

In fact, the parish constables came a-calling at the parsonage twice during that Tuesday. Thornhill was taken into custody for the first time shortly after 10am, but was released two hours later. Then, between 4pm and 5pm, as the coroner completed his preliminary inquiries, he was brought back for further questioning. At this stage Mr Hollins's suspicions appear to have been sufficiently strong for him to have Thornhill detained overnight at the Spread Eagle; yet, oddly, early the next morning – just a couple of hours before the inquest was due to begin – he was again set free.

Thornhill decided to make a run for it, but, with word of his departure having quickly reached the parish constables, he was overtaken about a mile beyond the village boundary. He was escorted back to Lymm and spent a second night under lock and key at the Spread Eagle.

The following day, Thursday 11 January, he gave his statement to the coroner (when it was written down and shown to him, he said it was a correct record but he refused to sign it) and was present when the inquest jury returned its unexpected verdict. He was once more free to go; this time he stayed overnight at the Spread Eagle voluntarily before returning to the parsonage on the Friday morning.

Later that day he took flight for the second time, reaching Knutsford where he booked a room at a public house in King Street. However, he was spotted outside the pub by one of Lymm's deputy constables and brought back to the village. The next day the Leighs committed their crucial testimony to writing. Thornhill remained in local custody until Tuesday 16 January, when he was committed to the County Gaol at Chester Castle.

His trial took place at Cheshire's Spring Assizes on Friday 20 April 1798, presided over by the Chief Justice of Chester, James Adair. In view of the medical dichotomy surrounding the cause of Sarah Malone's death, the indictment encompassed both possibilities. It charged Thornhill with killing Sarah firstly by striking her about the head – 'with a certain hammer of the value of sixpence' – and, secondly, by throwing her into the mill pool and drowning her. And, for good measure, it contained a third option of murdering the woman by battering her *and* throwing her into the water. He was found guilty on the first count after a trial that lasted from 8am until 10 o'clock at night.

The following court extracts were drawn from the Revd Thurston's rediscovered notebook – not without some difficulty, it should be said, since the whole of the court's deliberations, all 14 hours of them, were written out as one continuous passage, 35-pages long and with an almost total lack of punctuation. Additional evidence provided by Pass, the gardener, and coachman Harrison was particularly interesting.

John Pass recalled an incident at the parsonage on the day after Sarah's disappearance, its significance only becoming apparent in the light of subsequent events. At around 11am he and Harrison were working together on the west side of the grounds, where the land sloped steeply from the rector's garden down into The Dingle, when Thornhill came over and said his master wanted to see him.

As the gardener headed towards the house he glanced back to see Thornhill standing beside the garden wall gazing reflectively at the water in the hollow below. It was the spot where he had bundled Sarah Malone's body into the mill stream. Pass claimed Thornhill was thus engrossed in his private thoughts for 'about 15 or 20 minutes'.

On the morning of Wednesday 10 January, just before the butler made his first break for freedom, Pass and Harrison noticed Thornhill's hat on a table in the kitchen. It lay crown downwards and, when Harrison pointed to a mark on the rim, Pass said it looked as if it had been made by a 'bloody finger'.

On the subject of the murder weapon – which was never found – Pass told the court that Thornhill owned a claw hammer. It was normally kept in the butler's pantry, but, he said, since the murder it could not be found. Its disappearance piled even more suspicion on to the doomed butler – though the prisoner himself seemed the only one in court not to recognise the seriousness of his situation.

The Thurston transcript related, 'This unfortunate man, it is supposed, entertained the erroneous opinion that because nobody saw him commit the murder he was sure to be acquitted.' Just before the foreman announced the jury's verdict, he was said to have expressed his confidence to a person sitting near him.

Asked whether he had anything to say in his own defence, Thornhill replied belligerently, 'I am innocent and know nothing at all of the matter.' Even when the judge recited the 'awful sentence of death', a 'violent perspiration was the only alteration which appeared in him'.

His bravado deserted him once he had been returned to the castle cells below the courtroom – though the streak of arrogance that had sustained him in his more despairing moments since the murder survived to the end.

The *Chester Chronicle* of 27 April reported, 'After his condemnation, he became very penitent, but refused to confess to any person that he actually committed the murder, saying "he had already confessed to his Maker and would confess to no mortal."' It was a pledge he broke only in the final moments of his life, as he stood with the executioner's rope suspended from the scaffold above his head and death lurking beneath his feet.

The date was Monday 23 April, the time 1.30pm, the place Boughton. By now the old turned-off-the-ladder technique was no longer in fashion – Thornhill was hanged from the back of the cart that carried him to the 'fatal tree'. With the cart positioned underneath the scaffold and the noose tightened around his neck, the horse was whipped up and driven off, leaving the debonair butler dangling inelegantly in mid-air.

Moments before, the Revd Thurston's notebook recorded, Thornhill, who travelled all the way with a handkerchief covering his face, had finally confessed his guilt. 'He threw his head on the Ordinary's shoulder and said, "My good sire, there was too much reason for what my mistress said and for my behaviour to her." The minister said, "Then you confess to having committed the crime?" "Ah", replied he, deeply sighing, "'tis too true, but I hope God will forgive me". He was then exhorted to inform the multitude of it, but did not.'

The case had stirred up tremendous public interest, in great part due to the awfulness of the crime. But there were other enticing ingredients that went into making this something of a *cause célèbre*.

Take, for example, the contrasting backgrounds of the two main characters: the victim, a poor, deserted woman who was forced to take in washing to make ends meet, and her

The Butler and the Washerwoman

killer, a much younger man whose station in life gave him entrée into the upper strata of county society and who, doubtless, considered himself her social superior. Here, too, were those eternally fascinating elements of romance and sexual intrigue, in the ill-starred love affair between the butler and the upstairs maid, in the fatal attraction of the 'other woman' and the secret moment of passion that had such disastrous consequences for all three of them.

And at the very heart of the tragedy – as barbaric as the murder of Sarah Malone yet largely disregarded by history – the death of the baby, almost full term, who also perished in Lymm Mill's icy pool on that winter's night in 1798, the forgotten victim John Thornhill fathered with careless abandon and just as casually destroyed.

So, the butler did it…and no one reading the case file today could possibly doubt that. But how much can the dry bones of these timeworn and tattered court papers tell us about the real flesh-and-blood human being who was John Thornhill? We behold the manservant, but what of the man?

He has been described as 'not too bright' – and anyone pondering how he ever believed he could get away with murder, when he had the most obvious motive, might well come to that conclusion. While he had the nous to recognise that his best hope of an acquittal lay in the fact that no one had seen him commit the crime, such was his conceit that he couldn't prevent himself from boasting as much to two unimpeachable witnesses. Thornhill was not unintelligent, however – no employer mindful of his social standing would have given him such a high-profile place in the household had he not had a certain aptitude and presence.

And Thornhill was undoubtedly good at his job. His references were impeccable and his list of previous employers formidable. He also seems to have been popular with the other servants. Moving to Lymm was another step up the ladder of success…and it could well be here, in his impressive curriculum vitae, wherein lies the answer to the question of what turned the apparently mild-mannered butler into a cold-hearted killer.

John Thornhill, it is obvious, was an ambitious man. In his behaviour immediately before and after the murder, and in his dogged refusal to acknowledge his guilt until the very end, he demonstrated a single-mindedness that he would have needed to progress in his chosen profession, where the required standards were high and the tolerance level low. Having landed the job at the parsonage, he no doubt believed he would go on to better things: butler, perhaps, to one of the rich and powerful county families – a move, literally, to the top table of society, with all the rewards and status that would bring. He was not, therefore, going to allow one moment of sexual weakness destroy that dream.

However, the same obsessive, self-serving zeal that convinced him to see murder as his salvation also blinded him to the reality that once Sarah's body was discovered, and the secret of his illicit child was out, there was only ever going to be one outcome.

After Sarah and her baby, and then Thornhill himself, the ripples from the mill-pool Murder eventually spread out to claim a fourth victim. On 17 September 1798, five months after John Thornhill's execution closed the file on the case, the Revd Leigh died in his sleep, aged 66. Though in his later years he was in poor health, it was the view among his parishioners that the trauma and personal anguish he suffered as a result of the crime had hastened his death. He was interred in a place of honour in St Mary's

Church, where a plaque in the south aisle of the nave commemorates his 'enlightened example' and his 'charity and general benevolence' during his 40 years as rector.

The grave of Sarah Malone lies not far away, on the north side of the churchyard and just a few hundred yards from the murder scene. Her headstone, laid flat in a modern landscaping scheme, bears a rather more modest inscription, noting her burial on 12 January 1798 and the names of five others who followed her into the family plot.

Of the parsonage, where our story began and where much of the action took place, nothing now remains. Early in the 19th century it assumed the slightly grander sounding name of The Rectory, and in the 1920s, when a new rectory was established alongside the church (in what is now the Church Green Hotel), it became a private house. Soon afterwards, greatly enlarged by the addition of a ballroom and restaurant, the old Georgian parsonage took on a new life as the Dingle Hotel.

The building was eventually demolished in 1997 to make way for an exclusive housing development. Executive-style homes, with their carefully-tended lawns and neatly-ordered gardens, now overlook the wilder sweep of The Dingle and the site of the bloodiest murder in Lymm's history.

*　　*　　*

John Thornhill was hanged from a relatively-new scaffold on the opposite side of the Boughton road from Gallows Hill, where Cheshire's condemned felons had been executed for centuries. It was erected in 1791 but, in contrast to its venerable predecessor, it remained in use for only 10 years. One of the last two people to die on the old gallows was John Dean, who killed his wife in a fit of drunken rage. As with Thornhill, the squalid murder that occurred in the overcrowded heart of Stockport in the summer of 1790 also resulted in the slaughter of an innocent...

The old mill pool as it looks today, showing (right) the footpath along which Sarah Malone walked to her death on that dark and stormy winter's night. (Photograph by the author.)

Chapter Four

'Damn thy soul...aren't thou dead yet!'

Toccay it's little more than an alleyway, a narrow passage squeezed between the tall gables, backyard parking lots and rear exits of an untidy clutter of offices, shops and other assorted small business properties. In a street given over almost entirely to commercial occupation, the latest arrival, a corner block of smart new housing association units – a lean shoot of urban regeneration in a barren landscape – is now its only sign of residential life. Yet, for over 100 years, Watson Square in Stockport was a bustling thoroughfare of tenements and terrace cottages, its short, cobbled slope hemmed in on both sides by a huddle of closely-packed dwellings that, for their time, were also something of a monument to modern living.

When they were built, in the third quarter of the 18th century, Watson Square's two-up-two-downs were regarded as superior working-class homes. Among the first to be erected in the town, they were part of the initial phase of a massive housing programme that would gather momentum in the closing decades of the century, mainly in response to the influx of labour moving into the town to work in the budding cotton mills. In 1780 the population of Stockport was about 5,000; 20 years later it had mushroomed to around 15,000, making it Cheshire's largest town.

The most concentrated areas of development were on either side of Hillgate – the main route into the town from the south until Wellington Road was opened in 1826 – from where the new streets quickly spread outwards in gridiron profusion. Gradually, the whole area, now largely depopulated, became a teeming mass of humanity.

Watson Square, off Middle Hillgate – a cul-de-sac until Hopes Carr was constructed at its eastern end – was in the vanguard of Stockport's urban explosion...and, coincidentally, the scene of violent eruptions, 40-odd years apart, that sent two of its residents to the gallows.

The homes there were not much more than 20 years old – though many were seriously overcrowded and already slums – when mother-of-four Elizabeth (Betty) Dean was beaten to death in her living room in the early summer of 1790. She had been in the latter stages of pregnancy, and the child she was carrying also died as a result of the attack. Unbelievably, it was her husband – and the child's father – who did the doubly-foul deed as the couple's teenaged son pleaded in vain for his mother's life. Appropriately, John Dean was strung up twice for his crime: after his execution his caged corpse was hung on a gibbet on the outskirts of the town, a human scarecrow set to frighten off birds of a similarly wicked feather.

Nearly half-a-century later the continuing expansion of the cotton industry, by then supporting three-quarters of the population of Stockport and the surrounding areas, had turned the neighbourhood into a warren of cramped terraces and suffocating courts. Despite economic progress, living conditions, if not downright squalid, were invariably insanitary and unhealthy. And crime flourished: Cheshire's biggest boom town was also top of the county league table for lawlessness.

This was Stringers Yard, Stockport, but it could just as easily have been Watson Square, where the Dean family lived in similarly overcrowded conditions in one of the typical two-up two-downs that were crammed into narrow streets and suffocating courts during the town's late 18th-century/early 19th-century population explosion. (By permission of Stockport Heritage Library.)

Friction between the local population and the predominantly-Irish immigrant workers, and dissension among the Irish themselves – invariably inflamed by the drink that flowed from the multitude of local pubs and beer shops – frequently led to violence. Street fights were commonplace, and in Watson Square in the Autumn of 1833, in an affray involving at least 10 young men, one of the combatants had his neck so badly slashed with a reaping hook that for a time it looked as if this unremarkable little street would have a second murder on its record.

During a running brawl that spilled into the street late one Sunday night in September, Thomas Riley, a 20-year-old Irishman, attacked another young man with a sickle and almost decapitated him. The fight had begun outside the Old Admiral just around the corner in Middle Hillgate when, as Riley and four of his countrymen were leaving the pub, they clashed with another gang hanging around outside.

Against all expectations, the victim survived – by a stroke of good fortune the blade narrowly missed a vital artery. But nothing could save the life of Riley. He may have escaped a murder charge by an inch or so, but the mindless savagery of his crime – he was charged with 'cutting and maiming with intent to kill' – ensured he was hanged anyway.

Since the 1820s Stockport's Irish population had been growing steadily, as had the number of Irish workers employed in the town's cotton mills. This caused widespread resentment among the locals, who perceived the immigrants as depriving them of job opportunities. The ill-feeling led to periodic outbreaks of hostility, culminating in the infamous anti-Irish riot of June 1852, in which Irish homes were attacked and the town's two Roman Catholic churches ransacked, leaving 100 injured and one Irishman dead.

When John and Betty Dean moved into their two-storey, brick-built house at the bottom of Watson Square – it seems to have survived as a primarily-residential street until late in the 19th century but, after a steady decline, the last few houses were cleared in the 1960s – 'King' Cotton was still a princely heir apparent. Like many others before and after him, Dean, a cotton spinner who came originally from Stalybridge, was enticed into this expanding new sector of textile manufacturing by the prospect of steady work and high earnings.

Stockport's first cotton mills had been established in the late 1770s and, as the number of employers grew, many of them took over the former silk mills that had been the principal source of local employment for 40 years. It wasn't until the early 1790s, however, that the first major spurt of cotton factory building occurred, and by that time John Dean was in no position to benefit from the renewed prosperity it brought to the town.

The Dean family's lives were torn apart in the early hours of Sunday 20 June 1790. It's not known in which of the town's emergent mills John Dean was employed, but the previous day he had stopped work at noon, collected his wages and, after his tea-time meal, set out for an evening of serious drinking. It was his usual Saturday routine. He returned home around midnight and shortly afterwards he picked an argument with his wife and began beating her. Sadly, this was also a regular occurrence in the Dean household.

Up until Victorian times, wife beating was 'a fact of life in many working-class communities' says Clive Emsley in *Crime and Society in England 1750–1900*. And even on the rare occasions when such treatment resulted in death, he states, 'it was possible for a court to find mitigating circumstances'.

In the Deans' home in working-class Watson Square, however, John Dean's treatment of his wife Betty was about to go way beyond the bounds of mitigation. After the initial assault, in the couple's bedroom, his temper spiralled terrifyingly out of control and, in an alcohol-induced frenzy, he literally knocked the heavily-pregnant Betty from room to room, before a final hail of blows left her dying on the blood-saturated floor of the living room.

Dean, 39, punched and kicked his wife repeatedly about the head and body; according to local legend, he is supposed to have inflicted some of her injuries – even the fatal blows – with a heavy hearthbrush (although, as we shall see, there is some doubt about that). The poor woman's ordeal lasted for more than an hour; several times Dean paused to rest, exhausted by his exertions, before resuming his murderous onslaught.

When the row first flared, the couple's 14-year-old son Thomas tried to intervene and as he scuffled with his father they both went crashing down the stairs. Dean also turned on a female lodger who tried to calm him down, knocking her to the ground and threatening to kill her. Fearing for her life, she leapt from a first-floor window to escape the drink-crazed madman. She ran screaming down the street and eventually got help from a local constable, who rushed with her to the house.

Even after they arrived, along with several other people alerted by the commotion, Dean continued to strike his wife as she lay half-naked in front of the living room grate. He was heard to shout at her 'Damn thy soul, Bet, aren't thou dead yet?', or words to

Modern-day Watson Square. It's hard now to imagine the closely-packed terraces and tenements that teemed with life in former times. (Photograph by the author.)

that effect. Mrs Dean, who had been in her seventh month of pregnancy, was still alive at that stage – but only just. Despite prompt medical attention, she died less than an hour later. The surgeon who attended her was also unable to save her child.

Dean was eventually subdued, but it took four men to drag him the half-mile or so to the local lock-up on Mealhouse Brow. Known as 'The Dungeon', and situated below the old baronial courthouse, it contained five tiny cells hewn out of the sandstone hillside leading up to the market place. Dean is believed to have been the last person incarcerated there; The Dungeon was abandoned later that same year when work began on the New Bailey Prison in Melville Street.

At that time the old cell block was described as 'a very unhealthy and incommodious place for the confinement of any prisoners'. It was later incorporated into the sub-basement of No.8, Market Place. In the late 1990s, during an archaeological survey conducted as part of a major project to redevelop the site, an old blocked-off doorway, which once opened on to Mealhouse Brow, was removed and one of the cells – possibly the one that had held John Dean – was rediscovered. The narrow, arched chamber, roughly 12ft long and a little over 6ft high, contained a water spout bearing the date 1743.

A brief report of the murder appeared in the *Chester Courant* of 29 June 1790. Dean had by now been charged, but the *Courant*, operating under more liberal publishing laws than today, was moved to describe him as 'an inhuman Monster' and 'a man of infamous Character', who had 'frequently before, when in liquor, put her [his wife] in fear of her Life'.

In more measured tones, the paper said it believed there was a direct correlation between the proliferation of licensed premises and the rising tide of criminality. And it urged the county magistrates to consider 'the Necessity of still reducing further the Number of Pot-houses, the Encouragers of Idleness and Intoxication, from which Causes, in general, the Crimes which so much disgrace Humanity, at first proceed'.

Betty Dean's body was laid to rest in the graveyard of Stockport Parish Church on Tuesday 22 June, the day after her husband, heavily shackled to prevent his escape, had been escorted by coach to Chester Castle Gaol to stand trial for murder. Two months later, on Thursday 26 August 1790, the Summer Assizes began at Chester and the full story of her night of terror was recalled amid the mediaeval splendour of the castle's Great Hall. Also known as Hugh Lupus's Hall, and dating from the 13th century, the high open-raftered building, with its huge oak beams, stood on the east side of the castle's lower ward. It was the county's ancient seat of justice until it was replaced in the early years of the 19th century by Thomas Harrison's new Shire Hall (where the Crown Court sits today) in a major redevelopment of the castle site.

The jury was presented with an unassailable prosecution case: after all, at least four people had seen Dean striking his wife at various times during her hour-long ordeal. But the most devastating testimony was provided by young Thomas Dean. In his written statement, originally sworn before coroner John Hollins at the inquest into Mrs Dean's death at Stockport on 21 June, the boy told of his father's vicious temper when in drink, of his history of violence towards his wife and of the terrible chain of events Thomas was powerless to prevent the night his mother died. It was in every sense a blow-by-blow account that was all the more shocking for the matter-of-fact language in which the coroner's clerk had transcribed it.

Thomas's deposition, one of five remaining in the assize file in the National Archives, began, 'As long as he can remember his father has followed the practice of beating his mother when drunk, or intoxicated with liquor, which has been frequently the case.' Thomas said he could not remember his father hitting his mother when he was sober but that 'when anything she did displeased him when sober, he got drunk and beat her for it'.

He continued, 'On Saturday evening...he and the small children [a brother and two sisters] in a while went to bed in the same room in which his parents usually lay. He fell asleep for several hours but was awakened by the noise of his father beating his mother. A candle burned in the room and his mother and father stood near their bed, and he was beating her as hard as he could with both his hands.'

Thomas begged his father to stop and began to get out of bed; as he pushed back the covers the candle blew out and Dean went downstairs to relight it. Returning to the bedroom, issuing threats and curses, Dean momentarily forgot his quarrel with his wife and directed his anger towards his elder son. He dragged him out of the bedroom and on to the landing. The next thing the pair were tumbling down the stairs.

Mrs Dean, fearing the fall might have killed the boy, called out to Mary Bell, a lodger who shared an adjoining bedroom with her elderly parents. When she tried to placate Dean, he knocked her to the ground and then chased after her as she fled back upstairs. She managed to lock the bedroom door behind her but Dean was now so enraged that she was terrified he might break the door down. So she threw open the window and jumped down into the street below, a drop of about 12 feet.

By now Betty had gone downstairs into the 'house place' (living room) and was sitting with her back against a cupboard, clad only in her 'shift' (chemise). Dean went for her again. Thomas's deposition went on: '[He] began beating her again with both hands on her head and body as hard as he could. She called out to him not to kill her, but he continued cursing and beating her.'

When his mother broke free and ran into the back kitchen, his father followed her. Thomas stated, '[He] grabbed her by the hair and threw her to the floor and kicked her

When an old doorway on Mealhouse Brow was opened up during an archaeological survey in the late 1990s, 'The Dungeon', Stockport's mediaeval lock-up, was rediscovered, revealing (above) one of the cells – possibly the one that had held wife-murderer John Dean in 1790. (Photographs courtesy of Manchester University Archaeological Unit.)

on the back and head and hit her across the face with his hands. He then appeared tired and set himself down, cursing her, and as soon as he had rested himself a little he got up again, went to her and kicked her very violently.'

Dean repeated this several times – hitting her, then resting, then resuming the assault, like a cat tormenting a wounded bird. During one of his rest breaks he ordered his son to help his mother to her feet, but the lad was unable to get her to sit up, let alone stand. Dean dragged her by the hair back into the living room, where he continued beating and kicking her as she lay writhing on the floor. 'Several times,' Thomas said, 'he went back several yards and took a run at her and kicked her with even greater violence.'

Mrs Dean was by now lying crumpled up beside the fire. Then, said Thomas, someone yanked open a window shutter. It was one of the town constables, Thomas Thorniley. He, Mary Bell and several neighbours had gathered at the window and, as they strained to see what was going on inside the house, Dean once again laid into his wife. It was only when Mary Bell's father, William, came downstairs and unlocked the front door to let the constable in that Dean ended his orgy of violence.

Betty lay dying at his feet, but even then he seemed unable to grasp the magnitude of his actions. Thomas's statement concluded pathetically, '[His] father was told he had killed his mother…but his father mocked and laughed at them and said she was not killed, and he hit her upon the shoulder and bid her speak, but she was not able.'

Mary Bell told the court that it was about 1am when she became aware of a disturbance in the Deans' bedroom. She was sat up in bed and her mother and father were asleep nearby. She said she had heard Dean come in a little earlier and, from the manner in which he at first spoke to his wife, she had not thought him to be drunk. Then he started cursing Betty and calling her a whore, and all hell broke loose.

She said she then heard a noise 'as if he had pulled [Betty] upon the floor', followed by a cry from young Thomas. Leaving her room to investigate, she heard Dean 'swear he would murder the deceased', and she saw him and his son fall down the stairs.

'Damn thy soul...aren't thou dead yet!'

In her deposition, which also originated from the inquest, she said that when she tried to pacify Dean he 'struck her in the face, called her a whore and swore he would murder her, too'.

She also saw him 'beat and abuse the deceased very much' after she had returned to the house with Constable Thorniley.

Mary felt obliged to explain that her father had not got involved earlier because he was drunk and had only awoken when he heard the rumpus in the street below. Her mother, 'being very deaf', had slept through the whole noisy episode.

Thorniley said that after arriving at Dean's house and finding the door 'fast' (locked), he 'heard a noise like the sound of blows given by the hand'. A baker by trade, he seems to have been one of two constables serving the township of Stockport at this time. Appointed by the lord of the manor, constables were unpaid part-timers and usually served for a year, though some extended their period of duty by accepting payment to deputise for the official nominee.

His statement went on: 'He threw a shutter to the house window [off] its hinges, on which he saw John Dean sitting with his back against the window in his shirt and the deceased lying before him on the floor. The first thing he heard John Dean say, that he could understand, was "God almighty, damn her, I'll kill her" – then he struck her several times.' When Dean became aware of Thorniley at the window, he shouted at the constable, 'What do you want? You have no business here! Go about your business!'

After William Bell had finally stirred from his boozy slumber and gone downstairs to let the officer in, Thorniley went into the living room to find Betty Dean 'excessive bloody' and 'seemingly in a dying state'. She was lying in an undignified heap on the floor, the hem of her shift having ridden up around her waist as she slithered to the ground.

In an unexpected show of concern, Dean's final act before being dragged off to The Dungeon was to pull the garment down to 'hide her nakedness', said Thorniley.

Betty was immediately put to bed and surgeon Robert Clarke was summoned, but he told the coroner she was already 'in the agonies of death' when he arrived, and he could do nothing for her. He also tried in vain to save her unborn child by performing a caesarean section on her lifeless body. The child, he said, appeared to be naturally healthy, and from his postmortem examination he concluded that it had been killed by a blow to the abdomen.

Mrs Dean, he reported, had suffered a perforated liver and a branch of her auxiliary artery had also been ruptured, as had 'very many small blood vessels in different parts of the body'. There was extensive bleeding under the skin of the skull and 'particularly under that part of the skull on which there appeared to be a violent blow'. Her nose was broken and her whole body was 'bruised in a violent manner all over'.

The injuries, he had no doubt, caused Betty Dean's death, but he hazarded no opinion as to which were the most serious or how they might have been inflicted. The reports of Dean's trial that appeared in the two Chester papers (the only news journals published in the county at the time) claimed he had bludgeoned his wife with, alternatively, a handbrush or a hearthbrush, though both were prefaced with the words 'It appeared [that]', suggesting the content was not entirely based on first-hand reporting of the court proceedings.

Cheshire's Execution Files

In describing the scene in the Deans' living room when the constable and the others entered the house, the *Chester Chronicle* (3 September) had this to say: '[They] beheld the unfortunate woman lying stretch'd on the floor, one of her legs under the grate, her body uncover'd [*sic*] by any thing but the remains of a shift, and presenting a picture of savage barbarity indescribably shocking! Indeed, her body appeared to be one general wound! The monster, fatigued with the horrid work, sat in a chair near her, his hands, waistcoat, breeches, stockings and shoes nearly cover'd with the purple marks of his ferocity; the instrument of his cruelty (a handbrush) lying at his feet.'

The following week the *Chester Courant* (7 September) told its readers, 'It appeared on his Trial that he had perpetrated the horrid Deed in the most deliberate Manner – that without any Provocation given by the Deceased, he beat her with a Hearth brush, as long as he could stand, and then sat down and exercised his Barbarities, until he had beat out all her Fore-teeth (several of which were found in Different parts of the Room), cut her upper Lip in the most shocking Manner, broke all the internal bones of her Nose, and gave her a violent Wound on the temporal Artery.'

In the paper's original report of the murder, however, there had been no mention of a weapon, nor was there in the formal indictment against Dean. This charged that the defendant 'did make an assault...with his hands and feet...did cast and throw the said Betty Dean down unto and upon the ground with great force and violence...did strike, beat and kick [her] with his hands and feet upon the head, breast, back, belly, sides and other parts of the body...giving [her] several mortal strokes, wounds and bruises...from which she died.'

Likewise, the official record of the inquest jury's verdict, upon which Dean was committed for trial, and which has also survived, spoke only of him kicking and punching his wife.

The only reference to a bloodstained brush in the whole of the case file appears in a witness statement made two months after the murder and is resolutely non-committal. The statement, dated 21 August 1790, was sworn before the Revd Charles Prescot, rector of Stockport and a local magistrate, by William Hull. Hull, a weaver, had been walking down Watson Square on his way to his home in nearby Canal Street some time between 1 and 2 o'clock in the morning when he heard a woman 'crying murder' in the Deans' house. He tried the door, but it was locked.

He had gone in search of Constable Thorniley, but by the time he found out where he lived the officer was already on his way to Watson Square. Hull returned to the Dean house just as Thorniley was entering, and he followed him in. Hull deposed, '[He] saw John Dean violently kick his wife, who was lying naked to her shift on the floor, two or three times, and heard him say to her "Damn thy soul, Bet, thou art not dead yet, by God."' (In the *Chester Chronicle* trial report this came out as 'Damn thy soul, Bet, aren't thou dead yet!' and is the version quoted in most retellings of the story.)

We then come to the pivotal moment in Hull's testimony. He observed, 'A large hand-brush, about half-a-yard long, was lying at John Dean's feet.' It was a bald statement of fact: Hull expressed no opinion on the matter and, in his next sentence, moved swiftly on to tell of Dean's arrest and how he had helped the constable lock up his prisoner in The Dungeon.

'Damn thy soul...aren't thou dead yet!'

He did expand slightly on the subject at the end of his deposition, probably prompted by his JP inquisitor. But he would only add, 'The brush mentioned above was covered in blood from one end to the other and a great quantity of blood was on the floor. John Dean's right hand and arm up to the elbow were also covered with blood.'

What Hull seems to have taken great care *not* to say was that Dean struck his wife with the brush. He may have implied it, but he did not say it because he did not see it happen, nor did any of the other people who saw Dean assault his wife – Thomas Dean, Mary Bell and Thomas Thorniley. These three, plus the surgeon Robert Clarke, were the only witnesses named in the press reports yet, in their initial depositions at least, none so much as hinted at there being a weapon involved in the murder. Had this been the case, one would certainly have expected it to figure in the evidence of Thomas Dean, who was able to recall in painful detail every outpouring of his father's fury that night.

The implement, which would have been kept by the fireside, could easily have become bloodstained after coming into contact with the battered and bleeding Betty when she was hurled against the grate – as Hull testified, there was a large amount of her blood splashed about the living room floor by the time Dean had finished with her. And it was hardly surprising that Dean's right hand and forearm were covered in blood after the barrage of punches he had landed on Betty's mangled face and head.

If the news reports are to be believed, however, we can only surmise that the brush assumed a more sinister significance as the trial progressed and witnesses were cross-examined.

The only other explanation is that the *Chronicle* and *Courant* got it wrong. Like all provincial newspapers in the 18th century they were small-scale operations; they would not have had reporters, as we recognise them today, sat in court for days on end covering the assizes. It is almost certain that the accounts of Dean's trial were compiled at least in part from material obtained second hand, from court sources or from the case papers later (that the *Chronicle* was able to gain access to witness statements can be seen from the case of Joseph Allen described in chapter seven, while it is also clear from some of the crime broadsides published by its competitor that the court officials were prepared to extend the same level of co-operation to the *Courant*).

Also, the papers relied on 'freelance' correspondents and other outside contributors much more heavily than they do now – and routinely lifted stories from other newspapers. And, despite the sometimes fierce rivalry that existed between the two Chester weeklies, their assize court reports often betrayed the presence of the same hand. Could it have been that a resourceful 'stringer' with an eye for a good story seized on William Hull's cautiously-worded statement and put a rather more sensational construction on his mention of a blood-stained hearthbrush?

There is one further tiny clue to the mystery in the case files. It is contained in an inventory of John Dean's goods and chattels, attached to the report of the inquest findings. Also dated 21 June 1790, it is a comprehensive room-by-room listing of his possessions, the total value of which was put at £12 0s 5½d (which today would amount to well over £1,000). The report itself stated that the said goods and chattels were 'contained in the inventory of this Inquisition annexed' – then the following words were inserted as an afterthought – 'and in the possession of the constables of Stockport'.

The kind of hoop-iron cage in which the body of John Dean was suspended from a roadside gibbet on Stockport Moor following his execution for murder. It was a gruesome practice that was intended as both a dire public warning and a means of denying the victim a grave. (From the author's collection.)

Under the heading 'In the house place', the inventory noted fire irons, including tongs, a poker and a shovel – but no hearthbrush. Was this one of the things 'in the possession of the constables of Stockport'...taken away, perhaps, to be marked 'Exhibit A' in readiness for the trial?

Without a full transcript of the court hearing, we will never know the whole truth. But on the evidence of the official records alone, the belief that John Dean killed his wife with a fireside brush is without substance.

As expected, the outcome of Dean's trial was a foregone conclusion. He was convicted and sentenced to death and, said the *Chester Chronicle*, 'the better to perpetuate his ignominy, and render the example more permanent, the court afterwards ordered him to be hung in chains'.

It was the paper's conviction that 'seldom has the page of humanity been stained with a more horrible and ferocious murder'.

Throughout the trial, the *Chester Courant* recounted, Dean 'seemed unconcerned and when called on for his defence, replied he was quite innocent, knew nothing of the Matter, and left himself entirely to the Mercy of his Lordship'. The paper added, 'When Sentence was passed on him he did not make that Impression which naturally might be expected, for even then he persisted in his Innocence.'

Dean's execution was fixed for Thursday 2 September. After being handed over to Chester's city sheriffs outside the castle gates, he was taken in a cart to Boughton. The following day the *Chronicle* commented, 'The behaviour of Dean at the fatal tree was marked by every appearance of contrition; tho' at intervals his countenance betray'd those strong emotions of dread and horror inseparable from a departing spirit charged with so heavy an accusation. He acknowledged the commission of the fact; but solemnly denied having harbour'd the least intention of taking her life; ascribing it to the dangerous effects of drunkenness and passion.'

One dictionary definition of the latter is 'an outburst of anger', which was undeniably the immediate cause of Betty Dean's cruel death and the meaning the *Chronicle* report probably intended to convey. But the word also translates as 'intense sexual love', another powerful emotion. And it was this, it has been claimed, that was the real motivation for the murder – that it was not simply the result of a lethal combination of an evil-tempered husband maddened by drink and a marital row that got out of hand, but that there was another dangerous element in the equation...the all-too-familiar 'other woman'.

Dean himself is supposed to have admitted as much in a confession he was alleged to have made just before he died and which was printed as an execution broadside. The existence of the broadside (as has been noted before, this 'gallows literature' has to be viewed with circumspection) was revealed in an article by local historian James Hooley in the summer 1988 edition of the *Stockport Heritage Magazine*.

He quoted Dean as saying, 'I declare publicly to all the world that I have brought upon me this shameful end by following bad women. I had tarried late that night in company with one at Stockport, and getting upset in my mind came home and committed the horrid crime for which I am now just going to suffer.' Unfortunately, despite numerous inquiries, I have been unable to locate a copy of this document.

As Hillgate was the most popular beat of Stockport's streetwalkers, and its numerous pubs their main source of clients (then and throughout the next century as well, it seems), it is likely that Dean would have been acquainted with the local prostitutes. That he availed himself of their services – and one in particular – was affirmed by Didsbury historian Fletcher Moss, who seems to have been the first to put a name to the 'lady' in question.

In his book *Folklore – Old Customs and Tales of My Neighbours*, published in 1898, he identified her as 'Sal Fogg, a lady of easy virtue who lived at Cheadle'. He even accused her of inciting Dean to commit the murder. But, as with the missing 'confession' broadside, this frustratingly inadequate reference appears to be the only source of the claims.

The execution over, the scene shifted the 40-odd miles to Stockport, to another scaffold and another grisly show for the public's delectation. This time the vulgar street theatre was given an added touch of the macabre. As the cart carrying Dean's body approached the outskirts of the town, the county high sheriff ordered the cage containing the corpse to be hooked up to the gibbet, which was then hauled upright in the vehicle for maximum effect.

The gesture, no doubt appreciated by the crowd of spectators who were afforded an unrestricted view of the notorious murderer's iron-clad remains, was also applauded by the *Chester Chronicle*. 'If example is the object of punishment,' the paper commented, 'the conduct of the officers to whose care the body of Dean...was committed, deserves commendation.'

With Dean's body swinging grotesquely from the wooden gibbet, the procession wound its way from Brinksway via Hillgate to Stockport Great Moor – 'attended by more than fifty horsemen, with a prodigious concourse [on] foot', as the *Chronicle* recorded. It finally came to a halt on the edge of Black Lake, which was situated at the southern end of this vast wilderness in an area known as the Black Moor. The lake, which derived its name from the colour of the bog in which it was formed, was the largest of several sheets of water then dotted about the moor (which has now totally disappeared beneath suburban Stockport).

The gibbet, with its appropriately black-shrouded occupant, was erected at a spot close to modern Cherry Tree Lane, its prominent location chosen to post an unmissable warning signal to travellers entering the town along its southern approach.

Shortly afterwards a rumour spread that the gibbet had been removed and the corpse spirited away in the dead of night. But it proved to be a hoax. In fact, Dean seems to have 'hung around' for some time, judging by the words of local historian Henry Heginbotham, who referred briefly to Betty Dean's murder in his monumental two-volume history of the town, *Stockport: Ancient and Modern*, published in 1892.

Heginbotham, after repeating the line that she was beaten to death 'with a heavy hand-brush', maintained that Dean's body 'remained suspended on the gibbet until his bones had been picked clean by the birds'. He wrote, 'For several years passers-by avoided the spot, until at length the neighbours cut down and burnt the poles, buried the bones, and sold the irons to a neighbouring blacksmith!'

Some remnants of the iron 'suit' – and of the person for whom it was fitted out – may have been left behind, however, for pieces of hand-made chain, with what appeared to be human bone fragments attached to them, were dug up in the early 1980s in the garden of a cottage that was reputed to have stood on the gibbet site at the junction of Cherry Tree Lane and Castle Farm Lane. No expert assessment of the unearthed artefacts appears to have been carried out, however, and their fate is unknown.

From the body of folklore that has grown up around the story of John Dean and the Black Lake gibbet, one final anecdote is drawn. It comes courtesy of Fletcher Moss, who, in *Old Customs and Tales*, wrote, 'An old man says that his grandfather often told him how he, when a boy, had gone to see the murderer's body on the gibbet and thrown a stone at it. The results of the stone-throwing were rather startling, plainly showing that flies were no respecters of persons.'

* * *

The other Watson Square resident to be hanged at Chester was convicted in the spring of 1834, at what would become known as the 'Bloody Assize' due to the extreme violence reflected in the calendar, which involved everything from minor assaults to murder, and from stabbing and shooting to rape, aggravated burglary and grievous bodily harm. When it was over five men were put to death in the space of 13 days. It was a record for a single assize and provided a fitting climax to the extraordinary career of hangman Samuel Burrows. In his 24 years in office he was dogged by controversy and criticism, and even in death he could not escape the bitterness and recriminations...

Chapter Five

Memoirs of an Uncommon Hangman

On his deathbed Samuel Burrows looked back on his 24 years as a hangman with unabashed pride. To his 53 victims, he insisted, he had shown only kindness and courtesy. In return, he said, every one of them, in responding to the executioner's traditional parting request, had been prepared, at the end, to offer him the hand of forgiveness.

In between quoting from the scriptures and reciting the Lord's Prayer, he talked passionately about his life and work, saying, 'I know I have many enemies and when they rebuked me I laughed at them, for it was all folly, for I solemnly declare I never injured [wronged] any person in my life, but was always willing to advise them for their reformation who were straying from the paths of innocence and virtue. I never sent a poor person from my door, without relieving [*sic*], which is well known to them that applied in such cases, which I trust will be before me in heaven.'

He added, 'I am innocent of everything alleged to my charge respecting the unfortunate creatures, for they made their peace with me either before or on the drop, considering themselves no longer creatures of this world, it [being] well known that the sentence of the law must take its course.'

The words are from a contemporary broadside entitled 'The Conversion and Death of Samuel Burrows'. Printed privately, it includes what purports to be the record of an interview that took place on Monday 19 October 1835, the day before he died. The anonymous chronicler stated, 'It appears, according to his testimony while confined to his bed [that], during the last three months, he has been subject to the liver complaint, and was in great pain, which he bore with extreme fortitude, and paid every attention to his religious duties, imploring for mercy to his Redeemer, who desireth not the death of a sinner.

THE CONVERSION AND DEATH OF SAMUEL BURROWS.

Samuel Burrows is no more, he ended his career in the 63rd year of his age, at his residence, near Gorse Stacks, Chester, on the 20th October, 1835. It appears according to his testimony while confined to his bed during the last three months, he has been subject to the liver complaint, and was in great pain, which he bore with extreme fortitude, and paid every attention to his religious duties, imploring for mercy to his Redeemer, who desireth not the death of a sinner. He experienced his kindness to the unfortunate individuals 53 in number when on the scaffold in different places; he could not refrain trusting in his mercy, and we are happy to announce that the Bible and Prayer-book were his constant study, and gave up all worldly thoughts, and when he became unable to read, he was thankful to any person who rendered him scriptural advice, last week he was visited by the Rev. W. Clarke, of little St. John's, the excellent discourses from different passages of the scriptures took the the greatest impression on his mind and he joined in prayer during the whole of the ceremony. On Monday he said I know I have many enemies and when they rebuked me I laughed at them, for it was all folly, for I solemnly declare I never injured any person in my life but was always willing to advise them for their reformation, who were straying from the paths of innocence and virtue, I never sent a poor person from my door, without relieving, which is well known to them that applied in such cases, which I trust will be before me in heaven, I am innocent of every thing alledged to my charge respecting the unfortunate creatures, for they made their peace with me either before or on the drop, considering themselves no longer creatures of this world, it was well known the sentence of the law must take its course. He said many is desirous of taking the job, but thank God I am done, he then turned on his backin the bed, and lifting up his hands to heaven, he repeated the Lord's Prayer, and in conclusion with an audible voice for thine is the kingdom, the power and the glory, for ever and ever, Amen : exclaiming I die in peace with all mankind. On being questioned respecting his son Charles, he said he was a bad lad, and would not keep from evil company, he might be here to see the last of me, but he volunteered to go abroad from the Hulks, and if he remained he would get off for about four years, for all that was against him was stealing a pair of stockings, but I was the means of sending him off, for I could not screen such evils, for it would be the greatest injustice to mankind.

Henry his eldest son enlisted in Lord Combermere's Troops and died in the East Indies. Mary, the wife of Samuel died last March, of a decline, and he has made an assignment of his effects in the club, being 35 years a member, to his nephew. He was born at Haverton Moor, in the parish of Acton, near Nantwich, on his county, 28th June, 1772. He was 24 years in office, and executed 53 individuals.

Printed for W. Byrne, No. 169, Handbridge, Chester.

A privately-printed broadside recording the death-bed interview with Samuel Burrows, executioner extraordinaire, who hanged 53 criminals in his 24 years as Chester's Common Hangman. (By permission of CCALS.)

'He experienced his kindness [*sic*] to the unfortunate individuals, 53 in number, when on the scaffold in different places; he could not refrain [from] trusting in His mercy, and we are happy to announce that the Bible and Prayer-book were his constant study, and [he] gave up all worldly thoughts and when he became unable to read, he was thankful to any person who rendered him scriptural advice.'

As will have become apparent already, the text is a little incoherent in places; but, in the course of the interview, Burrows appears to have made the surprising admission that, such was his commitment to the rule of law and the pursuit of justice, he had even been prepared to 'shop' his own son, Charles, for theft. Sam was quoted as saying, 'He was a bad lad and would not keep from evil company.'

By his account, it would appear that the young man wound up in trouble with the law for stealing a pair of stockings (despite a lengthy search, I have been unable to turn up any details of his trial locally, though he may well have been dealt with by a court outside Cheshire, of course). Convicted and sentenced to seven years' transportation, he was sent to the hulks – the old abandoned and unseaworthy troop ships and men-o'-war moored in the River Thames and at the south coast naval ports, which had been converted into floating prisons when the outbreak of the War of Independence in 1775 brought a halt to transportation to America. Pressed into service as a stop-gap measure to hold convicts bound for the new penal settlements of New South Wales, Van Diemen's Land and Western Australia, they were to remain in 'temporary' use as both staging areas for transportees and places of imprisonment for the next 80 years.

In the same boat as Burrows were men who had committed crimes for which the death penalty could still be imposed, but who had been offered an alternative...a stark choice between execution and banishment 'beyond the seas' for the rest of their natural lives. Like him, though, most of them would have been serving sentences of seven or 14 years, for offences which they might once have been hanged but which, during the 1820s and 1830s, were reclassified in increasing numbers as 'transportable'.

For all of them, life aboard the hulks was the same brutalising round. Forced by day into hard labour, toiling in heavy irons in the dockyards or on some other public works project, they spent their nights crammed together in dark, dank and disease-ridden conditions, in which only cruelty and corruption thrived. Many ordered for transportation never reached their destinations – during the Napoleonic Wars period, for instance, there weren't the ships available to take them – and served their entire sentences on the hulks. At the best of times, convicts often had to wait months, even years, before embarking on the four-month voyage to the other side of the world.

Confronted by the prospect of an indefinite, unhealthy existence aboard the hulks, some of the minimum-term transportees – those from particularly-deprived backgrounds,

A prison hulk at Deptford about 1826. It was to one of these floating gaols, old abandoned warships pressed into service during the transportation crisis, that Samuel Burrows's son Charles was sent following his theft conviction. Engraving by George Cooke (1781–1834). (nla.pic-an9058437. National Library of Australia.)

perhaps, or more rootless types similarly disaffected with their homeland – would make it known they were willing to 'go abroad' sooner rather than later (there would doubtless be others equally content to give up their places in the queue). They saw, in the mysterious continent in the farthest-flung corner of the empire, the chance to make a better life for themselves once their servitude was over. For they knew that after four years' good conduct in the colonies they would become eligible for a 'ticket-of-leave'. This freed them from bondage and, although they had to remain in Australia until their sentences expired, allowed them to sell their labour and so gain a stake in the country's developing economy.

Charles Burrows may have opted for such a course. It would certainly explain his father's reported comments in the next passage of the broadside. In it, Sam regretted that his son would not be home 'to see the last of him', adding, '[But] he volunteered to go abroad from the Hulks, and if he remained he would get off for about four years, for all that was against him was stealing a pair of stockings.'

It was here that Sam – who had apparently become so concerned about Charles's wayward behaviour that he had decided drastic action was called for if he was to deter his son from a life of crime – intimated that he had either turned the boy in for the stockings' theft or, at least, persuaded him to give himself up. For he now confessed, 'I was the means of sending him off, for I could not screen such evils, for it would be the greatest injustice to mankind.'

If all this made Burrows sound the model of correctitude and restraint, even piety, the reality was quite different. Raised in the tough environment of a rural working-class home, he was a rough-and-ready fellow who first worked as a butcher and then, following spells as a domestic servant and a member of the press gang, became a catcher of rats and moles. It is open to speculation as to whether the kind of work he did – slaughtering and hacking-up livestock, exterminating vermin and dragooning men into military service – coarsened his life, or whether his natural disposition made him especially suited to those particular jobs.

When, as hangman, he first came to the public's attention, it was apparent that his behaviour, both on the scaffold and off it, depended on how much he had had to drink. But, again, the records do not show whether he was a hard drinker to begin with or whether he drank in order to fortify himself against the heavy responsibilities of his office – though the evidence suggests that his drinking became more of a liability in later years.

There is no doubt that, among the lower orders, the crude showmanship he brought to the job earned him a raffish celebrity that set him apart from the succession of unknowns who had held the office before him. Among the more sensitive majority of the public, however, he was regarded with a mixture of embarrassment and loathing. That the common hangman should inspire such extreme reactions might seem unfair, when it could be argued that he was as essential a part of the legal system of the day as the parish constable, the justice of the peace or the judge (and the prefix 'common' was applied not pejoratively but to indicate that he was a servant of the people).

But it is also true that many hangmen were pretty unsavoury characters, and right to the end the local press treated Burrows as an object of scorn and greeted his death with considerably more contempt than compassion. Typically, even this event was wreathed in acrimony...

Headlined 'DEATH OF AN IMPORTANT PERSONAGE', the *Chester Chronicle*'s obituary (23 October) wasn't too unkind, though its somewhat facetious introduction, cribbed from Shakespeare's *Hamlet*, set the less-than-respectful tone of the piece. It began, 'On Tuesday evening, at five minutes past 4 o'clock, Samuel Burrows set out upon his journey to that "bourne" whither he had dispatched many a reluctant explorer, but "whence no traveller returns".' Then, after the fine words, came the plain speaking, the article stating bluntly that 'Sam was better known than trusted, and more feared than beloved, in his progress through life.'

Returning to the Shakespearean theme, the *Chronicle* went on, 'In his time he "played many parts" on the great stage of life. He was bred a butcher, was afterwards servant to a surgeon, then employed in the press gang, and of late years his principal calling was that of a rat-catcher, or mole-catcher, in both of which he was very skilful. For the last 24 years he filled the dignified office of "finisher of the law" for this district, and in the course of that time he "turned off" 53 individuals, with as much *nonchalance* as if they were so many of his own superannuated, and therefore useless, rat-catcher's dogs.'

Sam's decline, it seems, started towards the end of 1834 when the condemned murderers Garside and Mosley were removed from his bailiwick for execution (see chapter 12). He made no attempt to hide his displeasure, and he was still brooding over that perceived threat to his career when he suffered another setback.

At the county assizes in the summer of 1835 a 56-year-old Macclesfield man, an ostler named William Booth, was indicted for what the newspapers described as 'an unnatural act with a mare'. Despite the dramatic reduction in the number of offences carrying the death penalty during the 1820s and 1830s, bestiality was still a capital crime, and on 15 August Booth was summarily tried, convicted and condemned.

In an editorial on 20 August, the *Chronicle*, describing the accused as 'a hoary headed sinner,' lamented the fact that Cheshire had acquired 'an unfortunate notoriety...for offences of this description' and insisted that an example should be made of Booth. However, nine days later he was reprieved and his sentence commuted to transportation for life.

Burrows went into a deep depression and, with his health already ravaged by alcohol, he took to his bed and died on 20 October at his home in Brook Street, Chester. He was 63. The *Chronicle*'s obituary writer reflected, 'Since the memorable decision of the judges in the case of the murderers Garside and Mosley, Sam was observed gradually to droop and pine away; but when Booth...obtained a commutation of his sentence, Sam exclaimed that his "occupation was gone", and he never held up his head afterwards.'

The report concluded, 'He is said to have died in peace with all the world, except the Editor of the *Courant*, whom he declared he would never forgive in this world or in the next.'

The *Chronicle*'s Chester rival had aroused the hangman's wrath by announcing his death before it occurred. The *Courant*'s brief 'news' item had appeared on the morning of 20 October and Sam got to know of it just before he died. What really wounded him, however, was the paper's withering dismissal of him. It stated, 'Sam Burrows, the notorious finisher of the law, died at an advanced age, last week, in this city. The

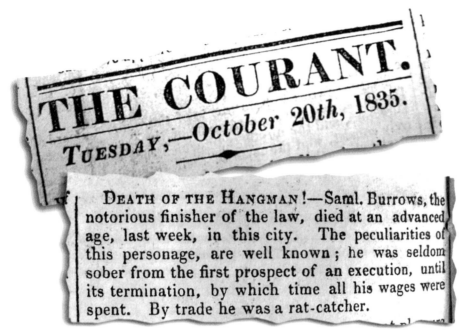

THE COURANT.

TUESDAY,—October 20th, 1835.

DEATH OF THE HANGMAN!—Saml. Burrows, the notorious finisher of the law, died at an advanced age, last week, in this city. The peculiarities of this personage, are well known; he was seldom sober from the first prospect of an execution, until its termination, by which time all his wages were spent. By trade he was a rat-catcher.

The 'news' item in the *Chester Courant* that so upset hangman Samuel Burrows. It was printed on the morning of 20 October 1835...hours before he actually died! (By permission of CCALS.)

peculiarities of this personage are well known; he was seldom sober from the first prospect of an execution, until its termination, by which time all his wages were spent. By trade he was a rat-catcher.' Full stop. End of story.

But if that upset the old boy, the *Courant*'s follow-up a week later must have had him spinning in his freshly-dug grave. Beneath the headline 'A REAL DESTRUCTIVE' was an even more venomous valediction. The paper stated, 'Sammy Burrows, the well-known finisher of the law...was, by profession, not only a pig-killer, a rat-killer, a mole-killer, and a man-killer, but also a self-destructionist, for by all accounts, he killed himself with ardent drink, which produced a serious complaint of the liver. We are creditably informed, that such was the obduracy of this man's feeling, occasioned by the execution of about 50 criminals, that he never heard of the probability of a hanging matter, without calculating on the profits which would be awarded him. In many instances, he was known to drink the amount of his wages on credit, before the execution took place.'

Samuel Burrows was laid to rest – with rather more Christian charity, one would like to think – on 23 October. He was buried in the same plot as his wife Mary (who had died the previous March at the age of 70) in the graveyard of St Oswald's Parish Church. At that time St Oswald's occupied the South Transept of Chester Cathedral, and the adjoining area, up to the city walls, was used as the church's burial ground. In 1881 the church was relocated in Parkgate Road, and the cemetery site is now part of the cathedral's landscaped precincts.

According to his obituaries, Burrows was born on 28 June 1772 at Ravensmoor in the parish of Acton, some three miles south west of Nantwich, though his baptism entry in the parish registers states that his parents were from Burland, about two miles further north. He was almost 40 when he began his official duties as Chester's (and, perforce, Cheshire's) hangman in 1812, having already served the city in one law-and-order capacity. At the back end of 1808 he was, briefly, a special constable, earning seven shillings a week.

In his new job the responsibilities were far more formidable...and so were the rewards (one city mayor would later describe them as 'extravagant'). He was paid £5 for each person he executed – about £225 today – and, as he was hired to flog 'em as well as hang 'em, he received an extra five shillings every time he was called in by the governor of the City Gaol to administer a dose of corporal punishment to one of his more recalcitrant charges.

On his debut as hangman Burrows executed two men at once. One of them took more than seven minutes to die – that is to say, he was more than seven minutes being slowly throttled to death. Sam, who, it could be said, was still learning the ropes, had positioned the noose so that the knot was at the back of the convict's head instead of under the left ear. It was not an auspicious start for the man who would become one of the country's longest-practising exponents of the executioner's black art. Nor was it the last spot of bother in the chequered career of Samuel Burrows.

The date was 15 June 1812, the unfortunate victim Joseph Thompson, aged 34, who was hanged along with Irishman John Temple (27). The two men, both weavers, were sentenced at the end of May at a rare special sitting of the county assizes, held to deal with around 50 people, men and women, charged in connection with the great blaze of civil and industrial unrest that had swept through the cotton manufacturing districts of north-east Cheshire and the adjoining counties during the preceding few months. A slump in the textile industry had brought a sharp reduction in wages, and the prevailing mood of militancy among the workforce, coupled with the wider public anger over rising food prices, erupted into lawlessness.

In March and April Luddites attacked two cotton mills in Stockport, but later the workers' cause was hijacked by more criminal elements. Consequently, as well as allegations of unlawful assembly and illegal oath-taking, the special assize calendar also contained numerous cases of machine breaking, rioting, violence and intimidation, house breaking, assault, highway robbery, looting and arson. When the sessions closed, 15 men had received death sentences and five were left for execution – though, in the end, only Temple and Thompson were made to pay the ultimate penalty.

Thompson, who was living at the time in Holmes Street, Stockport, had been among the Luddite mob which, on 14 April, rampaged through Stockport. After breaking the windows of several of the town's cotton mills, the rioters turned their attention to the factory of John Goodair at Edgeley, wrecking power-looms (the new automated machines that the weavers saw as a threat to their jobs) and setting fire to the building.

Then they broke into Goodair's home nearby and it was there that Thompson was recognised by one of the mill owner's servants. At the approach of the mob, the woman had taken refuge in the cellar, but when she smelled smoke she crept out and saw Thompson and several of his companions piling chairs and other pieces of furniture, including a piano, on to a fire that had been set in the middle of the front parlour floor. The crowd was finally dispersed by a detachment of the Scots Greys, after the town's anxious magistrates had called in the army. As well as arson, Thompson was also charged with stealing a silver plate from the Goodair house.

Temple was one of half-a-dozen or so men who, shortly after midnight on 9 May, forced their way into the home of Samuel Wagstaffe and his family at Adlington, in the parish of Prestbury, claiming they were 'General Ludd's men' looking for firearms. They found none; but, during their hour-long rampage, they terrorised the occupants and stole various items of silver and clothing. Armed with swords and pistols and with their faces masked by handkerchiefs, the gang carried out the raid in military-like fashion, responding by numbers to the orders barked out by their leader, the self-styled 'General Ludd' – described rather less grandly by the *Chronicle* as 'a stout man in a black coat and pantaloons'. This particular incarnation of the mythical 'General' turned out to be one William Walker, a 59-year-old collier from Gee Cross, who was sentenced to seven years' transportation at the same special assizes for rioting and stealing flour from a neighbour.

Temple, convicted of burglary and robbery, was recognised when his disguise slipped as he stooped to gather up a pair of shoes. He was apprehended with six or seven other men near Edgeley Chapel by one of the horse patrols that had been called up for duty during the emergency. Hidden inside his hat were a waistcoat and a silk handkerchief stolen from the Wagstaffes' house.

The *Chronicle* reported the double hanging on 19 June. 'Temple,' the paper said, 'was dead in about two minutes, but Thompson, owing to the executioner having placed the knot immediately on the back of the neck, was convulsed upwards of seven minutes.'

Burrows made a better job of executing John Lomas on Monday 24 August 1812, and by the following year he was already starting to display that swaggering, devil-may-care attitude that would be his trademark for the next 20-odd years. When, on 23 May 1813, he hanged Edith Morrey – the only woman to die at his hands – the *Chronicle* could not help noticing that Burrows (though he was not mentioned by name) 'did his duty in a manner that disposes us to think, at least, that he is not *ashamed* of his profession'.

Morrey, a 35-year-old farmer's wife and mother of five, had been tried with Lomas the previous summer on a joint charge of petty treason. They were both found guilty of murdering George Morrey – Edith Morrey's husband and Lomas's master – at the Morreys' farm in Hankelow, near Audlem. They had become lovers only a couple of months after the 20-year-old Lomas began working at the farm as a labourer. George Morrey was found murdered in his bed in the early hours of 12 April 1812. He had been battered about the head and body and his throat had been cut.

At the end of the trial, Mrs Morrey pleaded pregnancy and her execution was delayed until after her confinement. She was eventually put to death exactly 50 years to the day after Mary Heald suffered for the same traitorous crime – though burning at the stake was now no longer the statutory punishment.

While it was Lomas who carried out the murder – he had first bludgeoned his employer about the head with an axe as he lay sleeping, then finished him off by slitting his throat with a razor – Morrey was to emerge as the evil architect of the crime, the veritable 'black widow' who had incited her young lover to kill her husband and thereby remove the only obstacle standing in the way of their future happiness. Or so she led him to believe.

In the opinion of the trial judge, Chief Justice Robert Dallas, Lomas was 'the least guilty offender', his Lordship commenting that 'in the hardened heart of another was lodged that malice which hatched the [murder] plan'. The *Chronicle* (23 April) called her 'the wretched woman who instigated him [Lomas] into being a principal in the horrid crime'.

Not surprisingly, the case aroused intense public interest – and there was no let-up when Edith Morrey's day of reckoning arrived. Like all the executions at which Burrows officiated, hers was carried out at the City Gaol. Built next door to the old Chester Infirmary and opened in 1807, it also incorporated at its eastern end a House of Correction. It was on a temporary platform above the entrance to the latter that the gallows was erected.

With an estimated 6,000 spectators straining to catch a last glimpse of the wicked widow, her execution was an occasion ready-made for drama; but, as with Lomas before her, the final act contained no unexpected twist in the plot. And she was almost upstaged by that 'man of many parts' Samuel Burrows...

Cheshire author and playwright Maureen Nield describes the scene in *Rope Dance*, her definitive account of the Lomas-Morrey case:, 'At the top [of the scaffold steps] Edith turned towards the prison wall, as if, by removing the crowd from her field of vision, she could somehow become invisible. But their noise couldn't be blotted out. Much of it was being provoked by the hangman. Sammy Burrows habitually carried out preparations with a perky insolence that made him a darling of the masses, but which more sensitive souls found tasteless. He began his routine by balancing on a stool and trying to lasso the crossbar.'

A macabre postscript to the case was provided by James Hanshall in his book *Stranger in Chester* (1816), which revealed that, while John Lomas may have murdered out of love for Edith Morrey, she ultimately 'lost' her heart to someone else...anatomically-speaking, that is.

As usually happened with condemned murderers at this time, the judge ordered that, after her execution, Morrey's body was to be handed over to local medical men for dissection. The operation – the description 'open to the public' seemed grimly apt on these occasions – took place the following morning in a basement room at the castle. It was performed by a Mr Titley of Chester Infirmary and, wrote Hanshall, the surgeon kept the heart as a specimen.

That Morrey's execution went smoothly was plain for all to see – for, by judicial edict, the black curtains that previously encircled the scaffold had been removed. The drapes appear to have been in use since the execution in 1810 of Thomas Done, a 20-year-old barge master from Runcorn who murdered his girlfriend and dumped her body into the Bridgewater Canal at Lymm. The innovation was introduced after an excruciating incident in 1809, when, at a double hanging, both ropes broke and the two men had to submit to the ordeal a second time (see chapter eight).

But the curtains only seem to have been intended to screen the preliminary activity on the scaffold, for they were pulled back just as the bolt was about to be drawn, making the whole thing seem even more like a theatrical presentation. In 1813, however, the assize judges ruled that justice had to be seen to be done – in *all* its awful ceremony – if it was to have any redeeming effect on the watching public.

It should be pointed out here, too, that with the 'new drop' – which consisted of a double-leaf trapdoor set into the floor of a platform raised no higher than five feet above the base of the scaffold – victims of hanging did not fall out of sight into the void below, as they did when the 'long drop' was introduced in the 1870s. Because only a short length of rope was used, all but their feet and lower legs remained in sight the whole time, their every expiring twitch and spasm visible to the onlookers. Only the facial contortions – the pain-racked grimace, the bulging eyes, the protruding tongue – were deemed unsuitable for viewing, which is why a hood was placed over the victim's head in the final moments before the 'fatal bolt' was drawn.

In total, Burrows executed seven people in 1813, the busiest period of his career. And over the next seven years he added another dozen to his tally. From press reports of the executions, it would appear that he conducted himself with his customary zeal without attracting any undue criticism. But he caused an uproar at a double hanging following the Summer Assizes of 1820.

The two men involved were William Ricklington, a 24-year-old gardener from Durham, who had been indicted for breaking into Coddington Rectory, near Chester, and stealing various articles of men's clothing and then setting fire to the building, and Ralph Ellis (19), one of a gang who burgled a house in Elton, near Ellesmere Port. Ricklington's lover Esther Crewe, aged 27, appeared in the dock with him nursing their three-week-old baby. She was cleared of receiving stolen goods

The new purpose-built City Gaol and House of Correction (seen in the centre of this picture), which replaced the old Northgate Gaol in 1807. From 1826 the gallows was positioned above the front entrance, and the city walls opposite afforded a grandstand view of the hangings. Inset: Chester's notorious hangman Samuel Burrows.
(Prints by permission of CCALS.)

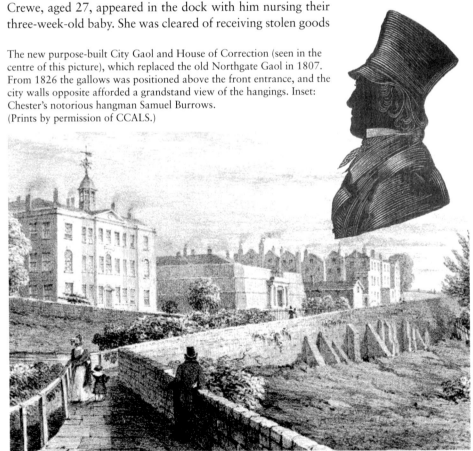

from Ricklington but was found guilty of stealing clothes from the rectory and was sentenced to seven years' transportation. Crewe had worked at the rectory as a laundry maid and housemaid until two months before the robbery. At the time the couple were living as man and wife in a lodging house in Boughton.

It was while he was carrying out his last-minute checks in readiness for the joint execution, on Saturday 16 September, that Burrows again showed his propensity for bad taste. As the *Chronicle* explained on 22 September, 'In affixing the ropes, the fellow who fills the disgusting office [of hangman], tried the length of them, by applying with the utmost *sang froid* the noose of one to his own neck; some person in the crowd cried out, "Shame, Shame!" The fellow repeated the motion, smiling at his own callosity of feeling, which called forth the execration of the multitude...'

By now Burrows was becoming as notorious as many of the villains he made away with and – the local press seemed to think so, at any rate – almost as bad. Whereas before the Chester papers had appeared content to protect the anonymity of the city's hangmen, the perennial Burrows had the kind of personality and presence they found impossible to ignore. They scrutinised his every move and reported each indiscretion – not just in his public role but in his private life as well.

A particular target for their barbs was his legendary drinking, and in this respect their concern was shared by the city sheriffs. Aware of the potentially calamitous effect that his intemperate habits could have on his official duties, the sheriffs eventually came up with a plan to help keep his head clear and his mind focused on his work. He was left in no doubt that he had to comply if he wanted to continue earning his money.

The scheme first came to light in 1826, following the execution of John Green, 31, who had been charged with breaking into the house of Samuel Dean at Bridgemere and stealing a pocket-book and about £16 in cash. Father-of-five Green was said to have threatened Dean with a pistol. His execution took place at the City Gaol on 26 August and, said the *Chronicle* (1 September), 'the executioner, Burrows, was kept in the Governor's house the day and night previous, to ensure his being sober (a rare thing) at the awful crisis'.

The arrangement could well have begun earlier in the year, for, as the *Courant* reported when covering the executions of Philip McGowan and Abraham Stones on Wednesday 26 April, Burrows had 'contrary to his usual custom, entered upon his duties that morning without being absolutely drunk!' It was not a flawless performance, however; the two men, both convicted of highway robbery, struggled violently for several minutes because, the *Courant* insisted, Burrows had not given them a long enough drop.

When the point was put to Burrows, his reply, said the *Courant*, was that 'if they [the ropes] were longer, the folks outside could not see the men hanging!'

In a parting swipe at the hangman the paper loved to hate, the *Courant* added, 'The men were scarcely dead before Burrows...begged permission of the sheriffs to retire "to get him a pint of beer."'

Stones, aged 20, a silk weaver from Liverpool, was convicted at Chester Quarter Sessions and has the distinction of being the last man to be hanged on the orders of one of the city courts.

For this double execution, the 'fatal engine' (as the papers liked to call it) was erected for the first time on the west side of the City Gaol, on the balcony that sat atop the colonnaded front entrance. The gallows, to which access seems to have been via the flat margins of the prison roof, stood in that same lofty position for all subsequent hangings; it was a popular move, for the adjoining city walls provided the public with a perfect vantage point.

The 'preventive detention' system, which was to keep Burrows out of temptation's way on the eve of an execution for the remainder of his career, was imposed next in 1829. Reporting the joint execution of John Proudlove and John Leir on 9 May, the *Chester Chronicle* noted that Burrows had been 'locked up all night in the prison, not only to insure his attendance but to keep him sober' (see chapter nine).

If, to his critics, Samuel Burrows was a heartless brute, a legalised serial killer desensitised by his regular employment in the business of death, there was one occasion in 1829 when he demonstrated that the genuinely tragic circumstances in the lives of many of his 'unfortunate creatures' were capable of touching his finer feelings. The (albeit brief) departure from his more familiar public persona was revealed by the *Chester Chronicle*, in an equally rare moment of press favour. It followed the execution of John Henshall and Joseph Woodhouse on 26 September. Woodhouse (40), from Newton, Stockport, had been convicted of raping his 11-year-old daughter and, by common consent, deserved his punishment. But Henshall (or Hanshall), a 20-year-old farmer's son from Dunham Massey, was an altogether more sympathetic figure.

He was one of a gang of about 10 men spotted poaching on the Earl of Stamford's estate at Ashley, near Altrincham, one night just before Christmas 1828. As they were being pursued by an even larger body of gamekeepers (some 15 in number), one of the poachers shot and wounded one of his lordship's men. An accomplice who turned King's evidence claimed Henshall had been armed with a gun called a 'detonator', but the young man insisted he had only carried the ammunition and that he had joined the gang for the first time that night after meeting them while drinking at a local pub.

The judge, the Honourable Thomas Jervis, it was reported, broke down in tears twice as he was sentencing Henshall, but, because of the severity of the game laws then in force, he said he had no choice but to impose the maximum penalty, despite the prisoner's youth. There were further emotional scenes when Henshall and Woodhouse arrived at the City Gaol and were taken into a room adjoining the scaffold to have their irons struck off. Both men immediately threw themselves on their knees, and on the drop Henshall again collapsed, begging for divine forgiveness and concluding with a fervent rendering of the Lord's Prayer.

The paper went on: 'Even the executioner [Burrows], hardened as he is by his natural disposition, and by his long familiarity with scenes of this nature, even he was moved to tears by the affecting scenes in the ante-room, as well as those whose painful duty it was to witness it.'

Whatever their feelings towards him as a person, the Chester papers recognised that Sammy Burrows was always likely to provide them with a good story, and they followed his public appearances even when he was working away from the city. One such instance occurred in Caernarfon, in September 1822, after he had executed a man convicted of highway robbery and attempted murder. On his way home by stagecoach, he found himself the target for an unexpected demonstration of public animosity.

The *Chronicle* reported, 'The hangman…was recognised by the passengers, who joined in a general *turn-out*; the coachman was obliged to give him an ejectment; and not till then would the passengers proceed.' How, or when, the unwelcome traveller made it back to Chester was not recorded.

The biggest and, as it turned out, final challenge of Burrows's career presented itself in April 1834, when he had to hang four men simultaneously. The gallows had been designed for no more than two people, so a second crossbeam was added. It was to spell double trouble.

The quartet, which included Thomas Riley, the sickle-wielding Irishman mentioned in the previous chapter, all appeared at the notorious 'Bloody Assize' that Spring. The others were: James Mason, aged 22, of Marple, condemned for a vile assault on his pregnant girlfriend with intent to procure a miscarriage (an offence that eventually led to the girl's death and which prompted the *Chronicle*, with some justification, to describe him as a 'monster in human shape'); William Nailor, a 38-year-old stone mason convicted of shooting at a cotton mill owner with intent to murder at Stalybridge; and John Carr, of Haslington, Crewe, a 27-year-old labourer, sentenced for cutting and maiming a man in a row over an unpaid debt. He was alleged to have knifed his victim 20 times in the head and body, all for the sake of tuppence.

The first problem occurred when Burrows pulled the lever to release the trapdoor. Nothing happened. The 'fatal bolt' would not budge. The combined weight of the convicts must have jammed it against its retaining mechanism and it took several attempts before it slid free and the trap fell. The executioner's frantic efforts, said the *Courant*, 'shook the malefactors'.

Then, because two of the condemned men were positioned closer to the edge of the trapdoor than usual, when the floor eventually fell away, leaving the four twitching and twirling like partners in a mid-air dance of death, Riley's feet could be seen scrabbling for purchase on the wooden framework. The *Courant* reported, 'He there struggled for some seconds before he got disentangled, and his punishment was consequently much protracted.'

The other member of the 'Infamous Five' to be executed following the 'Bloody Assize' was murderer Samuel Thorley, a 30-year-old nurseryman and seed dealer from Northwich. He slit his 21-year-old girlfriend's throat with a razor at nearby Leftwich, after an unsuccessful attempt to save their waning relationship. He was hanged by Burrows on Monday 7 April.

We know he was the overnight 'guest' of the city gaoler prior to these hangings, because by now each 'booking' was listed as an item of expenditure in the Chester Corporation accounts. For example, an entry in the Joint Treasurers' account book dated 8 April 1834, read, 'Paid Mr Jepson [the gaoler] for Board and Lodging of Samuel Burrows previous to the execution of S. Thorley – 10s 10d.' For the quadruple hanging, the ledger shows, the treasurers authorised payments totalling £1 17s 9d, but these were also to cover the costs of new ropes and 'expenses to Liverpool' (to where, presumably, Burrows had to travel to acquire them).

While Thomas Riley's protracted death struggles were regrettable, they don't seem to have led to any criticism of Burrows's preparations. He himself was more than satisfied with his afternoon's work, as subsequent events were to show. But, as ever with Burrows, controversy was never far away and, in an unpleasant sequel to the multiple hanging, he once again made himself the target of public odium. This time it was his off-duty behaviour that landed him in the papers…and in trouble with the law.

On Monday 19 May he was involved in a bizarre incident in the street, which ended with him being set upon by an angry mob and, to add insult to near injury, being summoned to appear at the Chester Mayor's Court on a charge of drunkenness. The *Chronicle* recounted the details, with undisguised glee, on 30 May. 'Sammy,' said the paper disdainfully, 'had indulged so freely in intoxicating draughts that he was rolling about the streets, boasting of his dexterity in carrying into effect the extreme penalty of the law, and at the same time exhibiting part of the apparel of one of the unfortunate individuals who recently suffered death in this city.' The right to claim the clothes worn by executed criminals was one of the perks of the hangman's job.

The *Chronicle* report went on: 'This excited the indignation of the spectators, who not only assailed Sam…but bustled and pelted him pretty severely.' When he ignored the mayor's summons (believing, said the *Chronicle*, that his 'exalted situation' put him above such trifling matters), he was arrested, clapped in gaol for contempt and hauled before the court.

The *Courant*, it will come as no surprise, took even greater delight in Sam's predicament. Its report began, 'That notable personage *Mister Sammy Burrows*, "yeoman of the halter", was brought up from the city gaol, in charge of an officer, and placed at the table to receive the judgement of the court.' With heavy-handed sarcasm, it went on: 'With great indignation at the conduct of this adjuster of hempen neckcloths, the mayor reprehended him very severely, in an emphatic address, from which we learned that on Monday last Sam had indulged his *penchant* for a glass until he became tipsy, and in that condition he recounted to a gaping and wondering auditory his various services, and their dexterous accomplishment, as "finisher of the law" – an important office truly in a civilized community…'

The mayor, said the *Courant*, railed at old Sam for 'his beastly drunkenness, and his disgusting boast of those duties which he ought to hold sacred and for which he was paid extravagantly'. For his 'abominable conduct' he was fined five shillings and ordered to be placed in the stocks if he failed to produce the money that day. Suitably contrite, Sam promptly paid up.

Burrows swore never to disgrace himself in such a manner again – and he didn't. He didn't get the chance. For, from that day until his alcohol-damaged liver gave out a year-and-a-half later, there was no further call for his services.

Though at the time he expressed his disappointment about 'the three that got away', his final thought on his quarter of a century of carrying the hangman's burden was that he was glad it was all over. He reportedly told his death-bed interviewer, 'Many [are] desirous of taking the job, but thank God I am done.'

If Burrows was right, the potential applicants queueing up to be his successor were all to be disappointed. When he died, the newly reconstituted Chester City Council (established under the 1835 Municipal Corporations Act) made no move to replace him. As the number of executions continued to decline following the penal reforms of the late

1830s – there were only nine hangings in Chester throughout the following three decades – different hangmen were brought in from outside the area as and when required.

At his departure, it must have been obvious that the city, and the county, of Chester would never see the like of Sammy Burrows again. At a time when society was at last emerging from the oppressive shadow of the hanging laws, even those who mourned his passing would not have been sorry about that.

*   *   *

When he was executed by Samuel Burrows in 1817, Joseph Allen was convulsed for almost 10 minutes, his agonies accentuated by the 'death rattle' of his leg irons. It was another jarring reminder of the deficiencies of the short-drop method of hanging, but, more clamorous still, was the reaction to the sentence. Allen had been convicted of passing forged banknotes, and, as had happened 30 years earlier in another case of currency crime, there was a press and public outcry over what was considered an unjustifiably-harsh punishment. John Oakes, like Allen, was a farmer, and in life – even unto death – the pair ploughed remarkably similar furrows…

Chapter Six

The Secret of the Sealed-up Stable

At the isolated farm where he was tending a lame carthorse, blacksmith John Hawkesworth stumbled on a tantalising mystery. One day, arriving to change the dressing on the animal's injured foot, he noticed that the doorway of an adjacent stable had been bricked up since his last visit. Puzzled, he went round to the back of the building where he knew, low down in the wall, there was a hole used for mucking out. This, he discovered, had also been blocked off, with loose bricks. Curiosity getting the better of him, he dislodged one and peeped through the gap.

What he saw inside was machinery, but, even from his restricted viewpoint, he could tell that it was not of the agricultural variety. Suspecting its purpose, Hawkesworth determined to find out for sure, and, on the not entirely false pretext of checking the horse's progress, he called at the farm several times the following week.

Watching and waiting for the right opportunity, he was eventually able to unlock the secret of the sealed-up stable. What he had uncovered in farmer John Oakes's converted outbuilding on that autumn day in 1783 was no less than the makeshift factory of a gang of coin forgers. And when, after some further sleuthing, he reported his detailed observations to the authorities, he had no hesitation in identifying Oakes as one of the ringleaders.

If it was true, the farmer was in serious trouble. Deadly serious. Counterfeiting was high treason and death the automatic penalty. And it was not just the manufacturers and major suppliers who risked losing their lives. Such was the extent of currency crime in 18th and early 19th century England, and so merciless the manner in which the courts dealt with offenders, that anyone caught dabbling in dud money stood a very real chance of being hanged.

The existence of this counterfeiting crimewave can be explained in part by the difficulties and deficiencies that beset the country's official currency during most of this time. It was a period in history when English coinage was in an especially sorry state. Although the Royal Mint issued a record amount of gold coins during the last quarter of the 18th century, silver was in drastically short supply. What coins were in circulation were old and worn, and those that had not deteriorated because of their inferior quality were invariably showing the effects of 'clipping'. This was one of the principal methods employed by the counterfeiters, in which the metal – silver mainly – was shaved off the edges of the coins, melted down and recast into new ones.

'The state of currency by the end of the 18th century', says Glyn Davies in *A History of Money: From Ancient Times to the Present Day* (1994), 'was once again deplorable.' In the midst of the great Industrial Revolution, a time when large amounts of capital were being invested in the new machine age technologies, the situation called for urgent measures. Glyn Davies records, 'It was in silver and copper coins, the bread and butter of everyday life, that the shortage was of crippling severity. Faced with a woefully inadequate and unreliable supply of official coinage, businessmen in the provinces in particular were forced increasingly to improvise.'

Five main methods were adopted in response to the monetary crisis: the use of metal tokens; the 'truck system' (payment in goods); paper notes issued by, and redeemable in, company shops and quasi-banks; the acceptance of foreign currency, especially silver, and the establishment of country banks, which issued their own notes and bills of exchange.

Operating under the same law of supply and demand that prompted legitimate businessmen into action, underworld entrepreneurs and assorted racketeers also 'improvised' to exploit the gap in the money market.

'The extensive circulation of counterfeit money,' declared George Theodore Wilkinson, in *The Newgate Calendar*, those great chronicles of crime and punishment in 18th century England, 'has become an enormous evil.' Writing around the turn of the century, he said of coining, 'Its extent almost exceeds credibility; and the dexterity and ingenuity of these counterfeit[er]s have, after considerable practice, enabled them to finish the different kinds of base money in so masterly a manner, that it has become extremely difficult for a common observer to distinguish their spurious manufacture from the worn-out silver of the mint. So systematic, indeed, has this nefarious traffic become of late, that the great dealers, who, in most instances, are the employers of the coiners, execute orders for the town and country, with the same regularity as manufacturers in fair branches of trade.'

John Oakes was the father of nine children (with another one on the way), but seems to have been only a minor producer when it came to counterfeit currency. When, on one of his veterinary visits to Oakes's farm, John Hawkesworth caught him and an accomplice in the act of fabricating shillings, however, it looked as if the forgers were about to put a considerable quantity of the homemade coins into circulation.

Oakes had little choice but to admit that the equipment in his stable – two stamping presses and a machine for producing round metal blanks – was for coin making. But the farmer, who was also in business as a carrier, claimed it was a consignment he had been hired to collect and store until arrangements could be made for it to be transported to its final destination in the Midlands. He had been unaware of the nature of his cargo when he accepted the contract, and he denied he had ever used the machines for counterfeiting. And, in a vigorous counter-attack, he charged his accuser with concocting a pack of lies to frame him.

Hawkesworth, he said, was out for revenge, trying to get his own back for the legal action that he (Oakes) claimed he had been forced to take to recover a debt of just over £11 – its modern value would be in excess of £1,000 – which the blacksmith had owed him. It was the basis of his defence when, on Monday 19 April 1784, Oakes stood trial at Chester Assizes on two separate indictments relating to counterfeiting 'the current coin of the realm'.

The Crown's case relied almost entirely on Hawkesworth's testimony, but it was a testimony of the most thoroughgoing and damaging kind. It survives today in the form of two depositions filed among the official court papers in the National Archives. The statements, sworn before a local magistrate, amount to a virtual prosecution brief of the case and demonstrate the lengths to which Hawkesworth was prepared to go to bring Oakes to justice...or, if we are to believe Oakes's version of events, to settle an old score.

His one-man crusade began in October 1783. By this time Oakes, his wife Mary and their sizeable brood were living in a small rented farm at Moss End in the old parish of Sutton, parts of which have since been absorbed into the southern suburbs of Macclesfield but which is still essentially rural in character. Approaching the age of 48, he seemed to be doing well. From the sale of his farm produce, and the extra money he earned as a carrier, he had – as the *Chester Courant* would later put it – 'procured a comfortable subsistence' for himself and his family.

Then, early in the month, one of his horses went lame. Needing a fully-fit team to operate his haulage business, he sent for his usual blacksmith. Hawkesworth, whose smithy was in Macclesfield, responded promptly to the call and, in the following weeks, made regular visits to the farm to treat the horse's injury. But that was not all he was keeping an eye on.

In a deposition dated 17 February 1784 (the second of the two statements he made to Macclesfield JP William Clowes), Hawkesworth said that it was on Friday 17 October that he first noticed the bricked-up stable. When, on closer inspection, he saw that both the doorway and the sluice hole in the rear wall had been blocked off, he concluded that the intention was 'to prevent persons looking through into the stable'.

By pushing out one of the bricks in the sluice hole, however, it was possible for him to see inside. There, said Hawkesworth, he spied 'several engines' partly covered with 'wrappering'. His deposition stated, 'This examinant, suspecting for what purpose they were intended, he attended to dress the horse several times the following week.'

Initially the self-appointed vigilante was thwarted in his detective work: three or four of Oakes's friends were constant visitors to the farm and there was always someone knocking about the place when he called. One of them he recognised as William Lowe, a fustian cutter from Manchester (the official case file describes him as a 'chapman' or pedlar); the others were strangers to him.

On Saturday 25 October, however, he arrived to find the farm deserted and he was at last able to get a closer look at the stable. He got in by going over the hayloft in the adjoining barn and climbing through a small opening at the far end, normally used for forking fodder and bedding down to the horses stabled below. On the floor of the stable, set up and seemingly ready for use, were two coin-stamping presses and a larger cutting machine for producing round metal blanks. Beside the latter was a sheet of copper, with small circular holes in it.

All the machinery, Hawkesworth deposed, had been 'freshly oiled and lately used'. Hidden in a manger in the stable, he said, he found four dies 'one for coining a shilling of King George and the others for half-pence'. He left all the incriminating evidence in place and exited the stable via the same hayloft route by which he had entered.

This might have been an appropriate juncture at which to report his findings to a constable or magistrate. But he seems to have been anxious to obtain more conclusive evidence against the counterfeiters before going to the law. So, about seven to 10 days later, he again dropped by Oakes's farm. One of the farm hands, Thomas Deane, was in the barn threshing corn. Hawkesworth asked him if he knew what was in the stable next door. When Deane professed ignorance, Hawkesworth – 'wanting to know the progress Oakes and his companions had made' – hung around until Deane went for his lunch and once again made his way across the hayloft and into the stable.

The cutting machine was now lying on its side, though from the perforated sheets of copper on the ground nearby it was obvious it had been busy since he last saw it. One of the coin presses had been fixed to a baulk of wood, which appeared to be broken. His deposition went on: 'He examined the stamping engine and found the die for making the impression of the head of a shilling fixed to the engine ready for use.'

Still Hawkesworth made no move to alert the authorities. Instead, he waited another week or so and then returned to the farm. This was on or about 12 November. As usual he first headed for the farmhouse to announce his arrival and went in through the back door. Carrying his mixing pot and various medicaments into the kitchen, where he was to prepare the latest batch of dressings for Oakes's still incapacitated nag, he found the farmer and his friend William Lowe sitting by the fire.

His statement continued, '[He] saw about two handsful of copper bits, some coloured white and others uncoloured, lying on the table. As soon as he entered John Oakes threw a handkerchief over them to hide them, and there was an earthen pot or crucible by the side of the fire which had something white in it. He asked them what they were doing and John Oakes said Mr Lowe had got some bad shillings and they were colouring them to make them payable.'

The hawk-eyed Hawkesworth noticed several uncoloured copper pieces, which were only partially covered by the handkerchief, and, picking one up, he found it bore 'an impression of the head of a shilling'. He said he asked Oakes and Lowe if they were colouring the pieces with the liquid in the crucible. Yes, they said, they were. 'They were both at work colouring the said pieces of metal,' Hawkesworth's deposition went on, 'and they continued at work the whole time he was there, which was about a quarter-of-an-hour or half-an-hour.'

Finally, just before he left, Hawkesworth mentioned to Oakes that he needed to buy further medication for the horse. Oakes, he said, 'gave him one of the new counterfeit shillings that lay on the table'. It was the evidence that could have tied Oakes to the stamping press in the stable, yet even then Hawkesworth held back from turning him in. It wasn't until Wednesday 10 December – a month later and more than seven weeks after his spying mission had begun – that he led two constables to Oakes's farm and the coin-making equipment.

The following day he made his first statement to magistrate William Clowes, in which he referred to two clandestine visits he had also made to the Moss End farm on the previous Thursday and Saturday (4 and 6 December). Both times, he said, he observed the cutting machine and one of the presses set up in Oakes's stable. His deposition added, 'On the Thursday before daylight he saw John Oakes in the stable with a lighted candle, and he then had two pieces of metal in his hand, one of which was of a whitish colour and the other copper coloured.' When Oakes looked as if he was about to leave the stable, the lurking blacksmith slipped away unseen.

When Oakes's farm was finally raided, the constables, armed with a search warrant

The Secret of the Sealed-up Stable

and accompanied by the ever-helpful Hawkesworth, discovered the machinery hidden underneath piles of straw and hay and various ancillary tools covered over with soil.

Oakes and Lowe were arrested and locked up in Chester Castle Gaol to await the start of the Spring Assizes. Contemporary press reports of their trial referred loosely to 'coining' and 'counterfeiting'. However, the court documents show that they were indicted jointly on a specimen charge of 'colouring base coins to make them resemble shillings, the current silver coin of this Kingdom'. Both men were found guilty and condemned to die, although Lowe was subsequently reprieved. Oakes had been charged on a second count of being in possession of coin-making equipment 'without any lawful authority or sufficient excuse' – an offence that also carried the death penalty.

Though he pleaded not guilty, Oakes was precluded from making a sworn statement by the court rules in force at that time (defendants were not allowed into the witness box until 1898). But his defence was the one he had persisted with from the start – that the coining implements had been on their way to Birmingham when Hawkesworth spotted them and that the blacksmith had lied to get even for the slight he felt at being sued for debt – and the one he stuck to right to the end. But, while it had its supporters, the jurors were obviously unable to accept its underlying premise: that, purely out of spite, Hawkesworth had made up the allegations knowing they would almost certainly result in Oakes's death.

Oakes was executed on Saturday 15 May 1784, at Boughton. Six days later the *Chester Chronicle* published the full text of a speech he wrote during his final days in prison, and which he made to the crowd as he stood in the very shadow of the gallows. It was a moving performance, by all accounts, and one which helped convince both Chester papers that he was innocent. Afterwards Oakes handed the message to the Ordinary of the Castle Gaol, the Revd J. Willan.

As his offence was considered treasonable, the condemned man had been dragged to the place of execution chained to the traditional traitor's hurdle. It was to be a straightforward hanging, however; the other ritual embellishments of evisceration, quartering and decapitation that were still part of the bloody tariff of official sanctions – the 'exquisitely aggravated' punishments, as V.A.C. Gatrell defines them so, well, exquisitely in *The Hanging Tree: Execution and the English People 1770–1868* – were, by this time, reserved for more politically-motivated acts of betrayal.

What was described by the *Chronicle* as 'the real declaration of the unfortunate John Oakes' began, 'Dear souls that are here present: I think it my duty in the presence of you all, and before the face of Almighty God, in whose mercy I have a firm hope, to declare

'Gallows Hill' (modern Barrel Well Hill) and the obelisk that marks the location of the county's original execution site at Boughton – Cheshire's 'Tyburn' from mediaeval times until 1801. (Photograph by the author.)

the whole truth respecting the charges laid against me, and for which I am to suffer death.' It then went on:

'John Hawkesworth, Blacksmith of Macclesfield, in this county (the evidence against me) deposed on oath that I had engines or pressers for the purpose of coining, and that he saw me at work colouring copper metal so as to appear like shillings.

'Now I John Oakes do solemnly declare before Almighty God, and you spectators, that at no time of my life did I ever counterfeit the silver, or other coin of this realm, or used the implements found in my possession, or was any way privy to their being used while in my custody – the reason of having them in my possession was being employed to convey them for hire as a carrier; part of which goods I received at Manchester and the other part at Latchford-bridge, near Warrington; which goods or implements I was to lay down at my own house in Sutton till called for, being in the road to Birmingham, whither they were to go. And I also declare that every thing that the said Hawkesworth swore against me is false, except that of the implements being in my custody, so help me God.

'Dear spectators: I have good reason to conclude that [Hawkesworth] did appear and swear against me with a premeditated determination to deprive me of my life. He was fully indebted to me 11 pounds six shillings and one penny, to recover which I was obliged to sue him; and accordingly I took out a Sheriff's warrant to force him to pay me – and he, knowing I had carried, and had in my keeping, the implements for which I am going to suffer, having seen them lie in my buildings, and knowing the use they were for, out of spite for my proceeding against him, laid an information against me for having them in my custody – but finding that the things being found on my premises was [sic] not sufficient to take away my life [he was mistaken in this belief: as has already been pointed out, simple possession of forging equipment could invoke the death penalty], he then swore that he saw me make, and afterwards colour, round pieces of copper, to make them appear like shillings, and even produced one which he swore I gave him to buy something to dress a horse's foot with.'

He concluded with an impassioned plea for public support to help ease his family's impoverished situation, urging that donations be handed to the Revd Willan, who would see that the money was 'properly applied to their use'.

The *Chester Courant*'s response was to publish an equally affecting 'declaration' on 18 May. It began, 'The Case of this unhappy Man was singularly lamentable and distressful.' The paper described how Oakes had worked hard to build up his business to provide a good living for his family, only to '[fall] an innocent Victim to the Malignity of a Neighbour'.

Waxing ever more grandiloquently, the paper went on: 'The Calmness and Serenity that attended the last Moments of this Man made such Impressions on the Minds of the Spectators as will not speedily be erased; and the Consciousness of his Innocence, he observed, gave him such an Assurance of eternal Felicity, that he felt no other Pain than what must naturally possess the Breast of a Husband and Father on leaving an affectionate Wife (now pregnant) and an infant Family in a State of Misery and Want.'

The Secret of the Sealed-up Stable

Two decades later, the *Chronicle* was even more certain that Oakes had not deserved to die. Recalling the case in an article published on 6 September 1805, the newspaper stated categorically that he had been 'merely the carrier of the raw material' and that it was Lowe who had been 'the actual maker of the base coin'.

The assertion may have been founded on information that came to light after the trial – it certainly was not the view of the presiding judge, the Hon. Richard Pepper Arden. Chester's Chief Justice sentenced William Lowe to death as well as Oakes, but subsequently reprieved him. Press speculation at the time was that he had got off on a technicality, some clerical error in the wording of the indictment, apparently.

But Judge Arden revealed the reason for his decision in a private memorandum to the Home Secretary (Lord Sydney). The letter was ostensibly about a third man convicted of a currency offence at the assizes, John Orme, of Rainow, who was condemned for possessing a mould used for making counterfeit shillings and half-crowns.

It was believed at first that Orme was a confederate of Oakes and Lowe. He was arrested on 18 October 1783 (the day after John Hawkesworth first glimpsed the coining equipment in Oakes's stable) following a routine house-to-house search by Rainow's parish constable Thomas Turner and special constable James Partington, who were investigating the theft of some cotton goods from a local mill. Under a bench in an upstairs bedroom at his cottage, the law officers found a trunk containing the mould together with some counterfeit shillings and a counterfeit half-crown, a crucible and some pieces of metal with holes cut in them.

Orme, a collier, was examined by a magistrate at Macclesfield, during the interrogation, Judge Arden noted, Partington 'saw the prisoner put something into his mouth and heard it ring against his teeth'. Turner also witnessed the incident. Orme's mouth was forced open and, the memorandum stated, 'there fell out two shillings, one of which fell into [Partington's] hand and the other upon the floor'. They were counterfeit shillings which, it was later proved, had been produced from the mould found at Orme's house.

Orme claimed he had recently let the room to a man called Oddie and that the trunk and its contents belonged to him. He discovered them in the room after this lodger had left.

Reporting Orme's death 21 years later, the *Chronicle* described him as 'a poor, hard-working man with a large family' and related, '[He] found a crucible for coining, with a few base shillings; the latter of which he put carelessly into his pocket; but, as he solemnly protested, did not attempt to utter them.' Arriving for his interview with the magistrate, Orme suddenly remembered he still had the coins on him.

The report went on: 'His fears got so much the ascendancy over his prudence, that he hastily put his hand into his pocket, and taking out the shillings, crammed them into his mouth…[a] circumstance so very strong, and apparently so conclusive against the prisoner, could not fail to have its weight with the jury, and the poor fellow was convicted.'

Orme was to have been hanged with John Oakes. But, due to the intervention of his brother Edward, a London cheese factor and hop merchant of some repute, and a petition endorsed by a prominent London MP, he was eventually reprieved – despite the fact that, after his conviction, he had tried (unsuccessfully) to break out of the Castle Gaol. Orme and his supporters continued the fight to clear his name and in 1789, after serving five years in the County Gaol, he was released and pardoned.

But if both Chester papers believed that Orme, like Oakes, had been wrongly convicted, Judge Arden (later Lord Alvanley) was equally sure he was guilty. In his confidential memorandum, dated 19 May 1784, he explained his thinking on the subject. It was written to the Home Secretary in response to Orme's mercy plea, but it also touched on the cases of Oakes and Lowe.

Regarding Orme, the Chief Justice stated that he had been 'perfectly satisfied' with the jury's guilty verdict. Then he went on to say, 'John Oakes, who lived in the same neighbourhood, was convicted at the same sessions of a capital offence under the same Act...under which Orme was indicted. I left Oakes and Orme for execution, having respited William Lowe, who was convicted of a similar offence, but against whom the proof was by no means so strong as against Oakes and Orme.'

Then came the key passage. Written before the Home Secretary ruled on Orme's petition, it seemed to be anticipating the minister's decision, when it offered the opinion that 'Oakes had by no means so good a character as Orme and, in case only one example ought to be made, was the properer [*sic*] object of severity'.

On such arbitrary reasoning was the life of John Oakes adjudged to be expendable – a classic example of what Robert Hughes, in *The Fatal Shore* (his masterly account of the convict transportation system), describes as 'the erratic mercy of the courts'. It might have been more relevant, and fairer, to toss a coin...

So was Oakes, as the jury decided, an active member of a counterfeiting gang? Or, as the local press and his other supporters believed, the object of a grave miscarriage of justice – an honest farmer who made a genuine mistake in handling illegal goods and became the innocent victim of another man's inordinate vindictiveness?

To favour the latter is to be persuaded that John Hawkesworth was so consumed by hatred after Oakes's civil action against him, and so unconscionably wicked, that he was prepared to see Oakes hang to satisfy his thirst for revenge. That, on a personal level, he was in the grip of such a powerful emotion – yet, when it came to business, he was able to put his feelings to one side and help Oakes out when the latter was in need of a horse doctor. It also begs the question: would Oakes have sent for him to attend to his injured animal in the first place if, as he claimed later, he was aware of the strength of Hawkesworth's enmity towards him? There must have been other blacksmiths he could have called upon.

For most of what Hawkesworth claimed to have seen at Oakes's farm during his two-month vigil, the assize jurors had only his word to go on. He obviously impressed them as a public-spirited citizen and a trustworthy witness; at the same time, the one part of his evidence that could be corroborated – the details of the Wednesday morning raid that turned up the coining equipment – must have made it difficult for them to believe that Oakes was telling the truth.

When the constables arrived at the farm, as they were able to confirm to the court, the cutting machine and the two presses had been covered up with hay and straw. Surely, if equipment of this highly-criminal nature was in transit awaiting onward delivery, as Oakes maintained, it would have been packed in crates or disguised within some sort of packaging, or, at the very least, more effectively concealed. Oakes said he was only looking after it for someone else. But if it was not being used for the purpose for which it was

The Secret of the Sealed-up Stable

The view from 'Gallows Hill' in 1827. It would have been the last earthly sight for countless numbers of condemned criminals who were 'launched into eternity' at Boughton, Chester. (From the author's collection.)

designed – that is, to manufacture counterfeit coins – why was it assembled and in full working order in his stable? Also, sealing up the building seems an elaborate precaution if the shipment was only being stored there temporarily. It suggests a rather longer-term arrangement...and that Oakes and his friends were going to some trouble to keep it hidden from prying eyes.

In the wall of evidence that Hawkesworth carefully constructed around the two defendants, one small but significant brick was the imitation shilling he said Oakes gave him that November morning in his kitchen. It was a tangible link between the farmer and the forgers...if it could be matched to one of the dies that were uncovered along with the coining presses in his stable. In his 17 February statement, Hawkesworth said he still had it 'in his custody'. But, judging by the newspaper coverage of the trial, no such connection was established.

In the end it made no difference. Hawkesworth was such a convincing witness that, on his say-so alone, the jurors found the 'colouring' charge proved. Had they not done so, it is almost certain that they would have convicted Oakes on the second capital count of possession – which did not rely solely on the blacksmith's testimony – and that the outcome would have been the same.

The judge had already sentenced one man to death for possessing coining equipment (John Orme), and, as he stated in his memorandum to the Home Secretary after the trial, having assessed the respective characters of the condemned pair, Mr Justice Arden took the view that Oakes was the more 'suitable' candidate to hang – or 'the properer object of severity', as he put it – should the minister decide to make an example of only one of them.

It was an opinion that was likely to bode ill for Oakes, whichever charge produced the guilty verdict. The farmer turned faker of shillings was – to coin a phrase – done for either way.

*　*　*

Joseph Allen was another farmer who, after struggling to make a living off the land, took to the road to supplement his income and support his growing family. He became a buyer and seller of farm produce, and it was while he was on his travels that he, too, became drawn into the dangerous world of currency crime. Whereas for John Oakes it had been forged coins, three decades later phoney pound-notes were the seeds of Allen's undoing. And, like Oakes, instead of a rich harvest, all he reaped was the whirlwind...

Chapter Seven

Money for New Rope

To everyone who knew him, farmer Joseph Allen was a man of unquestionable character: honest, industrious, reliable, a son of the soil and the salt of the earth. Such was his business reputation that he was able to obtain sizeable loans simply on the basis of a handshake and a gentleman's agreement.

Following in his father's wheel tracks, he had started farming in a small way in his native Acton (modern day Acton Bridge) in the parish of Weaverham, near Northwich. Later he began buying and selling local produce – meal, flour, cheese, potatoes and fruit mainly – and, with his horse and cart, trading at Manchester's weekly market. Then, in May 1816, at the age of 39, he took on a much bigger tenancy about a mile away in the village of Crowton. From having only two or three cows he now had a herd of 20 or more. But his rent shot up from around £30 a year to nearer £300…and he got into debt.

With the extra income he earned from his market trading – and no shortage of friends ready and willing to put their hands in their pockets to help him – there seemed no reason to believe that this would be anything more than a temporary cash-flow problem. Which made the solution he appears to have chosen to ease his financial worries drastic in the extreme.

Joseph Allen, for whom the term 'genuine' might have been invented, began spending money that was anything but. Through his regular trips to Manchester market, this rough-hewn rustic had come increasingly into contact with more streetwise wheeler-dealers – the hardened rogues and racketeers of the urban criminal fraternity – and with one area of illicit trade in particular. Tempted, it seems, by the promise of easy profits and a less strenuous way of boosting his earnings, he became involved with a gang of counterfeiters. As a result, he acquired a considerable number of forged £1 notes, and between the beginning of October and early December 1816 he paid his bills almost exclusively in the phoney money, palming off up to £25-worth at a time to his suppliers.

The judge at his trial would describe the case as the worst of its kind he had ever experienced, and the number of forged notes involved as 'frightful'. It was alleged that

Allen passed more than £100-worth during the two-and-a-half-month period – well over £6,000 at today's values.

The timber and brick cottages in this old photograph of Crowton have long since disappeared, but they would have been a familiar sight to Joseph Allen as he travelled to and from the village with his horse and cart. (Photograph courtesy of Crowton Women's Institute.)

Money for New Rope

It was indicative of the trust Allen commanded that he was able to get away with it for so long. As soon as the dud notes began circulating, several of his regular suppliers voiced their doubts about those he had paid to them, but, in the beginning at least, no one suspected him of any criminal intent. People believed him when he said he had come by them in the course of his business dealings and thought them to be good – an opinion that many of them continued to share even after his conviction.

In late November, however, traders with whom he had recently settled accounts began turning up at the office of attorney Peter Nicholson. Fearing they might have been paid in bad money, they took their concerns – and the suspect 'oncers' – to the Warrington lawyer, who was clerk to the local magistrates. A Bank of England expert was called in, and he quickly confirmed that the notes were forgeries, and very good ones at that.

Though he had not been the last person to tender all the notes, the paper trail led ultimately back to Allen, and on Monday 9 December William Tildesley and William Caldwell, Warrington's two borough constables, together with a third man, William Allsop, visited his Crowton farm. They searched the house, and on a desk they found about a dozen £1 notes; in the desk drawer there were a further half-dozen tied in a bundle and several more in a pocket book. They were all new notes that did not appear to have been in circulation. Many of them, like those handed over to Peter Nicholson, were numbered sequentially.

At a time when the provincial public had no great confidence in paper money, preferring the comforting feel of a gold sovereign to the flimsy pound note, it was a normal precaution to write on the back of each note the name of the person from whom it was received; the notes seized at Joseph Allen's home bore names such as 'Jelley', 'Heap' and 'Knott'. Allen, it appeared, had been busy endorsing them when the constables arrived, for the ink was still wet.

'Jelley', the name on most of the forged notes, was James Jelley, a shopkeeper and dealer who lived in Long Millgate in Manchester. He was also arrested along with Allen's brother Samuel, and the pair appeared at Lancaster Spring Assizes in March 1817. Jelley was charged with 'uttering' (putting into circulation) forged bank notes at Manchester, but was acquitted. Samuel Allen, 45, pleaded guilty to simple possession of forged bank notes at Warrington and – though it emerged later that he was probably a bigger player in the counterfeiting game than his brother – he was spared the rope and was sentenced to 14 years' transportation instead.

In all, 19 people were indicted at the Lancaster Assizes for currency crimes, the great majority of which involved uttering forged notes in Manchester. It was claimed that they changed hands regularly at the city's market, where Allen transacted much of his business.

Joseph Allen went on trial at Cheshire's Spring Assizes on Saturday 19 April 1817. Of the 80 prisoners before the court, more than 30 faced capital charges – a cause list which Chester's Second Justice, Mr William Draper Best, described as 'a calendar of depravity shocking to humanity [which] could not be looked at without fear and the most painful sensations'. Because of the volume of business, the presiding judge, Chief Justice Sir William Garrow, ordered that the court would sit until 5pm on the first day and begin at 8 o'clock each morning.

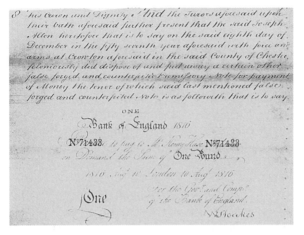

Detail from the indictment against Joseph Allen, identifying one of the forged £1 notes found in his possession during the raid on his farm. (By permission of the National Archives.)

Allen, who pleaded not guilty, was indicted with uttering bank notes 'knowing [them] to have been forged and counterfeited'. During his five-hour trial the Crown paraded some two dozen witnesses to testify against him – though many of them, the very people he had defrauded, were also willing to attest to his previous excellent character. Listening to their testimonials, it must have been difficult at times to distinguish them from the defence witnesses.

In its extensive coverage of the case on 2 May the *Chronicle* reported, 'The trial of this unfortunate man has excited an uncommon degree of interest amongst all classes of the community; and the melancholy fate which threatens him will, we hope, operate as a lasting example on those who, straying from the paths of honesty and virtue, may become the victims of avarice and ill-acquired wealth. Allen, it will appear from the trial, bore a character of extraordinary goodness; his integrity was supposed to be inflexible, and his trading character stood so singularly high that large sums of money have been advanced to him without any other security being demanded from him but his word.'

How and when Allen's involvement with the counterfeiters began are questions that remain unanswered to this day. But the *Chronicle* felt confident enough to state, 'We do not believe that it has existed long; but the time, nevertheless, has been sufficient to throw into public circulation, an unexampled mass of forged notes: the injury they would have done to the mercantile world is incalculable; and the hard earnings of the poor have been sacrificed to a pitiable extent.'

It would appear, said the *Chronicle*, that James Jelley and Samuel Allen 'were in some degree dealers and co-partners in this infamous traffic', whereas Joseph Allen 'it is clear from his mode of proceeding, was but a novice in the business'. The newspaper added, however, 'There is little doubt, from the regular succession of numbers in the notes paid by Allen, but what he received them in large quantities from the makers.'

One of the first to receive counterfeit notes from Allen – and one of the first to bring them to the attention of the law – was John Plumb, off whom Allen seems to have bought farm produce on a regular basis. He paid Plumb £10 on 21 October and a further £20 on 18 November. By this time, Plumb told the court, he had heard that Allen had been given some 'baddish' notes, so, in the defendant's presence, he got a pen and marked all 20 of the notes with the letter 'A'. When Allen arrived with his next payment (£16) on 25 November, Plumb was working in the fields and was unable to mark the money, commenting to the effect that 'he could not tell the good notes from bad ones'. Allen, he said, offered to change any that were found to be bad.

Money for New Rope

Plumb accepted the money but his doubts remained; so, later that day, he gave the £16 to his son, plus another £7 he had received from Allen previously, and asked him to take the notes to Mr Nicholson, whose office was in Sankey Street, Warrington, to have them checked. It was a journey of discovery that several more of Allen's business associates would make in the days ahead.

When he was asked by the defence to describe Allen's character, however, John Plumb had no hesitation in saying, 'I never met with a more honest man.' And so it went on...

Farmer's wife Mary Okell said she had considered Allen 'a very respectable character'. She had received eight of the nine forged £1 notes Allen had given to Samuel Woodward of Acton for a quantity of potatoes.

Mrs Margaret Hazlehurst, who farmed at nearby Grimsditch, said of him, 'I have known [him] for seven years as a decent farmer.' She had sold some cheese to Allen and he had paid her £38 10s 0d, which included 25 pound notes – all counterfeit.

William Dean had also 'never heard anything [bad] against Allen', whom he had known for many years. He had received two payments from Allen, one of £3 and the other £5, all in one-pound notes. Every one of them was confirmed as a forgery.

Dean's brother John, who had known Allen 'perhaps 12 years' and had many dealings with him, said, 'He always paid me honourably till late while.'

But the most glowing tribute came from Alex Thompson, clerk and cashier at the Trent and Mersey Canal Company warehouse at Preston Brook. He said Allen had been doing business with the canal company 'every week, more or less' for 20 years, and, said Thompson, 'His general character was one of the best that dealt with us: honest and honourable. He has paid me many hundred pounds.'

It was only a single pound that Allen gave to Mrs Elizabeth Harrison, licensee of the Mermaid in Bridge Street, Warrington, when he and two friends made a mid-day stop at the pub in December. But it was another valuable piece of evidence against the Crowton farmer. He offered her the note after having lunch at the pub. She told the court, 'I did not like it, and said if he would mark it I would take it. He marked it with his own name.'

The landlady took the note to Peter Nicholson (something like £50 of the bad money eventually found its way into the lawyer's possession in this way) and on 9 December the constables raided Allen's farm.

Tildesley said he saw a number of pound notes 'lying promiscuously' (carelessly?) on Allen's desk – he counted 11 – and there were other notes in a pocket book and a parcel of six in the desk drawer. The latter, said the constable, were all torn at the ends, 'as if done together', and Allen told him they were 'ragged' ones, which he intended to return to the people who had given them to him. The notes on Allen's desk had the names 'Jelley', 'Heap' and 'Knott' written on the backs – 'and the ink was wet, as if just done,' the officer added.

William Allsop uncovered further notes in the farmhouse search. 'They were all perfectly clean,' he said, 'and had no appearance of having been in circulation.'

All the recovered forgeries were subsequently examined by Bank of England inspector Thomas Glover. A currency expert with 24 years' experience, he said it was his opinion that they had been printed quite recently from the same plate. Although the ink had more of a brownish hue than black and the paper was rather coarser than the genuine article, the forgeries were very good, he told the court. The signatures on them appeared to be those of officials properly authorised by the bank to sign notes, but closer scrutiny revealed that they were all done in the same handwriting.

As well as Jelley, the prosecution also managed to trace two of the other people from whom Allen claimed he had received the counterfeit money. In court Robert Heap agreed he had had dealings with Allen, and Samuel Knott said he was acquainted with the prisoner. But neither would admit to paying him in £1 notes. Allen himself was unable to produce anyone who would.

When he was called upon for his defence, however, he continued to insist that he had come by the notes innocently while going about his lawful business. He declared, 'I received all the notes, [taking them] for good ones, from Jelley and others.'

In two statements he made to a Warrington magistrate, both taken down and read to the court by Mr Nicholson, Allen said he had received £29 in notes from Jelley on one occasion and £81 on another, that he had £90 from Heap, and that Knott, from Fairfield, had also paid him 'some notes'.

William Bailey, clerk at the Manchester Meal House, with whom Allen also traded regularly, confirmed that the defendant had conducted some business with James Jelley in November 1816. The farmer had had 13 loads of flour for sale, and, after first asking Bailey to sell it for him, he announced he had found a buyer. Shortly afterwards Jelley arrived at the Meal House with two carts and took away 'eight loads and a piece' at 50 shillings a load. At that time, said Bailey, there were 'many forged notes in circulation in Manchester market'.

Allen's nephew James Jameson (who had also been arrested in connection with the forged currency but was released without charge) said he lived in a basement in Long Millgate 'not above three roods from Jelley's house'. On Saturday night, 5 December, four days before he was taken up, he said he was at Jelley's shop and saw him pay Allen 'a quantity of notes' for some cheese. The notes appeared 'fresh ones'.

John Davies, a miller from Onston, between Crowton and Acton Bridge, claimed that Allen always preferred new notes to 'ragged' ones. But on the subject of paper money, he said of him, 'There never was a more ignorant man'. He had attended Manchester market with Allen on many occasions and had seen him paid in notes, and he would often ask his opinion on their authenticity. He had heard the prisoner say many times that he could not tell a good note from a bad one.

'He never liked to trust his own judgement,' said Davies. 'But he would take any sort of note if it looked fresh.' When he was shown the six torn notes found in Allen's desk drawer, Davies responded, 'I do not think he would take such notes as these.'

He and Allen had been doing business for 10 years. 'I have never dealt with a more honest man in my life,' he declared. Which was more or less the same view expressed by neighbouring farmers Thomas Gandy, Robert Witter and Thomas Fryer, who also spoke on his behalf. And Allen's landlord, Samuel Hignett, who had known him for more than 10 years, said he bore 'a very good character'.

Mr Hignett was able to confirm that Allen was paying him rent of 'between £200 and £300' a year (the latter the equivalent of over £18,000 today). And it is in that brief statement – and the evidence of another witness, James Harrison – that the best clues to Joseph Allen's suicidal slide into crime probably lie.

Money for New Rope

Harrison, a Weaverham trader, said he had been buying fruit, cheese and flour from Allen for the past two or three years, though he had known the farmer much longer. Then he stated, 'He owes me £108, within 11d, and promised to pay it before now.' Asked by the judge to elaborate, Harrison replied, 'He has owed me the £108 near two years, and could not pay me on account of taking his [new] farm.'

In debt due to the extra overheads of running a far larger farm, and well known for his ignorance of money and naïve faith in new notes, Joseph Allen, it seems, would have been an easy target for the counterfeiters and shady dealers he had become acquainted with in Manchester. And with a wife and seven children to support, he was no doubt in need of some 'ready cash'. Judge Garrow was unsympathetic, however. In his summing up, he practically dismantled every prop in Allen's defence.

Pointing to the fact that the notes found in his possession were in regular sequence, Sir William said it was for the members of the jury to determine whether they thought it possible that such a run of notes could have accrued to the prisoner after they had been in circulation. He had to say he thought it 'extremely improbable'.

Some of Allen's own witnesses had admitted that, at first sight, they had been suspicious of some of the notes he had given them. 'If he (Allen) was so cautious, as has been described, by what likelihood would he have taken them?' the judge asked.

It was a 'material feature' of the prosecution evidence, said His Lordship, that Allen was caught with forged notes endorsed so recently that the ink was hardly dry. The judge interpreted this as an attempt 'to convey an impression that such notes bore the names of those from whom they were received'. But Allen was unable to produce a single witness prepared to admit to paying him in £1 notes.

Ivy House Farm, Crowton, pictured in its early 20th-century heyday as a working farm. Evidence suggests that the farmhouse that stood on the site previously was where, in 1816, tenant Joseph Allen's involvement in a forged pound-notes racket was uncovered. (Photograph courtesy of Mr Robert Kinsey.)

Regarding James Jelley, and the possibility that Allen had acquired most of the notes from him 'in the common intercourse of trade', the judge remarked that 'all the dealings [with Jelley] that could be ascertained only amounted to eight loads of flour at 50 shillings each load'.

He commented, 'The immense number of notes paid by the prisoner, and found upon him, all new and fresh, exclude the possibility that they had ever been in circulation. If he knew such notes were forged, his guilt is clear, the indictment fully made out.'

The jury returned its guilty verdict after conferring for only 10 minutes. Passing sentence, Sir William told Allen he had been convicted on evidence that 'could not sanction the shadow of a doubt'. His duty was also clear: to impose the severest sentence 'in order that all now present may be acquainted with the awful fate which awaits on a crime which will shortly place you on the verge of eternity'.

He continued, 'Yours is a case of such enormity, of such exceeding magnitude, as far to exceed any that ever I was acquainted with. Your traffic was carried on to as amazing an extent as a man could possibly be tempted to engage in.'

He was satisfied that Allen had been 'in connection with others, forming a desperate gang, whose means of wealth were wrung from the plunder of the tradesman and the public generally, and whose pecuniary advantages were gained at the peril of their lives'. The judge went on: 'Founding your projects on a good character, you availed yourself of the unsuspicious impressions created thereby, and put out your spurious notes in frightful numbers – thus impoverishing others; and, by running the risk of such notes being found in their possession, putting their liberty and lives in jeopardy.'

And he added, 'Your conviction, therefore, involves in it such aggravated circumstances that as entirely to exclude the slightest participation in the hope of mercy.'

After listening to the evidence 'with considerable attention' and 'without evincing any signs of fear or apprehension', Allen heard the judge's words with mounting anxiety. And, with the solemn intonation of the death sentence ringing in his ears, he left the court 'in a state of extreme agitation', the *Chronicle*'s trial report concluded.

The execution was fixed for Saturday 10 May and for the first six days after his condemnation, it was said, Allen took no refreshment other than water. However, due apparently to the ministrations of the Castle Gaol's long-serving Ordinary, Revd Willan, and two brother clergymen, his moroseness gave way to 'calm placidity and resignation', and he began eating regularly, said the *Chronicle* on 16 May. The paper described the scenes as the prisoner – 'this misguided man', as it termed him – left the castle for his journey to the City Gaol...and the scaffold:

> 'About 11 o'clock he was brought up into the Constable's house and from thence through the Debtors' yard to the Turnkey's Lodge. Here a dreadful tremor took possession of his frame. He wept bitterly...About twenty minutes past 11 o'clock, the order from the city Sheriffs, demanding his body for execution, was received, and when this was communicated to him, and the door slowly opening, presented to his view the military guard, his fear almost overpowered his faculties. The ringing of a passing bell at St Mary's [the church adjoining the Castle], a few minutes before the culprit was brought out of the prison, had a very solemn effect. It was a melancholy accompaniment to the

scene. Immediately previous to leaving the Castle he exclaimed: "Eh! dear, dear – what a great change I shall shortly undergo!" This sentence was uttered with great solemnity; and Mr Armitstead [one of the three clergymen in attendance] recommended him, in his way through the city, to keep his eyes from the mob: this he promised to do, but on arriving at Glover's-stone, the county boundary, he took away the handkerchief which he had held to his eyes and, mounting the cart, surveyed the multitude with great attention. When the cavalcade had passed thro' Bridge-street [and] Watergate-street, at the bottom of Nicholas-street he recognised some person and held up his hands as if in a threatening manner. He made no observations, but shook his head. Arriving at the City Gaol…[his] near approach to the precipice of eternity did not in the slightest degree relax his steadiness.'

Standing beneath the gallows, he was exhorted to make a confession, but Allen stuck resolutely to his story. He stated again, and for the last time, that he 'did not know a good note from a bad one'.

Just like John Oakes before him, Allen had rigorously maintained his innocence throughout his time in custody, and from his condemned cell, as the final days of his life continued to follow the same strangely parallel course, he also issued a written declaration of his innocence, protesting, in the most fervent terms, that he had been unjustly convicted. As with Oakes, it was a claim that received a fair amount of public sympathy.

The *Chronicle*'s execution report went on: 'The preparations at the Drop being completed, he ascended the platform with much steadiness and the Executioner tied the rope round his neck. At this trying moment his fortitude forsook him – his knees trembled violently, and the cord by which he was about to be suspended, now served him as a support.'

The prayers and final rites over, Joseph Allen gave the signal and was 'ushered to that dread bourne from whence no traveller returns'. It was not, however, a quick and painless passage. And the executioner, Samuel Burrows (who else?), looked on helplessly as another victim endured an agonising end.

Said the *Chronicle*, 'We never recollect seeing a man so long convulsed. It was near 10 minutes before life was extinct; in the course of which he was dreadfully convulsed, so much so that the irons on his legs shook rapidly with an appalling clank!'

In the *Chester Courant*'s report (13 May) it was revealed that, after hanging for the usual time, Allen's body was taken down and 'deposited in a handsome coffin, furnished, we understand, at the joint expense of some gentlemen, who live in the neighbourhood of Weaverham'. The following day it was buried in the graveyard of Weaverham Parish Church, watched by a large congregation of Allen's relatives and friends.

To them, shortly before his execution, he had, with no little difficulty, penned a final message. Illiterate, at times almost unintelligible, it was reproduced in the *Chronicle* verbatim – 'in order that the world may judge of the writer's capacity, and the sincerity and truth of the document', the newspaper explained. The message read:

'dear frends there as ben great deal of false reports Concerning my triel And my life lourd [?] as Well thrown away iave been rongsfuly aqsed [accused] for idid not no good notes from bad iave done nothing in this World to nobody that i no ove that i should have had lost my life My dear friends i beg you Will not think ill of my dear Wife and Children throu my mis forten may the lord bless them and i hope you Will all be good towards them for i Canot do any thing for them any more but i hope god Will not for get them so i bed you all fear Well and god bless you all and i hope We shall all meet together in heven in alitle time so may god be With you all amen for my time is near done in this World but dear friends think of my dear Wife and my dear Children for my sake god bless you – Joseph Allen.'

And the *Chronicle*'s verdict on the case? After summing up the evidence, the paper's execution reporter pronounced, 'There is too much reason to fear that Jelley had dealt in the dangerous traffic in counterfeit notes – but of the guilt of Allen, it is not our province to make any observations, excepting that, if the word of a dying man might be believed, we would pronounce him the unconscious instrument in the hands of others, rather than the guilty principal himself.'

And 'guilty principals' there were aplenty at this time. In the years 1805–1818, of the 1,035 people executed in England and Wales 214 of them were convicted of currency offences – a remarkable one in five of the total. And, in the very week it reported Allen's execution, the *Chester Courant* was urging its readers to be on the lookout for the latest batch of forgeries, copies of a new set of silver coins only recently struck by the Royal Mint.

The warning, on 13 May 1817, was contained in a news item headlined 'Caution to the Public', which appeared directly alongside the paper's execution report. It began, 'A great number of counterfeit sixpences, shillings and half-crowns, in imitation of the new coinage, are now in circulation in this city which, at first view, appears [*sic*] tolerably well executed.'

It gave the following advice on how to spot the duds: 'The most obvious difference is in the countenance of His Majesty [King George III], which is more stern than in the

Crowton village today, with (in the background) the former Ivy House Farm. (Photograph by the author.)

good ones, and the muscles of the face more strongly marked. The dotting which encircles the letters is indistinct, especially on the reverse side, and the distance between the dotting and the extreme edge is of irregular width and broader. The letters of the motto *Honi soit qui mal y pense* ["Evil be to him who evil thinks", the motto of the Order of the Garter] are too large, the word "*qui*" seems nearly worn out, and the whole of the word "*pense*" is visible, whereas in the genuine coin the letters N. and S. are half covered by the scroll of the shield. The *fleur de lis* in the crown, and the George suspended from the collar of the Order of the Garter [the jewel set in the insignia] are clumsy and indistinct and the milling rough and irregular.'

With the breadwinner taken from them, Allen's family, the real victims of his foolhardy crime, were left in a 'deplorable and desolate state', according to the *Chronicle*. It was hoped, said the paper, that the public would rally round and support the appeal for subscriptions that had gone out locally to 'afford some relief' to his wife and children and his elderly mother, who also lived with them. However, with all the children under the age of 14, it was never going to be possible for the family to keep the farm going, and within days of Allen's execution it was reported that all their furniture and agricultural equipment had been sold at public auction.

All that can be ascertained from property records is that, 20 years later, there were no Allens living in Crowton. At that time the Hignett family owned five separate parcels of land in the village. Which one Joseph Allen tenanted is not known, and while it is tempting to think that the crooked farmer may have lived in Bent Lane, it is more likely to have been in what is today Station Road (the B5153). On an 1839 tithe map that is the only piece of Hignett land shown as having a dwelling attached. The old farmhouse may have survived until 1886, when the existing property was built on the site. Known as Ivy House Farm, it ceased to be a working farm in the 1980s, when the buildings were converted into residential accommodation.

*   *   *

Like Joseph and Samuel Allen, history records that William and John Proudlove were brothers who also ended up on the wrong side of the law. Unlike the Allens, the Proudloves, who were born and raised in Sandbach, were only interested in real money – though they weren't too particular about how they obtained it. The other big difference was that both Proudlove brothers were hanged for their crimes. In William's case, *twice…*

Chapter Eight

The Men they Hanged Twice

On a temporary platform, erected high up on the front wall of the building it stood...an unexpectedly elaborate-looking structure, at once unfamiliar yet unmistakable. Looming menacingly over the handsome Georgian-style doorway, the fancy new gallows had been sited for maximum impact. Shortly after noon the heavy, iron-studded door that gave directly on to the platform swung open and William Proudlove and George Glover stepped out of the dark, windowless passageway and blinked in the sunlight of a pleasant spring day. As they walked stiffly across the wooden boards, the people packed below ceased their jostling and craned their necks in eager anticipation.

It was Saturday 6 May 1809. The stage was set for an occasion to remember.

The men, shackled hand and foot, were poised to become the first capital convicts hanged at Chester's new purpose-built City Gaol and House of Correction, completed two years previously to replace the ruinous – and infamous – Northgate Gaol. They were also to be the first executed in Cheshire on the 'New Drop'.

With its raised platform and falling trapdoor mechanism, the newfangled killing machine was, in fact, of similar design to the one that had been in operation at Newgate Gaol in London since 1783. Constructed here over the entrance to the House of Correction, it was regarded as a more efficient means of dispatch than death by strangulation, which, for centuries past, had been the fate of countless condemned criminals strung up on the traditional roadside gallows.

Market-day visitors swelled the crowd that had assembled in carnival-like mood to share in the momentous event. The first execution in the city for eight years, it had been heralded as the dawn of a more humane and enlightened age of capital punishment. But it all went horribly wrong. For the third time in succession, a public execution in Chester descended into chaos and a degrading spectacle...and William Proudlove and George Glover went down in history, so to speak, as the only Cheshire convicts to experience 'the drop' and live to tell the tale.

The preliminaries had gone smoothly enough. The men were marched briskly on to the scaffold and positioned over the trapdoor, their heads were hooded, their nooses tightened and the executioner withdrew to one side to operate the 'fatal lever'. But then calamity struck. As the bolt securing the trapdoor was sprung, and the prisoners plummeted side by side through the wooden floor, astonishingly *both* ropes broke and the pair went crashing into the pit below.

The crowd was in uproar and the sheriffs and other officials, who had been seated at the back of the platform, rushed forward to see what had happened. Amid the pandemonium it was discovered that the prisoners, though half-throttled, had both survived the fall unscathed.

In a state of some distress they were helped back inside the gaol, where they had to suffer an interminable delay while fresh ropes were obtained and tested (more thoroughly

The Men they Hanged Twice

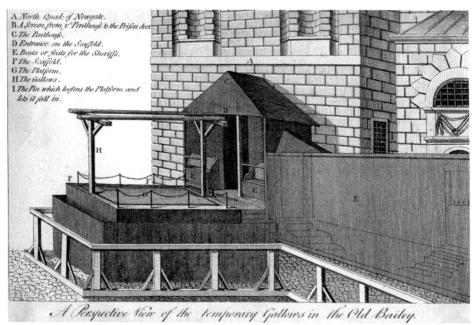

A *North Quad: of Newgate.*
B *A Screen from y.` Penthouse to the Prison door.*
C *The Penthouse.*
D *Entrance on the Scaffold.*
E *Boxes or seats for the Sheriffs.*
F *The Scaffold.*
G *The Platform.*
H *The Gallows.*
I *The Pin which loosens the Platform and lets it fall in.*

A Perspective View of the temporary Gallows in the Old Bailey.

The 'New Drop', introduced at Chester City Gaol in 1809, was based on the gallows at Newgate Gaol in London (above). Though it had a raised platform and falling trapdoor mechanism, the short length of rope used meant that victims remained almost completely in view during their last dying moments. (From the author's collection.)

this time, one supposes). Consequently, it was almost two hours later – their nerves steadied by liquor and some comforting words from the prison chaplain – when they were led out to face up to their ordeal once again. They mounted the scaffold steps with remarkable composure, under the circumstances, and were hanged at the second attempt in double-quick time.

'A most distressing circumstance' was how the *Chester Courant* described the affair in its edition of 9 May. 'Distressing and heart-rending' echoed the *Chronicle* three days later, commenting, 'The reader may here paint in his own mind the feelings of the spectators, but no language can describe it.'

There was no suggestion of sabotage – that the ropes had been tampered with by friends of the prisoners – so where did the blame lie for this frightful fiasco? Though the press did not state it in so many words, the inference was obvious enough: it was the hangman who provided and tested the ropes, the hangman who supervised the construction of the gallows and checked that it was working properly – so it was his fault if something went wrong. However, at a time when the local papers never named executioners, seemingly policy-bound to safeguard their identities for fear of inciting reprisals, they evidently felt constrained from making any personal accusations. All that would change, of course, when Samuel Burrows started his lengthy stint as the city's 'finisher of the law'.

The papers reported no hostility directed towards the anonymous functionary by the spectators, either. Among them the immediate reaction to the freak accident had ranged from loutish derision to shock and consternation, but at the end they had become uniformly subdued.

It was an expression of sympathy that would not otherwise have been extended to the two small-time thieves, who were part of a tough and determined gang, possibly as many as 13 in number, that had carried out a daring late night raid on Lawton Salt Works, near Alsager, the previous winter. When Officers of the Excise caught them red-handed removing bags of salt from a warehouse, a ferocious pitched battle ensued involving more than 20 men, during which one of the officers was shot and seriously wounded.

Proudlove, 32, and Glover, 23, sometime farm workers, were found guilty at Chester Spring Assizes of shooting at the exciseman with intent to kill and received the death penalty. Neither was the gunman, but, in the eyes of the law, they had conspired with others to commit a crime knowing one of their number was armed and were, therefore, just as culpable.

Four other men tried with them were acquitted. Three more alleged gang members were tracked down and brought before the court later. Of those, one was also cleared, and the other two were convicted on the lesser charge of stealing salt from the works and were sentenced to transportation. Another member of the gang turned King's evidence; the rest, including the man who actually shot the exciseman, seem to have evaded justice entirely.

While the case, and its improbable postscript, assured him of a special place in the history of Cheshire crime, the twice-hanged Proudlove also shares another claim to ill-fame. For, 20 years later almost to the day and more or less on the same spot, his brother John completed a unique, if unhappy, family double when he was hanged for highway robbery.

William Proudlove's journey to the gallows began on Monday 17 October 1808 when he left his home at Sandbach Heath to walk the three miles to Smallwood for an afternoon of drinking and gambling. With his mates William Newton and Joseph Beech, he arrived at the Bull's Head Inn around 1pm (a former toll house on the London-Edinburgh coaching route, the pub, considerably larger now, is on what is today the A50 Newcastle Road between Holmes Chapel and Kidsgrove). George Glover, who lived with his parents at their farm in Smallwood, was already there, as was Thomas Johnson, also of Sandbach, who had spent the previous night at the inn. For the next three hours the five friends supped ale and played cards.

At some point in the carousing, mention was made of the robbery that had been planned for that night at Lawton Salt Works. Salt, which, during the period of the Napoleonic Wars (1803–1815), was subject to a particularly heavy tax, was a valuable commodity and smuggling was rife at this time. Each works had its own Government-appointed salt officer to ensure all duties were paid and watchmen (excisemen) to prevent theft. Salt tax was abolished in 1825.

The Lawton works, which stood alongside the Trent and Mersey (or Grand Trunk) Canal at Odd Rode, two miles south of Smallwood, was the largest salt-making centre in the Nantwich group (or 'Collection') of salt works. It was built while the canal was being cut through the township during 1777–1778 to replace a much older works, which had been established about 100 years earlier in the little valley to the south, where the River Wheelock runs on a parallel course. The river is the boundary between the townships of Odd Rode and Lawton, and the original works was on the Lawton side of the river.

Following a major landslip in the valley bottom in 1937, the site of the new works was abandoned. Cleared and landscaped, it is now known as Rode Heath Rise, a countryside park managed by Cheshire County Council.

Thomas Johnson (22) would say later that the afternoon conversation in the Bulls Head was the first he knew about the robbery (despite the fact that his father Samuel and a brother, also called Samuel, were both in on it), and he maintained that he only agreed to join the others at the last minute. For someone so lately recruited to the gang he seems to have made a substantial contribution to the preparations for the robbery, for, by his own admission, he supplied most of the bags in which the stolen salt was to be carried away and, later, a horse on which to move them from their initial hiding place beside the canal to a safer location nearby.

However, it was understandable that he would want to play down his role in the crime, for by this time he had agreed to turn in the gang in exchange for immunity from prosecution and to testify against them at their trial.

At about 4 o'clock the five of them parted company to attend to their allotted tasks; Thomas Johnson returned to Sandbach, accompanied by Proudlove, and picked up nine bags from his house and a further five from the nearby home of another gang member, Joseph Lowe. Lowe was the 'getaway driver': his horse and cart would be used in the final stage of the operation, transporting the stolen salt to Manchester to be sold.

Lawton Saltworks at Odd Rode, where an exciseman was shot when a dozen-strong gang raided the premises in 1808. Two gang members, William Proudlove and George Glover, would become known as 'The Men They Hanged Twice' after an extraordinary incident at their double execution the following year. (Photograph courtesy of Mr George Twigg.)

The Lawton Salt Works site is now part of a countryside park known as Rode Heath Rise, managed by Cheshire County Council. (Photograph by the author.)

In the first phase of the plan, however, the robbers were to remove the salt from the works and stash it temporarily in premises belonging to boat builder Job Sproston. The boat yard, which was situated on the north bank of the canal close to Thurlwood Locks and about 200 yards from the salt works, was to be the rendezvous point for the robbers. The gang met up there as arranged at around 11pm. As well as the eight already mentioned, it also included at least four others: Robert Beech, James Harrison, William Whitehead and John Handford.

Some of what follows was revealed in the statement Johnson made in turning King's evidence, but most of the details are taken from the handwritten notes of the trial judge, Chester's then Chief Justice Robert Dallas. Both documents are among the official files on the case preserved in the National Archives.

On a night when the gang's plans were to go badly awry, there was a slight hitch even before they left their boatyard lair. A barge turned up unexpectedly and tied up at the entrance to the locks. Samuel Johnson senior was apparently delegated to deal with this unforeseen situation. Thomas Johnson stated, 'Samuel Johnson went up to the cabin of the boat and told the captain what he was going upon, but desired he would not say anything, and told the captain he would give him a couple of shillings.'

With the barge master bribed to turn a blind eye, the gang advanced under cover of darkness on the salt works. Using the walkway over the lock gates, they crossed to the south bank of the canal, where the works lay, and took the towpath to the edge of the site.

To understand what went on that night, it is necessary to know something of the layout of the works. The four main production buildings, each containing a pan house and a hot (or stove) house, were ranged in parallel rows, two on each side of a basin that ran off the canal at right angles and which provided access into the works for the salt barges. The pan houses were where the concentrated brine – steam pumped from the vast underground salt beds more than 200 feet beneath the Cheshire Plain and up to 10-times saltier than sea water – was boiled in large coal-fired open vessels. When salt crystals formed on the surface of the boiling brine and sank to the bottom of the pan, they were raked to the side and shoveled into tubs or moulds (originally made of wicker but later wood). Like sandpies, the salt lumps slowly set and were then moved into the adjoining hot house for the final drying process.

Each hot house had a storage area, or warehouse, at first-floor level, into which the dried salt lumps were eventually 'lofted' through trapdoors for milling or bagging, or, in later years, to be cut into smaller blocks and wrapped for domestic use. Hot House No.2 and Hot House No.3, which faced each other across the basin, were linked by an overhead gangway, and a flight of iron steps led up the outside of each building to the gangway. From chutes at opposite ends of the gangway, the milled or bagged salt was loaded in bulk into the holds of the vessels tied up in the basin below. A humpback bridge carried the towpath over the entrance to the basin.

Arriving at the works, the gang posted two lookouts. William Whitehead selected a vantage point on a bank at the eastern end, from where he could observe the Excise Office and canal bridge No. 139 (the main way in by road); James Harrison stood watch on the valley side. Here he would be able to see anyone approaching along the old road from Lawton Heath. The others, led by Joseph Beech, headed for Hot House No. 2. Beech had obtained a duplicate key to the door of the upstairs store room. A few paces behind came his brother Robert, carrying a gun. Thomas Johnson would later describe it as 'a pistol half-a-yard long' – possibly a horse pistol – loaded with shot. He was the only one of the gang known to be armed. Once inside, the thieves set to work by the light of candles.

After about an hour things seemed to be going well. Up to a dozen bags had been filled with salt, shouldered along the towpath and over the lock bridge, and then dumped safely in Sproston's building. But the intruders had not gone unnoticed. Exciseman

Plan of the Salt Works on the night of the raid. 1–4, hot houses; 5, gangway over the canal basin; 6, canal basin; 7, towpath bridge; 8, excise office; 9, Thurlwood Locks; 10, Sproston's boatyard; 11, canal bridge No.139 (main route into the works). (From a drawing by Mr George Twigg.)

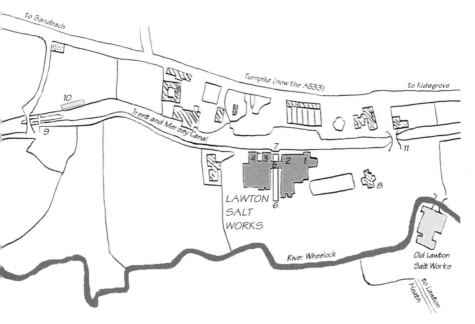

Cheshire's Execution Files

William Stockton, whose bravery would later result in him suffering serious gunshot wounds, was the senior officer on duty at the works that night. He had become aware of their presence after leaving the Excise Office on one of his regular security patrols and, ironically, spotting the crouching figure of look-out William Whitehead about 50 yards away.

Dousing his lantern, he roused two off-duty excisemen, John Tucker and Robert Thompson, who lived close by, and the three of them returned to the works to watch. At first they could see nothing amiss but, on moving closer to Hot House No. 2, they were able to make out six or seven men walking along the towpath. The men were carrying sacks and hugging the walls of the hot houses on the far side of the towpath bridge.

Realising they would need reinforcements, the excisemen withdrew and rounded up five more men who were employed at the works. Their number swelled to eight, they now felt able to tackle the robbers, though at that time they did not know how many they were up against. When they neared Hot House No. 2, Tucker pointed to a light in the first-floor warehouse and he and his colleagues made for the iron staircase. Stockton was armed with a sword and Tucker and Thompson each had a pistol. It was between midnight and 1am when the battle commenced.

Thomas Johnson said in his statement that he realised they had been rumbled shortly after he and Proudlove returned to the storeroom for their second loads of salt. Joseph Beech was inside the storeroom, and as Johnson reached the top of the external staircase he met Glover coming out carrying a bag of salt. 'Glover,' he said, 'had gone halfway down the steps when the officers met him.'

Stockton was the first on the scene. Reaching the bottom of the iron staircase, he raised his sword and jabbed it into Glover's side, as Tucker, pistol in hand, advanced on the steps followed by Thompson and their posse of salt workers, whereupon Glover 'threw the bag down the steps and ran back up again', said Johnson. As the four robbers crouched together in the storeroom doorway at the top of the steps, Johnson said he heard one of the officers call out from below, 'Now my lads, we have you. You have had a long run. Why don't you come down?' Another shouted to a colleague, 'If they don't come down, fire upon them.'

For the robbers, cornered in the salt store, there was now only one way out. Beech took the plunge first. Lifting up a trapdoor he lowered himself into one of the salt chutes and slid 20 feet into the basin below. Johnson and Glover quickly followed suit. The sound of them splashing into the water convinced the pursuing excisemen they had all got out that way and created the diversion by which Proudlove, still hiding in the storeroom, was able to slip out unnoticed and make his escape.

It was as officer Stockton rushed down the stairway to the canal basin that he was shot and wounded. In Judge Dallas's notes, the exciseman recalled the moment: 'I heard a noise as of persons going through the shoot [sic] into the water. I went to the bottom of the shoot to hear if anything more would come down, and in this situation, in about a minute, I received my wound. I did not see the person. The shot struck me in the arm, shoulder, neck and head, and also in my side. When I received the wound my back was almost towards the canal and my right side towards the basin. Tucker at this time was up in the gangway and had not to my knowledge come down before I was wounded.'

The Men they Hanged Twice

This latter comment was obviously intended to counter any suggestion that his fellow officer, known to be armed, had shot him by mistake in the darkness and confusion. His conviction that it was one of the salt raiders who had peppered him Stockton re-affirmed in his trial cross-examination, when he elaborated, 'I was under some alarm when the pistol was fired and cannot say the exact position in which the person stood from whom I received my wound. I can only make a vague guess. I received the wound from off the towing path, as I believe, not from above.'

His opinion was supported by the evidence of exciseman Thompson, who, in Judge Dallas's notes, was quoted as saying, 'I heard a man fire a pistol or gun. He was on the end of the [towpath] bridge and fired towards the place where the salt is thrown down into the boats.'

Either way, Stockton was lucky to survive. Recognising the seriousness of his situation, he staggered off to get help. He was eventually treated by a local surgeon, but was confined for eight weeks as a result of his injuries.

Forced to retire from front-line action, Stockton missed what might be termed the second phase of the engagement...and another burst of gunfire. After Glover, Joseph Beech and Thomas Johnson had made good their escape down the loading chute, the rest of the gang – who we must presume had been carrying salt to Sproston's yard during the initial exchanges at Hot House No. 2 – now returned to confront the excisemen and their workmates. It was a fierce set-to that saw the robbers temporarily turn the tables on their pursuers, and, for a few tense moments, the excisemen found themselves under attack and trapped in one of the salt works' buildings.

In the 'Dallas Report', Officer Tucker told how, after coming down from the gangway, he had seen one of the escapees (Glover) in the basin wading under the towpath bridge towards the canal. He said to his colleague Thompson, 'I have a mind to shoot him.' He went round the other side of the basin and pointed his weapon at the man's head, but Thompson restrained him. That was when the other gang members reappeared on the towpath beside the bridge.

Tucker stated, 'I told the men if they came forward I would fire. They abused and threatened us...They then came up within two or three yards and seemed determined to assault me, on which I fired at them. When I fired, this one man was standing on the towing path about two yards from me. I received a wound in my hand, by a stone or brick.'

The men kept on coming and Tucker fired again, but when he received a second blow he and the rest of his party retreated to storeroom No. 2 under a hail of missiles. For some time bricks and stones clattered against the doors and windows of the building and the robbers continued to shout threats at the excisemen cowering inside. Then, as suddenly as the attack began, the gang dispersed and it was all over.

Some of the raiders regrouped at Sproston's yard. Glover reached there by swimming the canal, while Proudlove, having first gathered up a bag of salt left behind by one of the fleeing gang members, made it back via canal bridge No. 139 and the main Sandbach road (the present A533). Discussing the night's work, Proudlove announced proudly that he had thrown a 'brick end' at the officers, while it was generally agreed that it must have been Robert Beech who had shot the exciseman.

In his lengthy statement, termed 'The confession of Thomas Johnson' and dated 13 February 1809, the turncoat informant said he believed 'nobody of his party had any firearms but Robert Beech'. The deposition went on: 'Robert Beech told this examinant...he had fired at the excise officers.'

Johnson also revealed that the stolen salt – amounting to some 400lb, apparently – was subsequently removed to another hiding place in Thurlwood (using the horse he had provided, presumably) and then taken, in Joseph Lowe's cart, to a barn in nearby Betchton. About a week afterwards Johnson helped Proudlove and two other members of the gang to load it into Lowe's cart once again, and Lowe and Newton took it to Manchester to sell. Before they could do so, however, the plan was uncovered and the salt was seized by law officers in the yard of the Crown and Thistle pub in the city.

While it seems clear that Johnson's information eventually put all the men in the frame for the robbery, it was not the main reason why George Glover was arrested. He was identified by at least three people as the man who had hurled the bag of salt at the excisemen on the steps of Hot House No. 2. Consequently, he was the first of the gang to be taken into custody. A single man, he was apprehended late in the evening of 18 October at the home in Smallwood he shared with his parents, farmer Samuel Glover and his wife Mary. Among the arresting party was exciseman John Tucker.

'I recognised him immediately,' Tucker stated. 'Glover is the man, I swear it.' His fellow officer Thompson had held a lantern close to Glover's face, he explained, 'and I was about a yard-and-a-half from him'.

John Smith and Thomas Smith, two of the salt works' employees who had been called up to help the excisemen foil the robbery, both knew Glover personally and also recognised him. The former stated' 'I was a yard-and-a-half away from him. It was Glover. I have no doubt.'

William Proudlove, a married man with a young family, was picked up on 15 February 1809, two days after Thomas Johnson signed his formal confession, naming him and all the other gang members. Samuel Arrowsmith, one of the Sandbach constables, went to his home accompanied by a deputy, John Ridgway, and the now fully-recovered William Stockton. Proudlove did not give in without a fight. When the officers forced their way into his house he tried to make a break for it, but Ridgway grabbed him and held on, exclaiming, 'I'll stick to thee as long as I've life left in me.' The two men were grappling on the floor, said Arrowsmith. The constable added, 'I drew a pistol and told him if he did not surrender I would shoot him.' Wisely, Proudlove stopped struggling.

He was handcuffed and taken to the Bulls Head in Sandbach, from where he was taken by post-chaise to Chester Castle Gaol. On the way he offered his captors five guineas to let him go. When they refused, said Arrowsmith, he increased the amount to 10 guineas, beseeching them 'not [to] be hard on a poor man'. Finally, the 'poor' man said he would also throw in his 10-guinea watch.

The same day, Joseph Latham, the constable of Smallwood, accompanied by his deputy, George Beckett, a wheelwright from Odd Rode, went to bring in Robert Beech, the gun-toting member of the gang. Latham had learned that he was lodging in Odd Rode at the house of John Hobson. As the constable tried to arrest Beech, he was attacked and assaulted by Hobson, and Beech got away. Hobson, 35, was charged with helping him escape when he, too, appeared at the county's Spring Assizes, but he was found not guilty and discharged.

When the sessions opened, on Monday 10 April 1809, according to Judge Dallas, 12 men had stood charged with shooting at the excise officer. However, the surviving indictment lists 10 names and records verdicts against six only: Proudlove and Glover, 'guilty'; Newton, aged 30, Harrison (19), Lowe (22) and Samuel Johnson (60), 'not guilty'.

It is possible that the grand jury had been unable to return 'true bills' against the other six, but it is more likely that they were not then in custody to answer the charge. At least one of the men listed on the indictment certainly was not: William Whitehead, aged 31, from Northwich, was not committed to the castle until 24 June. He was dealt with at the next sitting of the court.

As the judge's notes confirm, Thomas Johnson had blown the whistle on the robbery and the men he alleged had taken part in it. During the trial he had to admit, however, that in agreeing to appear as a Crown witness he had been 'given to understand that by accusing these men I shall save myself'. And the jurors seem to have been unprepared to accept the uncorroborated word of a self-confessed thief, deciding that they could safely convict only if there was reliable supporting evidence.

In Glover's case, three other prosecution witnesses were prepared to swear that he was one of the robbers; against Proudlove there was the testimony of the two Sandbach law officers that he had resisted arrest and attempted to bribe his way to freedom.

Chief Justice Dallas had no doubts about the two men's guilt. In what the newspaper described as a 'sketch' of the judge's comments on passing sentence, the *Chester Chronicle* of 21 April reported him as saying to the prisoners in the dock, 'Assembled in a gang of 12 persons or more on a settled scheme of depredation, you trusted to your numbers and set the laws at defiance...in the execution of your unlawful purposes, you fired a pistol and wounded an Officer of Excise. The administration of justice would be miserably defective indeed if it did not interpose its potent arm to discourage similar offences. You must answer for your crime with your lives.'

Following their sentences, petitions were sent to the Home Secretary, Lord Liverpool, on behalf of both men, to try to save them from the gallows. The minister called for a report from the trial judge to enable him to rule on the mercy pleas, and the Chief Justice's notes were part of his response.

In an accompanying private communiqué dated 28 April, Judge Dallas made it clear he was not prepared to support the petitions. 'I have nothing to state, with respect to the Convicts or the Case,' he wrote. Any alteration in the sentences, he said, would be for the Home Secretary alone to decide. 'I must beg leave to state,' he added, 'that I do not consider it as in any respect depending upon me.'

The main ground for the appeals was that when the officer was fired at, neither man was present. Proudlove, it was claimed, was 'near a building of one Job Sproston about 200 yards distant', while Glover was said to have been in 'a room within the said salt works'.

The Home Secretary rejected the petitions, however, and confirmed that Proudlove and Glover would hang as scheduled on 6 May. By the time the appointed hour arrived, it was reported, both men were ready to accept their punishment...though, as they emerged from

Cheshire's Execution Files

Cutting from the *Chester Chronicle* of 12 May 1809, advertising publication of a pamphlet, the profits from which were to be 'applied to the relief of the distressed and unfortunate widow and children of William Proudlove'. (By permission of CCALS.)

> ... a continuance of the same.
>
> N. B. Ladies waited on thirty miles from Chester.
>
> **IN THE PRESS,**
>
> *And in a few days will be published,*
>
> PRICE TWO SHILLINGS,
>
> *A SERMON,*
>
> Preached in the Chapel of the Castle of Chester, previous to the execution of the condemned criminals.
>
> *Geo. Glover and Wm. Proudlove,*
>
> Who suffered on Saturday the 6th of May.
>
> *By the Rev. Wm. Fish, A. M.*
>
> Subscribers will receive with the SERMON a short narrative of some interesting facts, communicated to the Constable of the Castle, by the unfortunate men, relative to themselves and their accomplices.
>
> The profits that may arise from the sale are intended to be applied to the relief of the distressed wife and children of William Proudlove.
>
> Subscribers' names will be received by Messrs. Broster and Son, and Mr. Poole, bookseller, Chester; by the printer of the Chester Chronicle, and the printer of the Chester Courant; also at the North Wales Gazette Office, Bangor.
>
> **Postscript.**

the City Gaol and strode out into the sunshine for the last time, they, like everybody else present that day, were totally unprepared for what happened next.

'At the place of execution,' the *Chester Chronicle* reported on 12 May, 'one of the most distressing and heart-rending circumstances occurred, that perhaps ever was seen on a similar occasion; they embraced and took leave of each other in the most affectionate manner and on being tied up and the fatal signal given, the platform fell and, shocking to relate, both the ropes broke, and the poor men were precipitated to the bottom of the scaffold!'

The *Chronicle* continued, 'They were taken into the [prison] chapel (neither of them materially hurt) till other ropes could be procured, each exclaiming "What a sad business is this!" They then requested the Revd Mr Fish to be again sent for, and after taking a little refreshment, joined him most fervently in prayer nearly two hours; when ropes being prepared, they met their unhappy fate with the most manly fortitude and resignation, amidst the commiserations of the surrounding crowd.'

It was the third successive execution – the third in a decade – to outrage press and public opinion.

On the previous occasion, on 3 October 1801, another experimental method was tried – with equally distressing results. It was the first execution to be carried out within the city walls and the first (and only) one at the old and dilapidated Northgate Gaol, Chester's common gaol since mediaeval times. It was certainly an appropriate setting for the barbaric act that was witnessed that day; George Ashdown Audsley, in *The Stranger's Handbook to Chester* (1909), described it as 'a terrible specimen of legalised corruption...[wherein] was practised those "tortures thrice refined" which might put even the great Inquisition to the blush.'

The main prison was situated above the gate's arched entrance, but the real chambers of horror were a pair of cells cut out of the sandstone rock some 30-feet below street level. One was the torture chamber and the other a dungeon called 'The Dead Man's Room', where the city's condemned criminals spent their last miserable hours before execution.

Some authors have identified the joint execution of Aaron Gee and Thomas Gibson, both of Stockport, as the first instance of the 'new drop' being used in Cheshire. Well, the two men were 'dropped' all right, and the technique was new. But there the similarities ended. Far from embracing the improvements embodied in the trapdoor type of gallows used for many years at London's Newgate Gaol, it seems the method employed here perpetuated the inept cruelties of the past.

Ropes were attached to a beam projecting from the outside wall of the attics on the south (city) side of the Northgate and the men, it seems, were simply heaved out of a window.

The Men they Hanged Twice

In his *History of the County Palatine of Cheshire* (1823), James Hanshall, a former editor of the *Chester Chronicle*, wrote, '[On] the signal being given by the unfortunate men, they were propelled from the aperture...forty feet from the level of the street; the rope having a run of about twenty inches, and their bodies beating against the walls and the windows below, in a truly frightful manner.'

It was 'stretching' at its most literal and the instrument was immediately nicknamed 'The Drag' – though, mercifully, it was never used again.

Earlier that same year had occurred what was probably the most lamentable sight seen at an execution in Chester since Mary Heald was burned at the stake in 1763. It was the day the city sheriffs hanged a dead man.

A classic of gallows lore, the story of John Morgan, Samuel Thompson and John Clare, the last felons to be hanged at Boughton, has been told many times. Their exits brought the curtain down on this ancient theatre of death in the most dramatic style. It happened on Saturday 9 May 1801, and another large crowd had gathered to witness the end of an era.

As the cart neared the 'fatal tree' the press of people forced it to a halt, and Clare, who had several times declared that he was 'not born to be hanged', leapt off the back and, though wearing shackles on his wrists and ankles, managed to break through the crowd. From the top of Gallows Hill he hurtled down the precipitous slope and half running, half tumbling, plunged into the Dee.

It was a fatal mistake. As the *Chester Chronicle* recorded on 15 May, '[From] the weight of his irons he was...drowned a few yards from where his body went in.'

As the other two convicts waited in the cart – 'with great propriety', as the *Chronicle* put it – their executions were temporarily stayed while efforts were made to retrieve their

Chester's infamous Northgate Gaol, the common gaol of the city from mediaeval times, which was demolished in 1808. It was here, on an improvised gallows nicknamed 'The Drag', that Aaron Gee and Thomas Gibson were crudely executed in 1801. (By permission of CCALS.)

unfortunate companion. Clare was finally brought out of the river about 20 minutes later; his lifeless body was returned to the cart and – 'in the most brutal manner', said the *Chronicle* – was strung up and turned off with the others. The city sheriffs knew their duty; the law had decreed that Clare should be 'hanged by the neck' and, dead or alive, hanged by the neck he was going to be.

The *Chronicle* was outraged. Not by Clare's treatment, however, but by the way Morgan and Thompson were kept waiting to die. The newspaper commented, 'Would it not have been better, and more consistent with humanity, to have let these men meet their fate, who were then prepared for their awful change, than to distract their attention by such a horrid sight, and afterwards, if it were necessary to put in force the execution of the law, to have suspended his [Clare's] body?'

The *Chronicle* added, 'We never heard any execution more universally execrated by all ranks than this, nor one that more deeply affected the feelings of the spectators.'

It was not the end of the men's indignities, either. For, as they were being taken back through Chester to be buried in St Mary's Ditch adjoining the castle, the three uncovered bodies were unceremoniously dumped in the street when the driver, displaying 'unwarrantable negligence' ('drunk' in another version of the story), ran the cart into a post at the corner of Pepper Street and Bridge Street and overturned it.

The *Chronicle*'s report ended with a plea that it would take up several times in the coming years: 'It would surely be more safe for the future, were a drop erected in the front of the castle, or on some convenient spot in the yard, without dragging the unfortunate sufferers through the streets of the city, which experience tells us daily is productive of no good as an example, and thus prevent the confusion naturally attendant on such lamentable occasions.'

The case of 'The Men They Hanged Twice' was in the headlines again in September 1809, after continuing inquiries into the salt works robbery led to three more alleged gang members appearing at the assizes. William Whitehead, together with Samuel Johnson [Jnr], aged 25, of Arclid, and Joseph Camm (27) of Sandbach, were charged with shooting at exciseman Stockton and also with stealing 400lbs of white salt from the works.

This was the first mention of Camm; he was not one of the men identified in Thomas Johnson's confession and his name does not appear in any of the official papers on the case. He was eventually acquitted. Whitehead and Johnson were convicted on the theft charge only, and they were each sentenced to seven years' transportation.

It seems, however, that the three other gang members – including Robert Beech, the man who actually fired the pistol – were never brought to court.

* * *

If William Proudlove's death sentence was intended to deter others from following in his lawless ways, the message could hardly be said to have hit home. For his brother John was among those who, clearly, had not been listening. He continued the family fashion for thieving and, in 1829, he became the second Proudlove to wind up wearing the 'hempen neckerchief'. On Cheshire's highway of crime, his execution was a milestone for another reason, too...

Chapter Nine

The Dreaded Middlewich Gang

He was, in a manner of speaking, the last of the highwaymen. But not for him the fleet-footed steed, the silver-filigreed flintlock and the daring, darkly-heroic aura of men like Edward Higgins, the one-time Knutsford 'squire' whose 18th-century exploits created a local legend to rival that of Dick Turpin. In an age when the masked and mounted adventurers of popular literature had long ago ridden off into the sunset, John Proudlove travelled on foot; his weapon of choice was more likely to be a broken-off tree branch crudely fashioned into a club, his 'style' closer to that of the modern street mugger than the romanticised road agents of old.

He was, more accurately, the last man to be hanged in Cheshire for highway robbery. In 1829, when the 25-year-old Sandbach shoemaker left his individual footprints on the path of criminal history, the distinction had yet to be recognised, of course – the crime was not removed from the diminishing list of capital offences until late in the following decade. At the time of his conviction – for robbing a farmer on the road from Sandbach to Betchton – that was the extent of his criminal record.

But, after his trial, he was exposed as something more than a common footpad; the man now recognised as one of the only pair of brothers to have been executed at Chester in modern times was a notorious outlaw and member of the so-called 'Middlewich Gang', a ruthless band of thieves and roughnecks that, for some time, had been terrorising the area around the mid-Cheshire town.

Another member of the gang was John Leir, 21, also of Sandbach, who was convicted at the same Spring Assizes on an unconnected charge of aggravated burglary. With five other men he had broken into and robbed the home of a retired clergyman near Middlewich, leaving the old man badly beaten and lying close to death in his blood-spattered bedroom. He and Proudlove were comrades to the end: they were both hanged on the same gallows less than three weeks later.

Although no official documentation exists to confirm the contemporary (mainly newspaper) reports that gave rise to their reputations, an article in the *Chester Chronicle* of 8 May 1829 was typical of the press comment of the day. It stated, 'These two unhappy men formed a part of what has long been known and dreaded as the Middlewich gang, and it is well known [they] have been concerned in most of the depredations which have been committed in that part of the county.'

It was an unequivocal statement that was repeated in almost identical, though naturally more sensational, terms in a 'penny broadside' rushed out by a Chester printing house to cash in on the double hanging. Copies of the broadside, whose text probably emanated from the same journalistic source, would have been hawked among the people crowding at the foot of the gallows in the manner of merchandisers at a modern-day pop concert. Bearing a stylised woodcut depicting two bodies hanging from the scaffold above the City Gaol's doric-columned front doorway, the broadside, in the usual melodramatic

Broadside relating the crimes of John Proudlove and John Leir, two members of the 'Dreaded Middlewich Gang', who terrorised this part of central Cheshire during the late 1820s. (By permission of CCALS.)

terms, gave a brief account of the men's crimes, their trials and their behaviour from the time of their convictions until their last 'fatal expiations'.

Its introduction declared extravagantly, 'The Criminal Annals of this Country [sic] have not on record Deeds of greater Atrocity than those which have been committed by the Gang of Thieves that these Unhappy Men were connected with, who had a long time infested the neighbourhood of Middlewich, and were well known to be concerned in most of the Depredations effected in that part.'

Unfortunately, neither publication thought fit to cite any specific evidence in support of its claims; a trawl through the news columns of the local papers also failed to identify positively these previous 'depredations', while there was little point, as it were, in looking for this particular needle in the haystack of official records since they are concerned only with prosecutions and, apart from the two cases with which we are concerned here, none of the other offences seems to have been brought to court.

However, through the crimes of known associates like John Proudlove and John Leir, which were covered extensively by the press, we can at least get some idea of the kind of men who made up the 'dreaded Middlewich gang' and the 'deeds of atrocity' that contributed to its reign of terror. With no other anecdotal information available, it is on those newspaper reports that, of necessity, our story must largely rest.

John Proudlove was about five or six when his brother William was hanged (see chapter eight) – just old enough to remember the devastating effect it must have had on his family. He was unlikely to have been present to witness the extraordinary scenes at the infamous 'broken ropes' execution, but the stories he would have heard afterwards – doubtless embellished in the telling – were calculated to act as a powerful warning to the impressionable youngster. Yet, vivid though they may have been, his childhood memories had ceased to exert any moderating influence by the time John Proudlove reached adulthood.

The Dreaded Middlewich Gang

At first it looked as if he might make something of himself. Having taken up the trade of shoemaker, he seemed to have had the good sense, and the necessary application, to acquire the skills to become a valued member of the community. But he had not learned the lesson of his brother's death. Instead he chose the same dangerous lifestyle and a similar sideline in thieving. If he thought he could make a better job of it than his brother and outsmart the law, however, he was wrong. As sibling rivalry went, this was one 'contest' that was always likely to end up level. Dead level.

The younger Proudlove lost his personal battle with authority after an ill-judged robbery on Christmas Eve, 1828. He had been enjoying a festive drink in the 15th-century Crown public house in Sandbach's market square with his pals James Harrop, aged 29, and James Statham (26) – also known members of the Middlewich Gang – when they singled out farmer Robert Moseley as their target. It was a seemingly spur-of-the-moment crime, but sufficiently well executed to suggest that it was not the first time they had worked the routine.

Moseley had been on his way home to Betchton after spending most of the evening at the town's weekly market (with Christmas Day falling on a Thursday that year, the market had been brought forward to the Wednesday). At around 10pm, after visiting two other pubs en route, he stopped off at the Crown for a nightcap. Discovering several of his friends there, he joined them for a couple more glasses of ale and left about half-an-hour before midnight.

In the Crown he had become aware of a group of four young men who were seated at a table on the opposite side of the bar. He could hardly have missed them: in youthful high spirits, they were drinking and talking animatedly and attracting a fair amount of attention. What he did not realise, however, was that the young men had also been watching him – and, in particular, the fat canvas purse which he produced from his breeches pocket when it was his turn to buy a round of drinks. It seemed to them to contain a great deal of money, the proceeds, possibly, from his dealings at the day's market.

Farmer Moseley also failed to notice, as he said his goodbyes and resumed his journey home, that three of the young bucks who had previously seemed in no hurry to call time on their roistering had suddenly drained their glasses and left the pub. Now, after reaching the end of the High Street and putting Sandbach's built-up town centre behind him, he was about to discover where they had got to.

Heading off into the countryside, he had gone no more than 200 yards along what is now known as The Hill (A533) – little more than a cart track and thinly populated, it was even then the main route to Newcastle-under-Lyme – when he became aware of someone skulking in the hedgerow just up ahead. 'Halloo, who is there?' he hailed as he drew near. There was no friendly response to his greeting, however.

Almost immediately, Moseley was whacked across the left side of his head – 'with either a stick or a bludgeon,' he testified at the trial – and he fell down dazed. Struggling to his knees, he tried to fight back, but his attacker (later identified as Harrop) threatened, 'Damn your blood! If you resist I'll knock your brains out!' Harrop then pulled the farmer's hat down over his eyes, threw him on his back and fell across his face.

With what looked like practised teamwork, the two other men, who had been lying in wait behind the hedge, joined their companion. One of them, Proudlove, held Moseley's legs and, with their victim now pinned firmly to the ground, lifted his purse, containing 10 sovereigns, from his left-hand breeches pocket, while Statham extracted a handful of silver and copper from the right-hand pocket. In total they got away with £10 8s 2d, more than £700 in today's money. It was all over in a matter of minutes.

Though he had been robbed around midnight on an unlit road, Moseley would claim in court later that a full moon was shining brightly out of a cloudless sky and so he was able to make out his assailants clearly. He recognised them as three of the four young men who had been drinking noisily together at the Crown.

The following Monday, therefore, when he spotted Harrop strolling brazenly through the streets of Sandbach, he informed one of the local constables and had him arrested. After questioning the suspect, the constable, James Faram, went with Moseley to the Red Lion, where a pigeon shoot was in progress. Shortly afterwards five men entered the pub and Moseley pointed out Proudlove among them. By the following Thursday, New Year's Day, Statham was also in custody.

At the trial, at Chester Castle on Monday 20 April, two defence witnesses claimed they were also in the Crown that night and had seen Harrop and Statham, together with Harrop's wife and brother and another man, walking towards Harrop's house – in the opposite direction to the route taken by the farmer – at around 12.30am on Christmas Day. This was a little more than half an hour after the robbery and the place was two miles from the scene of the crime.

Proudlove had nothing to say in his defence and did not call any witnesses. The jury was out for half an hour, returning with verdicts of 'guilty' against all three men. It was now early evening, and the judge (the Hon. Thomas Jervis) announced that he would defer sentencing so that he could give the case, as he put it, 'the most mature consideration'. After what must have been a nerve-jangling night in the cells, Proudlove, Harrop and Statham were brought up and placed at the bar early the next morning. When the judge donned the 'fatal black cap', the outcome of his overnight deliberations appeared painfully obvious, the convicted men's hopes seemingly dashed.

'The most death-like stillness pervaded the court', said the *Chronicle* in its 24 April trial report. It was the calm before the storm, however, for the judge's gesture was the signal for frantic scenes in the dock. In the tearful exchanges that followed, Harrop pleaded pitifully for his life while Proudlove, in arguing the innocence of his comrades, virtually put the noose around his own neck. According to the *Chronicle*, the dialogue went as follows:

> Harrop: 'Oh, my lord, I'm innocent. My lord, my lord, spare my life. I had nothing to do with the robbery.'
>
> Proudlove: 'May I speak, my lord? These men that stand on each side of me are innocent. That man (Moseley) is a false forsworn man.'
>
> Judge: 'What do you say of yourself?'
>
> Proudlove: 'My lord, I robbed him. I did it myself. There was no person with me. These men had no hand in it. They are both innocent.'

Proudlove's motive may have been well intentioned, but his assertion that this was a one-man robbery did not impress Mr Justice Jervis, who now turned his attention to the defence counsel, Mr Cottingham.

The Dreaded Middlewich Gang

Judge: 'Mr Cottingham, an alibi was set up for two of these men, which the jury did not believe, and which I did not believe. I am bound to make an example in this case.'

Harrop (with great emotion): 'Oh, my lord, my lord, do spare my life – transport me, but spare my life.'

Once Proudlove had made his public confession, it was a safe bet that, if the judge was going to make an example of anybody, it was going to be him. Proudlove was duly sentenced to death; the other two had death merely 'recorded' against them. Since 1823 judges had been allowed to reduce the penalty for what was still officially a capital offence in this way. It automatically commuted the men's sentences to transportation for life, the strict condition being that if they ever returned to these shores and were caught, they would not be given a second chance.

In a final comment on the case, the *Chronicle* made the first public statement linking the robbers with John Leir and Co, whose trial it had reported the previous week (see below). Airing a belief that was apparently held firmly by the authorities, the paper said of Proudlove, Harrop and Statham, 'There is little doubt that all three are part of the formidable gang of burglars and thieves that infest the neighbourhood of Middlewich – the same who committed the desperate burglary in the house of the Revd Matthew Bloor of Stublach.'

John Leir had been the 'fourth man' with whom Proudlove, Harrop and Statham were celebrating Christmas Eve at the Crown the night they robbed Robert Moseley. He was in no way involved in that crime, though he was certainly well qualified. The convicted burglar, by trade a silk weaver, was little more than 21 years old, yet, as he confessed shortly before he died, he had been breaking the law since he was nine.

Sandbach's busy Thursday market, *c.*1910, with the Crown public house in the middle background. It was after visiting the market – and the Crown – that Betchton farmer Robert Moseley was attacked and robbed by John Proudlove and two companions in 1828.
(By permission of CCALS.)

Leir was sentenced to death along with Samuel Patterson, aged 26, in the opening days of the assizes, which began on 9 April. With four other men they had been charged with breaking and entering the home of the Revd Bloor at Cross Lanes in the township of Stublach, about a mile-and-a-half north of Middlewich, and stealing various items of personal property, including silverware, and over £80 in money. They were also accused of assaulting the 86-year-old retired clergyman.

Their co-defendants were John Bostock, aged 33, James Walker (age unrecorded) and brothers Peter and John Alcock, 28 and 19 respectively. All six were said to have been part of the loose collective that was the Middlewich Gang.

The raid – part of the wave of robberies and burglaries that created a climate of fear in 1820s Cheshire – took place during the night of 14–15 March 1829. The Revd Bloor, 'a most respected clergyman' and formerly curate of Over and also of Pulford, shared his home with two other elderly people – his manservant John Foden, aged 80, and housekeeper Sarah Hanshall, who was 86 and 'in a state of complete dotage' – as well as Mrs Hanshall's daughter, Mary, who was 'deaf and dumb'. Mr John Hill, the Attorney-General, said he mentioned these facts to explain why the Revd Bloor alone of the house's occupants had been called to give evidence.

After securing all doors and windows, the four members of the household retired to bed late that Saturday night. The activities of the gang of thieves who had been spreading panic throughout the neighbourhood recently were obviously in Revd Bloor's thoughts as he bolted his bedroom door and barred the latch to prevent it being raised from the outside. As an extra precaution he wedged a garden spade under the doorknob. But it was not enough to stop this bunch of desperadoes.

Between midnight and 1am, said Mr Hill, Revd Bloor was awakened by the sound of the kitchen door being forced. As he got out of bed to investigate, his bedroom door was smashed open and three men, all armed with bludgeons, burst into the room. The first one felled him with a single blow, at which the others began beating him about the head and body.

'It would appear', said the Attorney-General, 'that the old gentleman made considerable resistance, for he contrived to get hold of a sword which hung by his bedside, and he succeeded in knocking one of the men down. But they eventually beat him insensible – and the floor of the room was covered with his blood.'

The old man was probably saved from more serious injury by the smallness of the bedroom, the intruders' makeshift clubs repeatedly striking its low ceiling, lessening the impact of the blows.

From a pocket in the Revd Bloor's breeches, which were under his pillow, the thieves removed a purse containing 20 shillings in silver, then they ransacked the rest of the house, stealing, among other things, a Bank of England note for £80, two or three sovereigns, six silver tablespoons, six silver teaspoons and two watches, one of silver and the other 'a metal one with a gold chain usually worn by the reverend gentleman himself'. The spoons belonged to Sarah Hanshall and were engraved with her initials.

Leir was apprehended four days later in Pendleton, near Manchester. With John Bostock, he had been trying to sell the Revd Bloor's watch and the stolen teaspoons to a dealer. The initials 'S' and 'H' were still just about visible on their handles, though an attempt had clearly been made to obliterate them. Two files, which could have been used for the purpose, were discovered in Bostock's pockets.

As expected, from the moment he appeared in the witness box, his wounds freshly dressed, it was the Revd Bloor who made the biggest impression on the jury. 'The old gentleman', observed the *Chronicle*, 'excited much sympathy…by his infirm and venerable appearance and owing to the bandages about his head.'

He turned out to be a far-from-reliable witness, however. Despite some intense cross-examination, he stood firm in his belief that the man who had first burst into his bedroom on the night of the burglary and knocked him to the floor was Samuel Patterson. It was undoubtedly the evidence that persuaded the jury to bring in a guilty verdict against Patterson, as well as Leir; only afterwards was it established that the elderly cleric had got it seriously wrong. Patterson was not one of the robbers. He was subsequently able to prove beyond doubt that he was elsewhere at the time and, on 1 May, eight days before he was due to hang, he was granted a royal pardon and released from custody.

It seemed the Revd Bloor had not so much recognised the man as his mode of dress; the clothes Patterson was wearing when he appeared before the committing magistrate, and which he wore at the trial, were, the *Chronicle* explained on 15 May, similar to those worn by one of the robbers. From the new evidence, the newspaper declared, it had been 'satisfactorily ascertained…that Patterson was elsewhere (no matter how occupied) on the night in question'.

Who, or what, provided him with such an unassailable alibi – and, more to the point, what prevented him from putting it forward in his defence at the trial – was never revealed, though the *Chronicle's* seemingly coded use of the words 'no matter how occupied' suggests Patterson had been up to no good elsewhere that night.

If, after all he had been through, the Revd Bloor had become confused, who could blame him? Indeed, his traumatic experience had affected his health much more seriously than anyone realised. That became apparent on 21 August, when, a little over five months after the robbery, the old man died. The crime, it seemed, was claiming its second victim. For Sarah Hanshall, the parson's disabled housekeeper, had passed away on 25 April.

Her short obituary in the *Chronicle* ended, 'It is said that she never recovered from the fright occasioned by the burglars' attack in March last.' Though it was never stated quite so publicly, the same was surely true of Revd Bloor.

At the start of the trial, the Attorney-General had accepted a formal verdict of not guilty against Bostock and, at the direction of the judge (Mr Justice Jervis), the jury also acquitted the Alcock brothers.

In his summing up, Judge Jervis said that Patterson had been 'positively sworn to' by the Revd Bloor, while Leir had 'very recent possession of the watch and spoons'. After 'a short consideration', said the *Chronicle*, the jury found Patterson and Leir guilty and the sixth man, James Walker, not guilty.

Leir and Proudlove were hanged on Saturday 9 May 1829. The previous day Leir claimed that he and three others had carried out the robbery. He conceded that the old man had been 'very badly used', and he added 'I hope God will forgive me.'

Cheshire's Execution Files

The *Chronicle* recorded the final moments of the two condemned men in some detail, including a brief conversation Leir had with the executioner (Burrows) as he was being pinioned:

'Leir said to the executioner, in a confident tone, "You have no occasion to tie me so tight – I shan't struggle much" – and he also required the fetters on his legs to be adjusted, in order that he might be more at ease. After he was pinioned, he said, "I say, won't you take off my handkerchief [neckerchief]" – and this being done, he next ordered his jacket to be buttoned, observing, as he looked at it, "I little thout [thought] when this was new, that it was made for this job." He then required the handkerchief to be put into his hand, which he was to drop as the signal for the execution, and declared, as his last words, that Patterson was innocent.

'Both the culprits walked to the scaffold and ascended the steps without assistance, and Leir with apparent alacrity. After the ropes were adjusted, and before the executioner could descend from the scaffold, Leir stooped as much as he could and dropped the handkerchief. It was now discovered that the cap was not pulled over his face, and the executioner accordingly again ascended the scaffold to perform that operation, which must have occasioned an interval of awful suspence [*sic*] in the minds of the culprits. At length the fatal bolt was drawn and both were launched into eternity. Proudlove died almost instantaneously, but Leir struggled dreadfully, and it was upwards of seven minutes before life appeared to be extinct.'

The *Chester Courant* explained the reason for John Leir's delayed death. 'As the executioner withdrew the bolt,' the newspaper said, 'Leir stooped down as far as the rope would permit, which weakened his fall, and had the effect of prolonging his sufferings.'

If, as Professor Clive Emsley has written, hanging was theatre, in Chester it had become high drama...with the emphasis on 'high'. Since executions were switched to the front of the City Gaol in 1826, the gallows was mounted on a platform erected on the balcony that crowned the building's imposing western portico, a stage set given a classical look by the four Grecian-style columns supporting it. It provided an unrestricted view for the audience, but, for the condemned prisoners, 'making an entrance' was now a potentially dizzying experience. As well as the roof-top walk from the cells to the platform, they (and the hangman) also had to contend with a climb up on to a drop that was not the most solidly-secured structure, it seems.

It was something noticed at the Proudlove-Leir hangings by the writer of the broadside referred to earlier. He described it as 'the tottering platform'. Despite the frequency with which it was used, the gallows was not a permanent fixture. A local carpenter was engaged to erect the apparatus each time it was needed and to dismantle it afterwards, for which, by 1834, the going rate was 27 shillings.

Delving into the backgrounds of the two condemned men, the *Chronicle* discovered that, while Leir was unmarried, Proudlove had 'left two children, and his wife far advanced in pregnancy, to mourn his untimely end'. And it was in the closing passage of its report of John Proudlove's execution that the paper first revealed that 'his brother,

The Dreaded Middlewich Gang

A somewhat distorted image of an execution at Chester City Gaol, as depicted in a woodcut from an 1857 broadside. At first the gallows was erected above the door of the adjoining House of Correction, then, after 1826, the main entrance of the gaol itself. (By permission of CCALS.)

Wm. Proudlove, was executed on the same spot twenty years ago…and was the first who suffered on the new drop'.

The broadside repeated the claim and supplied further family details. '[The] father,' it said, 'died about 10 years back, and the mother travels with a horse and cart, selling various goods.' The broadside also made the claim that another Proudlove brother had been transported for some unspecified crime, and furnished what are the few known facts of John Leir's young life. It stated that he was from 'a respectable family, who bestowed upon him an excellent education' and that he 'formerly worked for Messrs Bull & Co. of Sandbach' as a silk weaver.

One loose thread that neither the broadside nor the local press was able to tie up, however, was the identity of that significant other robber who shared Samuel Patterson's taste in clothes and whose distinctive garb almost caused a miscarriage of justice. Dressed to kill (or at least to inflict serious injury), he was the man who smashed his way into the Revd Bloor's bedroom and launched the vicious attack on the frail churchman. He may well have been the gang's leader; he certainly played as prominent a part in the crime as John Leir. But, like most of the Middlewich Gang, he seems to have got away with it.

* * *

It was during the 1820s that the hard-line, hang-'em-all authority of the 'Bloody Code' began its terminal decline as, increasingly, judges sought to deal with all but the most serious capital offenders in ways that were rather less permanent than death. Nationally, up to 95 percent of death sentences were being commuted, yet, in Cheshire in the third decade of the 19th century, hardly an assize passed without some poor wretch being carted off to the gallows.

In the 11 years from 1819 to 1829, a total of 22 people were executed at Chester, a rate of one death warrant per session. The situation prompted the *Chester Courant* to rail against what it described as 'those awful spectacles, which, alas, are too frequently exhibited in our land'.

Eight (more than a third) of those who ended up on this road to oblivion were highway robbers. These 'new highwaymen' – footpads and opportunist thieves who were the forerunners of the modern street mugger – were part of a distinct crimewave that peaked in Cheshire at a time when it was reported to be receding elsewhere. Circuit judge Thomas Jervis told the jury at the end of John Proudlove's trial that highway robbery was still 'alarmingly frequent' in the county.

The assize court calendars confirm that this was a well-trodden criminal path, yet few found the way paved with gold. And many risked their necks for a pittance, including men like George Groom, hanged for robbing a disabled pensioner of a handful of copper, and Edward Clarke, executed after committing two street robberies, from the first of which his share of the proceeds was said to be just sixpence.

Groom, a 32-year-old labourer and father of five from Alsager, held up the infirm old man as he was riding his horse and cart through the village of Odd Rode in the parish of Astbury at about 5 o'clock on the morning of 27 February 1822. He claimed he had been driven to commit the robbery in order to feed his family. But he brought home only scraps. His victim, James Kennerley, had just eight pence (8d) on him at the time, worth little more than £2 today. After threatening to 'blow his brains out' (though he was unarmed), Groom took the money anyway and beat up the old-timer for good measure – 'in a most brutal manner', according to contemporary press reports.

He was convicted at the Spring Assizes of 1822 and executed on Saturday 4 May. The *Chester Chronicle* (10 May) said, '[Groom] attributed all his course of wickedness to the grand beginning of all offences – Sabbath-breaking, and playing at pitch and toss, and other such games.' He had 'long been well known in the annals of crime'.

He was hanged alongside William Tongue of Stockport, convicted at the same assizes of rape. On the morning of the execution, the *Courant* reported, Groom claimed the reason he had ill-treated the old man was that 'he was so tardy in giving up his money'. He had turned to highway robbery, he said, because 'he had no bread in the house'.

A total of 67 prisoners were tried at the assizes that Spring. Of those, 29 received death sentences – an all-time record, according to the *Courant* – though in the end only Groom and Tonge went to the gallows. The rest were reprieved.

In tune with the new mood of scepticism towards the death penalty then prevailing in the nation's courts, Chester's justices were becoming more inclined to use the respite system to spare as many lives as possible. However, the process of deciding who should live and who should die seems to have remained firmly rooted in old-fashioned prejudice and intolerance. The more indigent, inadequate or unconforming the convicts, the more likely they were to be executed. Serial delinquents, even of the juvenile kind, could not expect to be shown mercy, while even a first offender's hopes of a reprieve could depend on whether he (only rarely was it a she) was able to produce a credible witness to speak up on his behalf. And where two or more people were convicted of the same offence, and it was considered politic to make an example of only one of them, a bad reputation could be enough to determine who was for the drop.

But if the sentencing system was a bit of a lottery, and death the (bad) luck of the draw, there was no lack of players willing to join in this judicial game of chance. It was a gamble Edward Clarke was prepared to take, even after one uncomfortably-close brush with the law.

At the county's Spring Assizes in April 1823, Clarke was said to have been one of a gang of five young men who, the previous December, had taken part in a highway robbery in his home town of Stockport. But he managed to talk his way out of trouble – by agreeing to turn King's evidence and testify against the others. His piece of good fortune was a warning he failed to heed, however. And when, little more than a month later, he committed a similar offence, he was not allowed to wriggle off the hook a second time.

The young man known by the nickname of 'The Boatsman', who admitted he had been 'many times in custody', had sailed close to the wind once too often. At Chester's Summer Assizes at the end of August he was found guilty of assault and robbery and sentenced to death. His share on this occasion was meagre, too, probably less than two shillings – about £6 in today's money. He was hanged outside the House of Correction, adjoining Chester City Gaol, on Saturday 13 September 1823. He was just four months past his 18th birthday.

*   *   *

If highway robbery was the scourge of 1820s Cheshire, it was the crime of murder – that 'crimson wand' by whose touch, wrote Scottish criminologist and writer William Roughead, 'things base and sordid, things ugly and of ill report, are transformed into matters wondrous, weird and tragical' – that conjured up the most public fascination during the decade. Two murders, in fact – each one possessing a 'peculiar alchemy' (as Roughead also defined it) to turn the unspeakable into the utterly irresistible. In the first, the sexual shenanigans of a handsome young farmer, a dead (and pregnant) serving woman and a broken razor displaying more than a touch of the crimson stuff were the seductive elements in the melting pot...

Chapter Ten

Shocking Affair of the Unfaithful Farmer

By his early 20s Samuel Fallows had secured the tenancy of a farm on one of the grandest country estates in Cheshire. And, remarkably for one so young, he quickly earned the respect and admiration of his neighbours, not least of whom was his venerable landlord, William Davenport, Gent., Squire of Bramall Hall and the head of a distinguished old county family.

The Davenports of Cheshire could trace their lineage back to the time of the Conquest, and the Davenports of Bramall Hall had been lords of the manor for over 400 years. Fallows was said to be 'esteemed and beloved' by the elderly squire, who, following the death of Fallows's father, had been only too happy to allow the youngest son of his late tenant to take over the 35-acre farm adjoining the grounds of the magnificent black and white timber-framed manor house.

Lately there had been the unfortunate business with Mary Coups, a serving girl up at the hall, who was pregnant by Fallows, but these things happened...and, in any case, he was going to 'do the decent thing' and marry her. And William Davenport of all people was in no position to moralise, for hadn't he himself sired two illegitimate children?

As 1822 drew to a close, and with a New Year marriage in prospect, the handsome bachelor appeared ready to accept his personal and social responsibilities – to do his duty as both husband and husbandman – and settle down to a good and useful life in his predominantly-agricultural local community. But all that was about to change...with horrifying consequences.

Barely a week into 1823 – on the eve of his wedding no less – Fallows suddenly announced he was not prepared to go through with it after all. The nuptials were cancelled, but at such short notice that most of the invited guests only learned that the wedding was off when they arrived at church the next day. The effect his last-minute change of heart had on Fallows's reputation was nothing, however, compared to the discovery that, for several years, he had been living something of a double life.

For, it was now revealed, while he had been busy wooing the winsome Mary from the village of Toft, near Knutsford, the perfidious farmer was also sowing his wild oats 18 miles away in Bredbury, where he had been carrying on a long-term relationship with an older lover, Betty Shallcross. Fallows, master of his own household, seems to have had a penchant for the

How the *Chester Courant* first brought the news of Betty Shallcross's death, and the murder charge against Samuel Fallows, to the attention of its readers.
(By permission of CCALS.)

servant class: Betty was also a 'domestic' and had previously been employed by Fallows. He had also procured her sexual favours with promises of marriage. She, too, was currently pregnant by him. And in her case it was not the first time, either. She had borne him a child three years before.

Among the good folk of Bramhall (unlike the name of the hall the place is, confusingly, spelled with an 'h') the reaction to the disclosures was, initially, one of shock mingled with disbelief, to be gradually replaced by either dismay or disgust when it finally became clear that the Fallowses' white-haired boy had turned into the black sheep of the family. What none of the 1,300 inhabitants could possibly have suspected, however, was that there was a much wilder beast lurking inside Samuel Fallows. And that it would not be long before it was unleashed…

In the early spring, just as the brouhaha over the young farmer's indiscretions seemed to be dying down, it all exploded sensationally back into life with the discovery of a ghastly murder at Woodley in the township of Bredbury, near Stockport. The victim: none other than Betty Shallcross. She had been found in a shippon at Woodley Manor, where she was then employed, lying in blood-soaked disarray with her throat cut. The murder weapon, a straight razor, lay on the straw-covered floor nearby, heavily bloodstained.

'It is impossible to describe the sensations of horror which this cruel murder has excited in the neighbourhood where it was committed,' the *Chester Courant* pronounced when it learned, somewhat belatedly, of the 'barbarous' crime.

It had quite a stunning effect in the neighbourhood of Bramhall, too, though it was more in the way of an after-shock. For on the following morning, Sunday 23 March, John Stapeley Barratt, Deputy Constable of Stockport, the town's gaoler and the man then in charge of the murder investigation, paid a visit to Fallows's farm to interview the dead woman's two-timing boyfriend. The parish law officer was not satisfied with his alibi…and before the day was out, to the astonishment of his family, friends and neighbours, Samuel Fallows was in custody on suspicion of murder.

Betty Shallcross, who was 26, had been killed in an apparently determined attack during the early hours of Saturday 22 March. Cause of death was a single razor slash, five inches long, on the left side of her neck just above the collar bone, which had severed the jugular, resulting in massive loss of blood. There were defensive wounds on her hands where she had tried desperately to fight off her attacker and a number of cuts and contusions on her head, hands, face and other parts of her body that seemed to suggest the killer had used *two* weapons, one to subdue her and the other to deliver the fatal blow. A spur-of-the-moment crime of passion this most certainly was not. It was cold-blooded, single-minded slaughter.

A 'cut-throat' razor like the one with which Samuel Fallows killed Betty Shallcross in a cowshed at Woodley Manor. He may have disabled her first by stabbing her while the blade was still enclosed in the handle. (From the author's collection.)

An artist's impression of Samuel Fallows, the handsome young Bramhall farmer who murdered one of his two pregnant lovers, as he appeared at his trial in 1823. (Taken from the *Manchester Mercury*, by permission of Manchester Archives and Local Studies.)

The murdered woman, said the *Chester Chronicle* (4 April), had been found 'in a sad, bloody state, cold and stiff, and mangled in the most horrible manner'. The paper added, 'She was lying on her face without cap or handkerchief to cover her bosom and [with] her apron partly thrown over her mutilated shoulder'.

The reference to her absent clothing seems to have been the *Chronicle*'s subtle way of saying that Betty was not properly dressed – the kind of period press innuendo that usually implied the woman was not entirely respectable – though whether this, and the mention of her disarranged apron, carried any sexual imputation as well is a moot point that will be looked at in due course.

It was public knowledge, the papers agreed, that farmer's daughter Betty was pregnant by Fallows who, said the *Chronicle*, had 'paid his addresses to her' (courted her) for several years.

The inquest into Betty's death was conducted by Cheshire coroner John Hollins on Monday 24 March, at the White Bear pub (it stood on the site of the modern Lowes Arms), half a mile away in Butterhouse Green. The *Courant* noted, 'The fact of the prisoner and the deceased having been seen together a short time before the murder is supposed to have been committed, and their prior intimacy – her being in a state of pregnancy by him – and a powerful body of circumstantial evidence tending to the presumption of the prisoner's guilt, was gone into.'

The paper's correspondent had also done some digging around on Betty's home ground of Slack Hall, near Chapel-en-le-Frith, Derbyshire – where her father was reported to have farmed for over 30 years – and unearthed a local whisper that 'her acquaintance with the prisoner has been for a considerable time the source of great uneasiness to her family, who are highly respectable'.

If all this was not damaging enough, on 28 March the *Stockport Advertiser*, the first Cheshire paper to break the news of the murder, had made another highly-prejudicial comment about the accused man when it reported, 'When apprehended he evinced the most perfect indifference, and accounted for his absence from home on the Friday night in a manner quite improbable.'

After sitting through almost 10 hours of testimony, the inquest jury hardly gave it a moment's thought before returning their verdict, 'Wilful Murder against Samuel Fallows.' As was his duty at that time, the coroner committed the accused to the County Gaol at Chester Castle to stand trial at the next assizes.

Amid great public excitement, the spring sessions began on Monday 7 April 1823; by Friday the 11th, when Fallows's trial was down to be heard, the mood of anticipation had reached fever pitch and court officials braced themselves for the expected crush of spectators. They were not disappointed.

Shocking Affair of the Unfaithful Farmer

The *Courant* (15 April) described the amazing scenes both outside and inside the stately Shire Hall: 'It had been announced that the Court would enter upon the trial at 9 o'clock in the morning; and by seven, groups were seen moving towards the County Hall, under a well-founded impression that it would be difficult to gain a convenient seat. Long before eight, the grand jury boxes and those seats on the opposite side of the court, not immediately occupied by the petty jury, as well as the benches...below the bar, were crowdedly filled with respectable persons, among whom was a large proportion of elegantly dressed ladies. When the Judges and Counsel entered the Court, and the doors were thrown open for general admission, the rush into the Hall was tremendous; in a few minutes it was filled almost to suffocation. Those seats usually appropriated to attorneys and their clerks were taken possession of, and the avenues within the bar completely blocked-up...'

According to one estimate, it was almost an hour before order was restored and the trial could begin.

Fallows, now aged 25, cut an imposing figure. He was, observed the *Courant*, 'a good looking young man...of a fair complexion, seemingly 5 feet 10 inches high...genteelly dressed in a blue coat and trowsers [*sic*], and a black waistcoat with a black handkerchief round his neck'.

In the peculiarly precise wording of the indictment, it was alleged that Fallows had 'made an assault upon Betty Shallcross...with a certain razor made of iron and steel of the value of six pence, which the said Samuel Fallows...held in his right hand...[that] the throat of her the said Betty Shallcross...[he] did strike and cut...and did...give her...one mortal wound of the length of three inches and of the depth of one inch, of which she instantly died...[that] Samuel Fallows...did kill and murder the said Betty Shallcross.' In a strong, clear voice the defendant pleaded 'Not Guilty'.

Apart from Fallows, the most striking presence in the courtroom that day was that of Captain Salusbury Pryce Humphreys, RN (retired), the son-in-law of William Davenport.

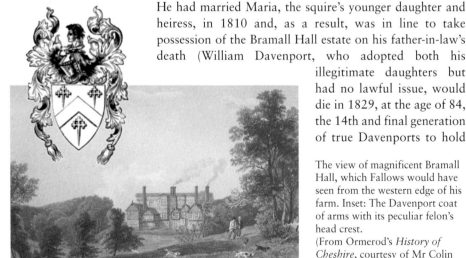

He had married Maria, the squire's younger daughter and heiress, in 1810 and, as a result, was in line to take possession of the Bramall Hall estate on his father-in-law's death (William Davenport, who adopted both his illegitimate daughters but had no lawful issue, would die in 1829, at the age of 84, the 14th and final generation of true Davenports to hold

The view of magnificent Bramall Hall, which Fallows would have seen from the western edge of his farm. Inset: The Davenport coat of arms with its peculiar felon's head crest.
(From Ormerod's *History of Cheshire*, courtesy of Mr Colin Lynch.)

Bramall Hall, though Capt. Humphreys eventually assumed the name of Davenport to continue the family line).

By 1823 old Mr Davenport seems to have left the day-to-day running of the estate to Capt. Humphreys; so, when the behaviour of one of their tenants became an embarrassment to the family, it was he who had to deal with the situation. The matter of Mary Coups's pregnancy and Fallows's ungallant behaviour towards her was introduced in the early part of the prosecution's evidence. But the most revealing perspective on this important prelude to the awful events to come – and the most reliable – had already been supplied by Capt. Humphreys in a couple of letters he wrote just after Fallows had jilted his unsuspecting young fiancée.

The female recipient of the letters was a family friend who was a benefactor of Mary, having been instrumental, apparently, in finding her employment at the hall. Though intended to be private, the letters (or copies of them) appear to have been made available exclusively to the *Courant*, on condition that the name of the lady in question remained confidential. They were reproduced alongside the paper's trial report.

In the first, dated 8 January 1823 – the day on which Fallows should have wed Mary – Capt. Humphreys referred to the 'dishonourable conduct of the person to whom she was engaged', to the visit Fallows had made to the hall 'on the evening preceding the supposed nuptials' and the letter he brought with him giving his reasons for backing out of the marriage.

The 44-year-old ex-naval commander, a senior local magistrate and a leading member of the county's political establishment, went on: 'I have done and said everything in my power to him, but in vain, and I have issued my warrant to apprehend him on his return this day from Manchester, to which place he set out this morning with his cart, doubtless for the express purpose of avoiding joining the party at Church.'

He, personally, had conducted Mary through the formal process of 'filiation' (i.e. identifying Fallows as the father of her unborn baby and making him liable to meet the cost of the child's birth and upkeep) to save her the distress of having to face the entire bench and a courtroom full of strangers.

He further disclosed that, under the same bastardy laws, he had ordered the young man to be held in gaol until he obtained the necessary sureties to guarantee that he made the maintenance payments, thus indemnifying the Overseers of the Poor against any financial liability 'resulting from his base and improper conduct'. Illegitimate children were otherwise a charge on the local rates of the mother's parish or township.

Capt. Humphreys – who would have the rare, if not unique, experience of appearing as a witness for both the prosecution and the defence at Fallows's trial – added that he had 'already put matters in train for getting rid of him as a Tenant'. However, in this respect he was to be thwarted, as he explained in a second letter he sent the good lady on 15 January. It seems that the previous day, while he was in his study attending to his correspondence, Fallows had turned up at the hall unexpectedly and, unbeknown to him, managed to speak to Mr Davenport in private. It seems the old man had not been fully apprised of his visitor's recent fall from grace, and Fallows was able to persuade him to agree, in writing, to renew the tenancy of his farm for another year.

'Mr Davenport now laments as much as ourselves that he should have committed himself to such a man,' said the captain. By this time – as they learned of the extent of his promiscuity and duplicity – a lot of other people were also having to revise their opinions of 'that nice Mr Fallows'.

Confirming that his long-running affair with Betty Shallcross was only now becoming common knowledge, Capt. Humphreys wrote to his female confidante, 'You may, dear madam, possibly have heard that another young woman, who formerly lived under his own roof as servant, has, in every particular, experienced the same fate as poor Mary, and another family made equally miserable.'

Little could he have anticipated what would be poor Betty's ultimate fate and that for *her* family the misery was only just beginning...

At the start of his trial evidence, Capt. Humphreys had explained that he was involved in the case as both the committing magistrate and as William Davenport's estate manager. For the record, he stated that he was related to the owner of Bramall Hall through marriage – though few of the leading lights of Cheshire's legal and society circles present in court would have been unfamiliar with the Davenport family's pedigree or with his place in it.

No doubt some were also aware that the Davenports once possessed the right to execute criminals: that, in the 13th century, the head of the senior branch of the family had been granted the hereditary office of Grand Serjeant of the Forest of Macclesfield, and with it the authority to hang any thieves and vagabonds caught in the forest. Which accounts for the rather unusual crest on the Davenports' coat of arms. Its form is a felon's head...with a golden rope around his neck.

Samuel Fallows had probably heard something of the family's ancestral history – he would certainly have seen the distinctive coat of arms – on his visits to the manor house. Now, here he was being accused by the representative and *de facto* heir of a landlord, whose personal insignia bore a hangman's noose and whose forbears exercised the power of life and death over those who offended against their laws. It was not a happy augury.

Salusbury Pryce Humphreys – who was knighted in 1831 and, although retired, made a Rear Admiral in 1837 – told the court of the night the prisoner arrived unannounced at Bramall Hall to break the news that he had changed his mind about marrying Mary Coups. Fallows said he would not marry her the next day as planned. Capt. Humphreys remonstrated with him and asked when he would fulfil his promise. Fallows replied that 'he would marry her, but could not fix a time because his uncle and his relations were opposed to the marriage'.

However, as Attorney-General John Hill (prosecuting) confirmed in his opening speech, Fallows had also proposed to Betty Shallcross. The farmer's promises, it soon became clear, were not worth a straw.

At the start of the trial Mr Hill conceded that all the evidence against Fallows was circumstantial. But he argued, 'Murder is seldom, if ever, perpetrated...in the presence of witnesses. It is almost always committed in private and, therefore, the bringing home of the charge to the accused will mainly depend on evidence of a circumstantial nature.' And he added, 'It has been observed in evidence of this description, where the chain is preserved, entire, connected and unbroken, there is none so strong.'

The prosecutor's comments are taken from the *Chester Chronicle* edition of 18 April, and it is from that source and the reports in the two other main newspapers covering the trial, the *Chester Courant* and the *Stockport Advertiser*, that the details of the court case are culled (the assize records afford no official corroboration, as all the witness statements have disappeared from the case file). Although much of the evidence printed was virtually identical, the direct quotations are from the *Chronicle* unless otherwise stated.

Betty Shallcross was in her second spell of employment at Woodley Manor when she died. The large farmhouse, built by colliery owner Mr Robert Cheetham Morrey in more recent times, stood on land that once formed part of the ancient manor of 'Wodlegh' (as it was first recorded in the late 14th century) and close to the site of the original mediaeval manor house. Betty had previously worked as a live-in servant to Mr Morrey for about a year, then left for some undisclosed reason (was it, one wonders, after she became pregnant by Fallows the first time?).

She had been back only four months when, on the morning of Friday 21 March, she asked her friend Rebecca Leigh to deliver a letter to Fallows, addressed care of the Plough Vaults public house in Lower Hillgate, Stockport. Betty knew Rebecca was going to Stockport that day and, it being market day, she also knew Fallows would be there and that he usually called at the Plough for refreshment (it was claimed later that she knew this because it was at the weekly market that she and Fallows used to meet). Betty's instructions to her friend were to hand the letter to the landlady, Mrs Ann Hickman, and to ask her to give it to Fallows personally or to 'send it with speed' to him if he did not come into the pub that day.

Fallows did call in at the Plough and Mrs Hickman handed him the letter, which he read without comment. Mrs Hickman described Fallows as wearing a black coat and a black waistcoat – his preferred mode of dress since the death of his father three years before, she said – light cord 'small-clothes' (knee-breeches) and gaiters.

The description, later confirmed by other witnesses, was significant: the issue of Fallows's clothing was to have a material bearing on the outcome of the trial.

The purport of Betty Shallcross's letter was revealed by Fallows himself during the interview he had with Constable Barratt the day after the murder. In court, Barratt said Fallows explained that Betty had written to ask him for money towards the upkeep of the child she had had by him. The child, a girl, had been born at the Shallcross family home at Slack Hall around the beginning of February 1820. It would appear that, although he had previously contributed a weekly amount, Fallows was now in arrears. The outstanding sum was about 11 or 12 shillings.

Betty also expressed the wish to see him, presumably to discuss her financial situation. Whether she had specified the time and place in her letter or he picked the moment, it was the prosecution's case that Fallows met her that night. Twice, in fact. And that on the second occasion, in the unlikely, pungent surroundings of that moonlit shippon – the meeting place may have been chosen because it was a little distance from the main house and empty at the time – he settled up with the bothersome Betty once and for all, eliminating both his present and future burdens at a stroke. A razor stroke.

That Betty had been out of the house earlier in the evening we know from the evidence of Robert Thorniley, of Bredbury, another servant at Woodley Manor. He testified that she had left him instructions to leave the outer door unlocked so that she would be able to get back in again. However, she seems to have been careful not to tell anyone where she was going. Thorniley, 35, said he did not know what time it was when she went out, but that she came in at about 10 or 15 minutes to 12.

Some time after midnight she went out again. The prosecution alleged that it was for a second rendezvous with Fallows – without offering any explanation as to what was important enough to have induced Betty to sneak out of the house in the small hours to meet him again. It is one of the case's most tantalising unanswered questions.

After all this time it seems unlikely that their ongoing dialogue about money and marriage had reached such a pitch of urgency that it could not wait until a more reasonable hour. It is a distinct possibility, of course, that Betty was persuaded to return to their cattle-shed hideaway for more, shall we say, animal reasons. Had Fallows – who, after all, had had a long and intimate relationship with her – turned on the old seductive charm, and she went back expecting to resume their stolen night of passion? And in the act of love-making he had reached for the razor and committed the hateful deed?

The *Courant* was clearly hinting as much when, in its post-trial report, it envisioned Fallows employing the murder weapon 'more than probably...at a moment of unsuspecting endearment and tenderness'. The prosecution at Fallows's trial also seemed to be suggesting that there had been some sexual activity prior to Betty's death.

Betty Shallcross was reported missing early on the Saturday morning and a search began. At about 10am a young serving boy called Joseph Barker opened the door to the shippon and saw her lying face-down on the floor. The shippon was one of several outbuildings belonging to Woodley Manor; Barker described it as 'a back building...just out of the [farm]yard'. It could not be seen from the house as there was a large barn in the way. Too frightened to approach the bloody corpse, Barker immediately pulled the door to and ran to fetch Mr Morrey's manservant, James Pollitt. However, said Attorney-General Hill, the body was 'so shocking to the sight' that he, too, was 'afraid to go near it' and it fell to friend and neighbour Mary Tweedle to be the first to venture into the cowshed.

Mrs Tweedle said in court that, because the deceased's long hair was obscuring her features and was so 'clotted together' with blood, she at first could not make out the extent of her injuries. But her subsequent examination revealed that Betty's throat was cut on the left side. Pathetically, Betty's right hand was still raised to her neck as if frozen in her final despairing effort to protect herself. Her instinctive reactions had left her right thumb sliced open and the back part of her hand badly bruised. There were two deep wounds on the upper part of her head and one on the back. She also had a bruise on her forehead and her top lip was black and swollen. Betty had obviously taken quite a beating. There was a large pool of blood under her and another about half a yard from her feet.

Mrs Tweedle was closely quizzed by the prosecution about the state of Betty's clothing. She testified, '[Her cap] was lying by her side. She had no handkerchief over her breast...her breast was all uncovered. She had an apron fast about her neck...it was over her right shoulder. It was not as they usually wear them.'

In her frantic struggle to save herself, it would have been no surprise if Betty's clothes had become dishevelled or that, when she sneaked out of the farmhouse the second time, she had not dressed to quite her normal standard of neatness and modesty. The prosecution's purpose in pursuing this line of questioning, therefore, seems to have been to imply that there was a sexual element to the crime: that maybe Fallows had forced himself upon her, she resisted and he killed her. Or, alternatively, that he had lulled his old flame into a vulnerable position by feigning affection and this time the foreplay was the overture not to more fleshly pleasures but to murder.

The questions remain no more than a series of cryptic clues, however, for the prosecution left the matter deliberately ambiguous, safe in the knowledge that there was only one person alive who could refute their insinuations…and he was in no position to argue.

The various wounds found on Betty's body were detailed by John Cheetham, the Gee Cross surgeon who examined her on the Saturday afternoon after she had been laid out on a table in the Morreys' kitchen. His view was that the three head wounds had been inflicted with a *blunt* instrument – and he then confused the issue by suggesting it could have been a knife. He may have had in mind something like the blunt-*ended* blade of a penknife, which would have made a less clean cut if wielded with a stabbing motion.

There was no doubt about the other injuries, however. The fatal gash in her throat – contrary to the wording of the indictment, the surgeon, who presumably measured it, said the wound was *five* inches long – and the longitudinal cut on her right thumb had been caused by a sharp instrument. Such as a man's razor.

But did that necessarily mean Betty Shallcross's killer was armed with two different weapons? Maybe not. It seems entirely possible that the head wounds, which were obviously sustained before the fatal gash, were also caused by the razor – it was of the type known, appropriately enough, as a 'cut-throat' – while the blade was still folded into its long handle. The half-moon finger grip, or 'tang', at the hinged end would have protruded by almost an inch and could have done a lot of damage in the hands of someone bent on murder. Also, if there was a second weapon, would the killer have gone to the trouble of retrieving it while leaving the razor behind?

No matter: the murder of Betty Shallcross bore all the hallmarks of a pitilessly purposeful mind, a cold-hearted individual who was not deflected from his homicidal intent by the fact that his victim was conspicuously pregnant. John Cheetham's estimate was that she was 'five or six months gone'. It seemed she had conceived around the same time as Mary Coups.

Of all the witnesses to appear for the Crown, none cast more suspicion on Fallows than Fallows himself. In the days immediately following the discovery of the murder, he made two statements in which he set out conflicting alibis. Both proved to be false. Then there was the story of his disappearing clothes. He gave two different versions of that, too.

As a result, while he admitted that he was away from his farm throughout the whole night of Betty Shallcross's murder, Samuel Fallows was never able to explain satisfactorily where he was at the time she was killed. Instead, he spun a web of lies that, in the end, made it impossible for the jury to disentangle him from the crime.

Fittingly, the key witness in all this was the gaoler, John Barratt. He first recalled the Sunday morning interview he had with Fallows at his Bramhall home. The defendant's

Shocking Affair of the Unfaithful Farmer

farm was actually located in Bramhall Green, where today's sprawling dormitory town on the southern edge of Greater Manchester had its origins. The farmhouse stood close to the eastern entrance to Bramall Hall, on the site of what is now the major roundabout at the junction of Bramhall Lane South (A5102) and Bridge Lane (A5143).

When Constable Barratt asked him to account for his whereabouts on the previous Friday night, Fallows said that after he had finished milking he set out to walk to Toft to see Mary Coups. However, it was raining so hard that, after reaching Mobberley – a distance of about 10 miles – he turned back, arriving home around 2 o'clock in the morning. As he had not wanted to disturb his household at such an hour, he spent the night – in his soaking wet clothes – sleeping in his hay loft. He said he lay there until 10 o'clock the next morning, when he finally went into the house to get changed.

If that didn't stretch Barratt's credulity, Fallows now came up with a couple of out-and-out lies. Along with several other witnesses, the constable had himself seen Fallows in Stockport on the Friday wearing a black coat and black waistcoat (he had known the defendant for about five years). Keen to check them out for signs of blood, he asked to see the garments, whereupon Fallows insisted he did not own a black coat and that the waistcoat he had had on that day was a striped one.

The Bramhall farmer seemed to be digging himself deeper and deeper into trouble. Where, Barratt next inquired, were his cord breeches? Fallows replied that they had been so wet that, on the Saturday morning, he put them on a hedge close to the farm to dry and when he went to collect them later, he found someone had stolen them. Had he made inquiries about the theft among his household? No, he said, he had mentioned it to no one.

The New Bailey prison (arrowed), on the banks of the River Mersey at Stockport, where Samuel Fallows and the Ashton murder suspects were incarcerated prior to their trials. The last remnants of the building were demolished in the mid-1970s.
(By permission of Stockport Heritage Library.)

Unconvinced by his explanation, Barratt arrested Fallows and hauled him off to Stockport's New Bailey Prison. The following day, Monday 24 March, he brought him up before the coroner at the inquest into Betty Shallcross's death. As Mr Hollins was reading out what he had allegedly said to the constable, Fallows dramatically halted the proceedings and retracted his statement.

'It's all a lie', he interrupted. 'There is no truth in it.' The coroner wanted to know why he had said such things. According to the *Courant*, Fallows replied mysteriously, 'I cannot tell, but I have been informed that people would come against me and say anything.' After Mr Hollins had cautioned him to 'tell the truth this time', he made a second statement that sounded even less plausible than the first. What was significant about this one, though, was that at least part of the story could easily be checked and corroborated. Or not, as the case proved to be.

According to Barratt, his revised alibi was that he had gone out on Friday night to hunt poachers. The gamekeeper at Bramall Hall, Fallows said, suspected him of trapping hares on his farm: the keeper had found gins laid for the purpose and had pointed the finger at his young neighbour. So he had gone 'into the fields' to keep a lookout in case the real poachers returned and he would be able to 'clear himself'.

He said he had 'watched all night till five in the morning' and then gone home. Once again, he said he did not care to awake his household at that hour and so he had slept in the hayloft. This time, he said it was about 9am when he awoke and went indoors to change his clothes. His coat, waistcoat, breeches and leggings had become soaked during his all-night vigil in the fields, he explained, and he had put them on the hedge to dry. He had forgotten to bring them in on the Saturday night and – lo and behold – by next morning they had all been stolen.

Unfortunately for Fallows, his talk of gin traps and poaching allegations was shot to pieces by the Bramall Hall gamekeeper William Hamilton. In court Mr Hamilton stated categorically, 'I never told him there were any gins set on his farm by poachers, nor [accused him] of destroying game there.'

As for his conveniently vanished clothing, the court heard that the hedge on which Fallows had hung his wet things was used regularly for drying clothes. It was close to the back door of the farmhouse, in sight of the farm workers who were in and out all day long. But, while Fallows had indicated his clothes were adorning the hedge throughout most of Saturday, not one of his four live-in servants could remember seeing them.

On the subject of his relationship with Betty Shallcross, Barratt, again harking back to the inquest, said that Fallows had told the coroner he had only ever been to see her at Woodley Manor once in January. He had apparently called to give her some money and, he said, she had informed him that 'she had got a fresh sweetheart and would have no more to do with him'. When he agreed that he had stayed there for two-to-three hours, the coroner wondered what had detained him so long. The *Courant* reported, 'To this the prisoner made no reply. It was enquired whether they had since renewed their acquaintance; he denied it...'

By the time of his trial, the duration of that January visit to Woodley Manor had increased to over four hours. Mary Morrey, sister of Robert Morrey and the woman in overall charge of his household, told the court that he was there from 'almost three till

Shocking Affair of the Unfaithful Farmer

Happy Valley, Bramhall, and, in the background, the old Womanscroft Bridge, where a 10-year-old boy testified that he had seen Fallows on the morning after the murder of Betty Shallcross, providing crucial evidence that helped send her killer to the gallows.
(From the author's collection.)

7 o'clock'. And rather than cold-shouldering him with talk of 'another sweetheart,' Betty had walked part-way home with him. Miss Morrey stated, 'She was, to the best of my knowledge, followed [courted] by no one but the prisoner.' She also believed, contrary to Fallows's evidence, that he had called at the manor for her on previous occasions.

As his lengthy period in the witness box drew to a close, Constable Barratt returned to the events surrounding Mary Coups's pregnancy. He claimed that while Fallows was in his custody, following the warrant issued by Capt. Humphreys, he had 'persuaded him to marry her, as she was a woman of good character'. Fallows said he would marry Mary 'on the Tuesday following' and had asked Barratt to intercede with Capt. Humphreys to get him discharged for 'he should not like to be married in handcuffs'.

As it happened he *was* released when, after 24 hours in gaol, two friends from Stockport stood bail for him. But his latest 'marriage vow' was another promise he failed to keep and poor Mary was left in the lurch once more.

After gamekeeper William Hamilton's demolition of his hare-poachers claim, it was left to a 10-year-old boy to put perhaps the biggest dent in Samuel Fallows's revised alibi. If they were prepared to accept the word of a minor on a matter of such vital importance, the jurors may just have considered the evidence of young James Ridgeway to be the most convincing indicator of Fallows's guilt they had heard so far.

James, who lived in Bramhall with his father, told of a strange incident on the morning after the murder near Womanscroft Bridge. The bridge carried what was then Mill Lane (now Bridge Lane) over The Ladybrook; the latter, after winding its way through the picturesque Happy Valley and under the bridge, swung north and then west around the back of Fallows's farm and through the Bramall Hall estate. James saw Fallows emerge from under the bridge walking along the brook side. It was around 7am – even by his amended alibi that was two hours after Fallows said he had gone to sleep in his hayloft – and was already fully light, so the lad had no problem recognising the farmer, whom he had known for two years.

The bridge, which was replaced when the road was widened and straightened in 1931, was about 200 yards from Fallows's home, and he was heading that way. When he saw the boy, however, he immediately turned tail and ran off in the opposite direction.

Said James, 'He turned his head and looked at me. He had a black coat and light-coloured breeches on. He ran along the brook side [away] from me. He looked at me maybe about a minute. He ran from [the direction of] his house.'

To questions from the judge, the Hon. Charles Warren, James replied, 'He was about 20 yards from me when he ran away...I saw his face clearly...He ran swiftly.'

Fallows was last seen at the farm at about 6.30pm the previous evening. Labourer John Walton, one of his servants, said that, after the evening's milking session, his master 'came into the stable to me and then went out of the yard gate and turned to the left towards the Stockport road'.

Esther Brown, possibly the housekeeper, revealed how her master had told her that he was going out that evening and asked her to lock the doors if he was not in by the time she was ready for bed. He did not return and she locked up at about 9 o'clock. Between 9 and 10 o'clock the next morning he came in and went straight upstairs. When he came down he put on a fresh pair of stockings, then he washed his garters.

Fallows slept in the same room as Walton and his two other male servants, Thomas Oakes and Daniel Hallworth, sharing a bed with the latter. Significantly (in the context of the defendant's revised alibi), Oakes said he got out of bed on the Saturday morning as usual at about 4.30 and Hallworth was up just after five.

That Samuel Fallows returned to Stockport on the Friday evening was attested by David Clarke, a farmer from Cheadle Hulme, who met Fallows regularly at the market. It was between 6 and 7 o'clock (the apparent time discrepancy is explained by the fact that the clocks in Stockport were generally about an hour behind Bramhall time) when, said Clarke, he saw the accused going down Millgate 'in the direction of Bredbury'.

Much of the trial was taken up by the prosecution's attempts to put the murder weapon in Fallows's hands. In the days before the development of forensic science, when there was no classification of blood or fingerprints or proper understanding of the concept of contact trace evidence, unless the culprit was caught with the proverbial smoking gun – or, in this case, the dripping blade – the chances of establishing a direct link between the murderer and murder scene were slim.

In all, the Crown prosecutors examined five witnesses on the subject, recalling no fewer than three of them to ensure the jury got the message. Yet, for all their assertions, the evidence they offered was ultimately unsatisfactory and inconclusive.

The murder weapon was found by farmer Ralph Saxon, the Morreys' next-door neighbour, who lived at what is now called Manor Farm Cottage. The 16th-century three-storey Tudor building, which stands just across the main Hyde Road (A560) from Woodley railway station, is now all that remains of the old Woodley Manor estate. The manor house site today is occupied by a large haulage company depot. The last remnants of the house itself were demolished in the 1960s. The shippon in which Betty Shallcross met her grisly end is believed to have been pulled down in the 1970s, after becoming unsafe.

Saxon said of the razor, 'A bit of the haft near the rivet was falling off. I marked it and gave it to Mr Hollins [the coroner]. I showed it to Thorniley. It was very bloody.' In the witness box he was shown a razor by Constable Barratt and he swore it was the same one.

James Hodgkinson, a former employee of Fallows, said that when he lived with the defendant during the previous year he had often shaved with one of his razors. 'It was an old one,' he said, '[and] the rivet near the blade was loose.'

When he was interviewed by Barratt, Hodgkinson added, he was shown two razors, and he picked out one that 'looked very much' like the razor he had used. It was the razor Betty Shallcross's murderer left behind in the shippon at Woodley Manor. However, shown the implement in court, Hodgkinson would only say, 'It is very much like it but I cannot swear to it.'

Shocking Affair of the Unfaithful Farmer

During his original testimony, Officer Barratt said he had searched Fallows's house for the old razor but could not find it, though he did turn up two new ones.

Could the razor with the broken handle have belonged to someone at Woodley Manor? Certainly not, said housekeeper Mary Morrey. She declared, 'I had all the management of my brother's house. I know the razors which were used there. I can of my own knowledge positively state there was no such razor in the house.'

In response to all this, Fallows seems to have preferred to remain silent rather than to offer anything meaningful in his defence. If he had had such a razor, as James Hodgkinson testified, why did he not produce it and put an end to the speculation? If he had thrown it away because it was broken, and had bought himself two new ones, why did he not offer this perfectly reasonable explanation? And if his ex-employee was mistaken (or lying), why did he not say so?

In criminal trials of his period, defendants were not allowed the option of going into the witness box and giving evidence on oath, and the defence counsel did not have the right to make closing speeches. They could only question witnesses on their clients' behalf. But Samuel Fallows does not appear to have provided his lawyers with much ammunition with which to return the prosecution's fire.

Instead, he opted for silence, convincing himself that the weight of circumstantial evidence would be insufficient to convict him. From his demeanour in court, it was a belief he held right up to the moment the foreman announced the jury's verdict. He was aware, however, of the importance juries attached to the evidence of character witnesses in such restricted circumstances. He produced four (two others were called but did not appear, apparently), all of whom spoke in glowing terms about his previous exemplary conduct.

And that was how prosecution witness Capt. Salusbury Pryce Humphreys – the magistrate who had had him locked up for getting Mary Coups pregnant and who later bound over a number of witnesses to testify against him at his trial – came to give evidence in Fallows's defence as well. It was a brief, but laudatory, statement. He told the court, 'I have known the prisoner 12 or 14 years. He is a near neighbour of mine. I saw him almost daily, and he was justly esteemed and beloved by all who knew him.'

As for hard facts, however, Samuel Fallows could muster nothing in his defence. And the judge, in seeking to present a balanced review of the evidence to the jury, struggled to find any convincing arguments in his favour.

Mr Justice Warren first touched on the question 'Why did he do it?' No motive had been put forward at any time in the trial, and, he said, the jury would have to draw their own conclusions about 'the relative connection in which the prisoner stood between Betty Shallcross and Mary Coups'.

Referring to the defendant's mysteriously disappearing clothes, the judge said he found it 'most extraordinary' that Fallows had made no inquiries about the missing garments. He also described as 'rather extraordinary' the claim in his second alibi statement that he had slept in the hayloft because he didn't want to disturb the people in his house at 5am. Said the judge, '[Far] from his family being likely to be disturbed...part of them [sic] were actually up at that time.'

Judge Warren went on: 'He palliates one falsehood by telling another. He says he slept on the hay till 10 o'clock, whilst a witness proves he saw him near a brook bridge at 7 o'clock in the morning...He tells one story to the constable, which he flatly contradicts before the coroner; he then frames another [story] before the coroner, which, like the other, is proved to be false.'

The boy who saw Fallows at Womanscroft Bridge on the Saturday morning was, said the judge, a 'most important' witness and the thrust of his evidence – 'he looks at the prisoner and the prisoner runs away' – an 'important fact'.

And so to the murder weapon. Chief Justice Warren commented, 'The rivet of the one, which it was proved the prisoner once possessed, is loose. So was the rivet of the one found in the shippon. The hafts also were similar. It was not positively sworn to, although the witness [James Hodgkinson] swears to the best of his knowledge that it is very like the prisoner's.' If the members of the jury were of the opinion that the razors were the same, he said, the case would be 'strong indeed against the prisoner'.

Though the court had heard of his 'intimacy' with two different women, and that he had been leading the kind of life he personally regarded as 'disgraceful', the judge reminded the jury that the defence witnesses had all declared that Fallows had 'an unexceptionable character'. That, however, had been the only evidence the defendant had produced.

The judge concluded, '[He] has set up no defence whatsoever by the introduction of opposing testimony. The [prosecution] case remains untouched, untainted in every feature of it.'

It was a pretty devastating résumé, though, in the light of Fallows's impenetrable silence, it is difficult to see how Mr Justice Warren could have been more even-handed. The only surprise was that the jurors, who retired at 4.30pm after a trial lasting more than seven hours, were out for almost half an hour considering their verdict.

Fallows, meanwhile, continued to present an untroubled face to the world. He spent the period of the jury's absence sitting in the dock watching with apparent interest the opening proceedings of a civil case while sucking an orange and eating a biscuit with, as one reporter observed, 'perfect *sang froid*'.

When the jury pronounced him 'guilty', however, it was a rather different Samuel Fallows who stood – or rather tottered – before the judge awaiting sentence. As if genuinely shocked by the verdict, 'his legs trembled beneath him and his whole frame seemed convulsed'. When asked by the prothonotary, Mr John Lloyd, why sentence of death should not be passed upon him, he burst into tears.

As he pronounced the sentence, Judge Warren could not help but express some sense of sorrow at Fallows's situation. However, he went on, 'A more atrocious crime or one more abhorrent in the frightful circumstances of its perpetration never came before a British Court of Justice...You stand here as a double murderer, for the same hand that destroyed the mother destroyed also the infant in her womb...Your crime calls for the heaviest punishment...the blood of her that you mutilated and murdered demands it.'

Fallows, the *Chronicle* noted, had to be carried from the bar 'completely broken in mind and body...a miserable contrast to the bold, undaunted front he displayed when he was first placed at it'.

The *Courant*'s correspondent had also observed Fallows at close quarters during the trial. In his dramatic, not to say theatrical, dispatch, he wrote, 'While the fatal instrument he had employed – and more than probably employed at a moment of unsuspecting endearment and tenderness – while this weapon of blood and death was bandying about [sic] among the witnesses and immediately placed before his view, not a muscle of his face, not a feature of his countenance, was affected. The affecting description of the mangled and lacerated body of his devoted victim, the recital of the lakes of blood which lay under and near to her mangled corpse, the horrifying exhibition of her long hair clotted with coagulated blood, the story of her dishevelled fragments of dress lying scattered around her [sic], the history of the mortal wound in her throat, her bruises [on] the head, and the less serious, but not less interesting, cuts in her hands, which she had ineffectually lifted up to implore pity or avert cruelty – these tales of horror, which thrilled through the bosom of numberless individuals present, appeared to have no influence in moving the feelings of the man who had been the author of the awful history.'

After only a short period in the cells Fallows was back to his old intractable self. He was due to hang on the following Monday – the law at this time decreed that condemned persons should be executed within 48 hours or three days if the second day was a Sunday – and throughout the weekend, the *Courant* related, he 'remained reserved and sullen' and 'studiously eluded all questions aimed at extorting an ingenuous confession of the murder'.

In the same 15 April edition the *Courant* printed the third and final instalment of the 'private' correspondence between Capt. Humphreys and the lady with a personal interest in the welfare of Mary Coups. Dated Saturday 12 April, the letter explained why, in view of his previous 'excellent' character, he had had 'no hesitation' in speaking up for the prisoner – whom he felt constrained to describe as 'decidedly the handsomest man in court'.

Capt. Humphreys wrote, 'I have seen him *alone* in his cell...and the interview, as you will, dear Madam, imagine, was most affecting. We talked of the advice I had given him to marry Mary, which he now, alas! too late, laments most bitterly he did not follow. When I left him and shook him by the hand, he was crying aloud, and his sorrow and repentance are sincere. Whatever might have been my feelings towards him, for his perfidious conduct towards Mary Coups, they are now entirely subdued.'

He also revealed that Mary Coups (by now heavily pregnant, one assumes) had been in court throughout the trial, even though she was not expected to be called upon to give evidence. She seems to have moved away to have her baby, possibly with the assistance of her Lady Bountiful.

Twenty-four hours before he was due to hang, Fallows, it was reported, tried to bribe his way out of prison. He was said to have first offered the Castle Gaol governor more than £1,000 to connive at his escape. Then, stated the *Chronicle*, 'a person evidently acquainted with the Prisoner' approached the turnkey (the senior warder) with a similar proposition, though his promised pay-off was a more modest £500.

It was all to no avail, however, and the execution went ahead on Monday 14 April. Though it was still only about 5 o'clock in the morning when he took the short cart ride to the City Gaol, a crowd estimated at 2,000 accompanied the slow-moving procession.

At the prison the chaplain also tried unsuccessfully to get Fallows to confess. His only constructive comment on the subject, made somewhat irritably in response to this latest appeal, was, 'I have confessed to God. It is done.' Even on the scaffold, he made no answer when he was offered one last chance to unburden himself.

'Thus terminated the life of Samuel Fallows and, we fear, in a way too dreadful to be contemplated without "fear and trembling"', the *Chronicle* reflected. Reviewing the case, the paper declared that if anyone still harboured doubts about the guilt of this 'wretched man,' they must be 'put to rest by circumstances which have come to our knowledge subsequently to the Murderer's execution'.

Foremost among this new evidence was the 'full and ample confession of his guilt' the paper claimed Fallows had made to a brother and a sister who visited him in the City Gaol just before he died. 'They, and they alone, were the depositories of the dreadful secret,' the *Chronicle* commented, adding, 'If he thought that by maintaining so obstinate a silence he was rescuing his family from any odium that might fall on them by his death, he deceived himself.'

Then there was the razor found beside the body of the murdered woman. That it had belonged to Fallows was now 'equally doubtless', said the *Chronicle* – though its reporter felt that it would not be 'proper under existing circumstances' to name the source of his information.

For the first time, too, the paper made a stab at formulating some kind of motive for the killing. It continued, 'We have heard that Fallows was a young man of abstemious habits, and was not, therefore, likely to be excited to such a deed of desperation by applying "hot and rebellious liquors to the blood".' In other words, he didn't do it in a drunken rage. No, the root of his evil, suggested the *Chronicle*, was money.

'He was, we understand, remarkable for an avaricious closeness of disposition in money matters' – translation: he was tight-fisted – 'and it is conjectured (although well able to pay the weekly stipend in support of the child he had by the deceased) that he might have been stimulated to the horrible crime from a desire to avoid her future importunities! It will be seen that, on the trial, there is the admission of 10 or 12 shillings being due to her from him.'

A further example of Fallows's meanness, the *Chronicle* claimed, was his instruction to his sister to bring him some old clothes in which to be hanged. The gesture, said the paper, was intended solely to 'bereave the hangman of the suit he then wore'. In place of the 'genteel' ensemble of blue coat and trousers, black waistcoat and black handkerchief, that he had worn in court, Fallows appeared on the scaffold in 'an old blue coat, an old waistcoat and a pair of ragged blue stocking pantaloons'.

Whether executioner Burrows grieved over his loss was not recorded, though it would not have been the first time that his customary perk amounted to no more than a pile of rags.

If Samuel Fallows had, to say the least, a hard-headed attitude towards money, it was something he may have inherited from his father James, who had died in 1820, aged 74. His will, which records that his estate was valued at 'under eight hundred pounds', is filed at the CRO in Chester. And in both its terms and tenor, James Fallows showed he was not a man to let sentiment cloud his financial judgement. In one clause of the document, he made it clear that those children to whom he had advanced loans 'in his lifetime' would have their legacies reduced by the equivalent amounts. And another condition was that if any of his children sued for a bigger share of his estate (became

Shocking Affair of the Unfaithful Farmer

'litigious or troublesome', as he put it) they would forfeit all claims and 'in lieu thereof shall have only one shilling apiece and no more'.

With Fallows gone to his account, there the story seemed to have ended, and, with it, all further speculation as to his motive for murder. In the absence of a more compelling theory, we are left only with the possibility that it was about money after all. Already legally bound to maintain the baby Mary Coups was expecting, and with Betty Shallcross about to present him with a third dependent child, Fallows could see his paternal commitments stretching far into the future, placing a substantial drain on his income from the farm. Disposing of Betty and her unborn baby was an effective, if extreme, means of reducing his outgoings. But if avarice *was* the influencing factor, it can only have been supreme arrogance coupled with blind ignorance that persuaded him – the obvious suspect once the details of his wanton lifestyle emerged – that he could get away with it.

Fallows's death was not quite the end of the affair, however. There were still a few more 'shocks' to come.

At the end of Fallows's trial, Judge Warren had invoked the provisions of the 1752 Murder Act, under which the cadavers of all executed murderers could be handed over to surgeons for anatomical study. This, however, was to be no ordinary 'slice-'em-up' dissection; instead, the surgeons at Chester Infirmary took the opportunity to indulge in a relatively-new area of scientific interest known as 'galvanism'. It involved the use of the current from an electrical battery to stimulate various parts of the body into activity. The justification for such undignified, almost freak-show-like displays was that they provided opportunities to study the interaction between human nerves and muscles, and, ultimately, to advance the development of resuscitation techniques.

The experiments took place on Wednesday 16 April, in the less-than-perfect surroundings of the prison basement at the castle where, along with local medical men and their eager young students, a few members of the public managed to squeeze into the cramped 'operating room'. Some were no doubt hoping for a repeat of the wondrous sights witnessed in the famous Scottish case five years earlier, when, by passing an electrical current through the body of an Airdrie murderer named Clydesdale, surgeons in Glasgow had animated the corpse with such startlingly realistic results that one of the spectators fainted and others fled in terror. Or in the 1803 experiments on a double murderer condemned at the Old Bailey in London, which had also led onlookers to believe the corpse had come back to life and a beadle, who had been present, was reported to have died of fright.

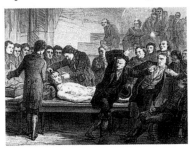

Following Fallows's execution, anatomist Dr Andrew Ure of Glasgow University carried out various experiments on his body using electricity in scenes reminiscent of those witnessed in 1818, when he subjected the corpse of a Scottish murderer to similar indignities. Spectators thought he had brought the man back to life and one of them (front extreme right?) fainted.
(By permission of Carol Trager-Cowan and David A. Stevenson.)

The *Chronicle* recorded, 'In the first experiment, an attempt was made to restore the action of the respiratory function, according to the suggestion of Dr Ure, the distinguished professor at Glasgow [Dr Andrew Ure was one of the two anatomists who had experimented on the body of Clydesdale]. For this purpose, Dr Jones [of the Infirmary] laid bare, and brought into view, the phrenic nerve as it runs down under the muscles about the middle part of the side of the neck.

'One of the poles of the battery was placed in contact with the phrenic nerve, the other in contact with the diaphragm through [an] incision under the rib – *a slight but unequivocal respiratory movement followed*. This movement was several times repeated – sufficient to prove the value of Dr Ure's suggestion...In the subsequent experiments, the muscles of the arm and leg performed their natural movements to an extent commensurate with the power of the battery, in a manner that excited the wonder of the uninstructed bystanders. The muscles of the face were made to contract with much effect, particularly those of the eyes and mouth, giving rise to a variety of painful expressions.'

It had been the *Chronicle*'s hope to procure 'a more enlarged and scientific account' of the experiments. But the paper, a tad peeved, pointed out that the good doctor had chosen instead to publish his findings in 'some Philosophical Journals'.

*   *   *

As shocking crimes went, there was none more so than the second murder to electrify the public of Cheshire in 1823. At once sensational and controversial, it involved a highway robbery that escalated into bloody violence, leaving a brave businessman lying battered to death at the roadside and a remote rural community deeply traumatised. Such was its lasting effect on the local population that, half-a-century later, the public responded generously to an appeal to provide a lasting reminder of the terrible event...

Chapter Eleven

The Stones that Cried Out 'Murder!'

The slab of chiselled rock lying half hidden behind a tangle of grass and thistle at the highway's edge could, at first sight, be mistaken for a weathered old milestone, or some long-forgotten boundary marker. The majority of those who travel this windswept stretch of moorland road – mostly in cars, mostly in a hurry – are probably unaware of its existence, however, let alone its significance.

Set into one of the dry-stone walls that are the stitching on the patchwork of fells, fields and cloughs that characterises Cheshire's Pennine fringe, the inscribed tablet, alongside Buxton Old Road, close to the county's easternmost boundary at Higher Disley, is a memorial to a murder victim. It records that near this spot in 1823 – after being attacked and robbed – William Wood, a textile manufacturer from neighbouring Derbyshire, was brutally slain. It was the bloody and shocking climax to a crime whose impact was still being felt locally 50 years later when the public fund launched to create this unique landmark was substantially over-subscribed.

The group of prominent Victorian gentlemen behind the enterprise – citizens as solid, sober and upstanding as the object of their beneficence – also intended the 'indication stone' (as they termed it) to be a warning sign, its formal inscription ending with the solemn exhortation to 'Prepare To Meet Thy God'.

Its text was inspired by chapter 24 of the Gospel of St Matthew, and, in particular, verse 44: 'Therefore be ye also ready: for in such an hour as ye think not, the Son of man cometh.' In its original context, the quotation foreshadowed the end of the world and the last judgement of God. Here, beside the snaking switchback route that climbs steeply out of Disley village and over Whaley Moor before descending equally dramatically into Whaley Bridge, the words written in stone were meant to remind travellers on the precarious highway of life of the need for moral vigilance. Never knowing what might lie around the corner – so their message went – everyone should be in a constant state of spiritual readiness for that unpredictable moment when the Angel of Death steals in like a thief in the night. Or, as in William Wood's case, three thieves in broad daylight.

The roadside 'Murder Stone' on the outskirts of Disley, where William Wood was slain in 1823. The memorial was paid for by local residents following a generously-supported public appeal 50 years later. (Photograph by the author.)

As a spokesman for the fundraising committee commented at the time of the stone's unveiling, 'Little would William Wood think, when he left his home and family that morning, that he would never see them again. So uncertain is human life, that we cannot too often, and in too many places, be reminded of the fact [that]…in such an hour as you think not, "the Son of man cometh".'

The unusual ceremony took place – 'in the presence of a large concourse of people,' according to a report in the *Stockport Advertiser* – on Saturday 11 April 1874, when it was also revealed that the public appeal had produced a cash surplus. The extra money, it was announced, would be put towards the repair of Disley's village fountain, then said to be in 'a most dilapidated condition'.

Other marker stones had been placed in the wall over the years since the murder, apparently, but some had borne the wrong date and the most recent, engraved with the initials 'W. W.', had been vandalised along with the surrounding wall. The committee's aim in erecting the new memorial, the *Advertiser* explained, was to set the record straight and provide a more substantial 'memento' of the 'atrocious crime'.

That the campaign should generate so much interest, and prompt such a remarkably generous response (the whole thing was organised and completed within four weeks, it was reported), demonstrated the continuing effect on the collective conscience of the local community of an event that occurred before most of its inhabitants were born…a truly sensational murder memorable not just for its improvised brutality but for the youthfulness of the three alleged perpetrators, all of them under 20 and the youngest just 17 years old.

It was a case made all the more notable by some inept policing – at one stage the investigation looked to be heading for scandalous failure – and a controversial prosecution that saw the legal proceedings drag on for eight months. In the course of the murder hunt, the constables missed at least two opportunities to nab the culprits, the ringleader slipped through the net altogether (he was never caught) and another of the robbers was allowed to cheat the law by committing suicide…while the only one brought to trial for the crime was widely believed to have had no hand in the actual killing.

William Wood was murdered on the evening of Wednesday 16 July 1823. A 32-year-old master weaver, he owned a small factory in Eyam in Derbyshire, operating a dozen looms and manufacturing cotton cloths such as calicoes and checks. He had left his wife and child on the Monday to travel to Manchester with a consignment of cloth to sell at the following day's market; now, after conducting further business in Stockport, he was on his way home on what was the original turnpike road between Disley and Whaley.

A new turnpike, winding through the Goyt valley along the line of the modern A6 trunk route between Manchester and Buxton, had been opened some three years earlier, but it was part of the routine of Mr Wood's weekly market visit to make the return trip on foot, knowing that by taking the old road 'over the top' he could knock at least a mile off the journey. Although it involved a steep ascent through some fairly wild terrain, with only the occasional habitation – and he was carrying a large sum of money at a time when highway robbery was occurring with frightening regularity in the county – he seems to have had few qualms about going that way.

It was reported at the time that friends had recently expressed concerns about his safety, but Wood, a fit and muscular man, had shrugged them aside, saying he would not be afraid of tackling one man or even two. If he was attacked by more, however, he had to concede that he 'knew not what might be his fate'.

Shortly after 7 o'clock he was observed on the outskirts of Disley by two 'neighbours', whose homes stood alongside the road about half a mile apart. He was walking towards Whaley and nearing the boundary between the two townships. Following him, some 20 yards behind, were three young men. They were all poorly dressed, though one wore a noticeably tidier-looking suit.

About half-an-hour later, farm labourer John Mellor, on his way back to Whaley from 'Bullock Smithy' (modern Hazel Grove) in his employer's cart, was travelling the same route when, at a place called Longside, he came upon the body of the businessman stretched out on the grass verge. Tradition places it in the neighbourhood of Higher Disley, but the exact location was about 20 yards over the boundary in the township of Yeardsley cum Whaley, part of the ancient parish of Taxal (Taxal was then in Cheshire; in 1936 it was transferred to Derbyshire and the old township boundary is now the border between the two counties).

William Wood was lying face down under the gritstone wall that flanked the highway and opposite a large fir plantation. A section of the wall had been pulled down in an apparently hasty – and unsuccessful – attempt to cover up the body. Some of the stones lying closest to it had blood and what turned out to be human hair adhering to them. There was a large pool of blood under the murdered man's head and splashes on the wall and the ground for some distance around. It appeared that the fearless Mr Wood – staunch Methodist, devout churchgoer and pillar of his local community – had put up a spirited fight.

Mellor alighted from his cart and was examining the body when two other drivers, who had been following closely behind him on the road, also stopped to take a look. He later described the dead man's appearance to the jury at Chester Assizes. 'He had a terrible wound on the back of his head and two [further wounds] on his forehead,' he would recall. 'They seemed to have been knocked in with a stone.'

One of the other carters, Edmund Pott, from Kettleshulme, said he felt the body and it was still warm. And, from the severity of the injuries and the extent of the bloodstains, he concluded, 'The man that did the murder [sic] must have used great violence.'

It was also obvious what the motive was. The pockets of the dead man's breeches had been turned inside out and when Pott searched the deceased's clothing all he could find was an old penny. From the transactions he completed during his three-day business trip, it was subsequently calculated that Mr Wood should have had on him at least £110, its spending power the equivalent today of more than £8,000.

By this time the three suspected robbers were no more than half a mile away at Stoneheads, where they had a brief encounter with labourer Thomas Etchells. He was at the front gate of his house – which was also beside the old road, on the hill by which it makes its final descent into Whaley Bridge – when they came towards him 'running very fast'. As they drew level they slowed to walking pace and asked him how far it was to Chapel-en-le-Frith. Etchells later stated in evidence, 'I told them it was four miles and they said "Thank you, sir" [and] then went running away...abreast of each other.'

Two of them wore dark coats – one blue and one black – while the third, as well as being the tallest of the three, also stood out as he had on a jacket and matching trousers made of 'pillow fustian' and dyed an unusually-light colour. On the jacket's left sleeve, between the shoulder and elbow, Etchells said there was 'a red mark' about four or five inches long – a bloodstain seemingly.

A few minutes later, still not quite 8 o'clock, the runaways were seen by wheelwright John Johnson as he stood at the door of Whaley smithy, which was situated at the point, at the northern end of the town, where the old and new turnpikes met. The men passed within 20 yards of him as they turned into Market Street and headed towards the River Goyt (then the boundary between Cheshire and Derbyshire) and the ancient crossing that gave Whaley Bridge its name.

On the other side of the bridge they tried to board a post-chaise waiting in front of a public house called The Buck, but were told by the post-boy that the carriage was already taken. Contrary to their inquiry to Thomas Etchells, instead of making for Chapel-en-le-Frith the three were last seen legging it down the Buxton road.

They arrived in the Derbyshire spa town as night fell, but early the next morning they moved on to Macclesfield (one of them walking at least some of the way barefooted, apparently). There they blew a large slice of the booty on new clothes, shoes and a couple of watches – seemingly unconcerned about the amount of attention they were attracting – before travelling by stagecoach to Manchester. It was their home town, but if they felt safe now they were back on familiar territory they had reckoned without the intervention of a public-spirited barman.

At around 5.15pm the same day, Thursday 17 July, less than 24 hours after they had left William Wood lying dead in a pool of his own blood, they strutted like peacocks into the taproom of The Greyhounds in Oak Street. Waiter Thomas Bowcock, who knew the men and had seen them in the pub two days earlier, could not help but notice their apparent change of fortunes. In place of their previously shabby clothing, they now wore smart new threads, and whereas before they had little money, now their pockets bulged with it.

Bowcock, believing they may have committed a robbery, shared his suspicions with the pub's landlord, who promptly dispatched his son to the local police office in Back King Street. However, by the time the lad returned with two officers, only one of the young men was still in the pub. He was arrested without resistance. He at first gave his name as 'Bradley' but, under interrogation, he revealed that he was Charles Taylor and that he lived in Oldfield Road in Salford. He admitted being involved in William Wood's robbery but insisted that he had played no part in his murder.

Although only 17 years of age, Taylor had already served two prison terms for felony. For his second offence he was sentenced to six months in Chester Castle Gaol and, the police now discovered, had only been released the day before the murder. A report in the *Manchester Mercury* claimed that, even among his fellow prisoners, Taylor was considered 'a very evil-disposed youth'.

He was locked up in the New Bailey Prison (it stood on the banks of the Irwell near Albert Bridge), where he readily identified his accomplices as John Platt, aged 19, and Joseph Dale, aged 18. It meant names could now be added to the descriptions of the murder suspects, which were already circulating among police offices and the public.

The Stones that Cried Out 'Murder!'

'[A] diligent search was made in all directions during the night in quest for the other two, but without success,' said the *Mercury*. The following morning Platt and Dale were seen drinking with some women at the Coach and Horses in St George's Road on the north-east side of the city. The landlord, 'being struck with their appearance,' sent word to the police office, but the pair seem to have got wind of what was going on and, once again, managed to escape before the law arrived.

The *Mercury* was critical of what it saw as a lack of police co-operation, after learning that John Frost, one of the Macclesfield constables, had also been tipped off about the suspects shortly after they left the east Cheshire silk town. Alerted to the news of the robbery and murder, and hearing about their local spending spree, he had followed the three strangers to Manchester by the first available coach. But, once there, rather than seek the help of the city police, he chose to pursue his inquiries alone and, it was suggested, in a less than professional manner.

'We cannot help thinking,' the *Mercury* reproached, 'that if Mr Frost…had immediately on his arrival here communicated with Mr Lavender, at our Police-office, where he might have expected much important assistance, the result would have been far more satisfactory; instead of which he arrived by the Mail [coach], and without giving any information whatever, stopped about an hour in town, and then returned home.'

If the investigation was not going well, things were about to get worse. At about 1pm on Friday 18 July a warder making his rounds at the New Bailey checked on Charles Taylor and found him hanging from an overhead heating pipe that ran through his cell.

In a news item headed 'THE LATE DREADFUL MURDER and Suicide of one of the Suspected Assassins', the *Chester Chronicle*, in its issue of 25 July, reported indignantly, 'The wretched murderer, it appears, had tied his stockings together, and with the assistance of his garters, was enabled to make them sufficient for the fatal purpose. He was not quite dead when found, but had so far effected his fatal purpose, that he died on Sunday morning about 3 o'clock.'

It was an act of self-destruction that probably saved the hangman a job (in Cheshire at this time a highway robber, especially one with past 'form', was as likely to receive the death penalty as a convicted murderer), but before placing himself beyond the reach of justice he did his best to put a rope around the neck of one of the other 'Suspected Assassins'.

The *Manchester Guardian* (26 July) informed its readers that Taylor had made 'a full confession of the circumstances attending the robbery and murder'. According to the paper's source, Platt, Taylor and Dale had left Manchester on the 16th to attend the Wakes Week celebrations at Chapel-en-le-Frith and met Mr Wood by chance on the road. At 'How-lane' (High Lane) they joined him for a drink at a public house (where they would no doubt have had an opportunity to weigh up the size of his purse) and then walked with him 'for some distance'.

'At length,' the *Guardian* report stated unequivocally, 'one of the three, whose name is Platt, struck him a violent blow and knocked him down. Platt then took a large stone from the wall, and threw it upon his head, which killed him on the spot.'

Taylor 'denied that he at all participated in the murder' (by omission he appears to have exonerated Dale from that charge, too), the *Guardian* stated, '[but] as three stones were found, which evidently had all been used to effect the horrid purpose, there is some reason to doubt the truth of his statement.'

In fact, *four* bloodstained gritstones were recovered from the murder site and, as we shall see, they were to have a recurring impact on the case (one of them was said to have been reinstated in the wall as an early 'memorial', though the source of this information, an article in the *Stockport Advertiser* of 27 March 1874, contains a number of inaccuracies). They were first produced in evidence when Cheshire coroner John Hollins opened the inquest into William Wood's death at The Cock Inn in Whaley Bridge, on Saturday 19 July.

The *Manchester Guardian* reported, 'The stones...[were] all very bloody with hair still sticking to [two of] them; one was of an oblong shape, and had the appearance of bloody finger marks at one end.' The jury returned a verdict of 'murder by certain persons unknown'.

In the same 26 July edition, the *Guardian* (then published weekly) joined in the press criticism of the way in which the investigation was being conducted. It commented, 'We understand that a very culpable negligence has been displayed...by the constables of the township where the murder was committed. They have not offered any reward for the apprehension of the murderers, nor (as we are informed) taken any steps to find them out. All that has been hitherto done for this purpose, has, we believe, been at the expense of G.W. Newton Esq. [magistrate George Newton of Taxal Lodge, Whaley] and of the constables of Manchester.'

There was one Cheshire officer busy on the case, however. John Frost, the Macclesfield constable admonished for his covert (and unproductive) visit to Manchester in pursuit of the murder suspects, was to have more success when he continued his inquiries closer to home. He discovered that on their arrival in Macclesfield, the three young men had spent some time at the Golden Lion in Mill Street, and that after kitting themselves out in new clothes and shoes bought at shops in nearby Chestergate, they had left some of their old clothing at the pub.

He examined the garments along with, apparently, the editor of the *Macclesfield Courier*, who afterwards wrote, 'We have seen the clothes of these men; they are much smeared with dirt, evidently from a lime road, to conceal the blood on them, which in many places is very visible...and we have not the smallest doubt that the owners of them are the assassins who committed the horrid murder' (the owners were Platt and Taylor; Dale, it will be shown, gave away his old clothes to a street urchin).

By now, having learned no doubt of the arrest of Charles Taylor, and knowing they had twice come close to being captured themselves, the two wanted men had decided it was too dangerous to remain in Manchester. So they split up and went their separate ways. Platt may have headed for Chester, after which he seems to have disappeared completely. The suspect subsequently identified as 'the man in the light suit', he remains the case's darkest figure: a young but apparently incorrigible offender who, if he was not the lone killer, almost certainly instigated the attack on William Wood. Like Taylor, he had 'done time' and had only recently been released from prison, in his case the New Bailey in Manchester.

Press reports suggested later that 'Platt' was an alias, though there was some confusion

The Stones that Cried Out 'Murder!'

as to what his real name might have been. Dale was at different times quoted as saying he believed it was Pratt, Bratt and Brett. One thing is certain, however: he was never charged in connection with William Wood's murder.

While the inquiry limped on, a memorial service with a difference was being organised for the murder victim. In several respects it was a rehearsal for the 'indication stone' ceremony of 1874. The *Manchester Mercury* of 5 August 1823 reported, 'On Sunday week [27 July], after a short notice, given in the Sunday Schools of Disley and the neighbouring places, an excellent and appropriate sermon was delivered by the Revd Luke Barlow, of the Wesleyan Methodist Connection, of New Mills, on the spot where the unfortunate Mr Wood, of Eyam, was so barbarously and inhumanly put to death.' The minister's 'very suitable text' was the same verse from Matthew chapter 24, whose message would ring out from this lonely hilltop half a century later.

Teenager Joseph Dale, who was hanged for his part in the murder of William Wood, though few people thought he had been involved in the actual assault. (Portrait taken from a contemporary pamphlet, by permission of the British Library.)

The paper added, 'It is calculated that there were not less than 2,000 persons present. After the sermon, a collection was made for the widow of the unfortunate man, amounting to the sum of £4 10s 4d, a handsome sum, considering the class of the population of the neighbourhood.'

Joseph Dale, meanwhile, had decamped to Liverpool. He had arrived there on the morning of Friday 18 July, and for a couple of weeks he dropped out of sight. He resurfaced at the beginning of August when, according to a report in the *Chester Chronicle* (15 August), he tried to enlist in the army. But, after he had been interviewed by a recruiting team then on a visit to the city, his application was turned down on medical grounds – 'on account of a hurt in one of his hands, which unfitted him for the service', as the paper explained it.

The recruiting team's senior officer, a Sergeant Major Eyre, remembered him, however, and after reading an advertisement giving details of the two men wanted in connection with the Cheshire murder, he joined the search for the military reject. Dale was finally captured on Friday 8 August on board the *Mary*, of Great Yarmouth, as she lay in the Salthouse Dock making ready to sail.

'When first taken into custody, he denied any knowledge of the transaction,' the *Chronicle* stated, 'but in the course of the day he related the circumstances of the robbery and murder, and admitted that he had received from John Bratt, alias Platt, three pounds and seven shillings out of the money taken from Mr Wood...but firmly denied being present at the perpetration of the atrocious deed.'

Dale's arrest was a major breakthrough in the case – and big news. But there was little in the papers at this time about the captive himself. It would be many months before the press managed to root out any personal details about the anonymous young man who was suspected of being involved in one of the most sensational murders in Cheshire's recent history and about what the *Chronicle* later described as his 'short and miserable existence'.

He was reported to have been born on 15 August 1804 in Longsight, Manchester, but spent most of his young life in 'Chorlton Row' (now Chorlton-on-Medlock). The child of respectable parents, he received an elementary education before being placed 'in service' with a local family. When his mistress died he became a 'factory lad', working at different times for several employers in the Manchester area. It was during this latter period, he apparently admitted, that he rebelled against his Methodist upbringing and became involved with 'gambling and loose and abandoned women' – the twin vices to which, ultimately, he 'attributed his ruin'.

It was at this time, too, that he seems to have first met Platt, though from the evidence it appears he was only a casual acquaintance. There is no reason, either, to doubt his claim that he met Taylor for the first time the day before the three of them set out on their ill-fated trip to Derbyshire. Dale's brief association with the other two would be put forward as a major mitigating factor in his favour after his trial, when, for obvious reasons, he sought to distance himself from the two ex-convicts.

Later that Friday Stephen Lavender, of the Manchester police, arrived in Liverpool to take charge of the prisoner. They returned to Manchester the following morning and Dale was lodged in the New Bailey. On the Monday Lavender escorted him to Whaley Bridge, where he spent the night before being examined by Mr Newton, the magistrate.

That same day, Tuesday 12 August, just three days before his 19th birthday, he was taken to Chester Castle Gaol to await trial. The start of the Summer Assizes was less than two weeks away but, for the young man about to get his first, harsh taste of prison life, it would be more than eight months before he finally learned his fate.

His trial took place on Monday 25 August before the Chief Justice, the Honourable Charles Warren, and the Honourable Samuel Marshall. As the witness depositions are missing from the assize court files, the following trial sequence is drawn from two publications: the *Chester Courant* of Tuesday 2 September 1823 and a pamphlet, whose abridged title is *A Full Report of the Trial of Joseph Dale for the Murder of Wm. Wood*, which was published in the spring of 1824. The latter reproduces (often verbatim) much of the content of the *Courant*'s more contemporary account. However, unless stated otherwise, the quoted source is the pamphlet – 'Printed and Sold by Joseph Pratt, 11, Bridge-Street [Manchester], and Sold also by all the Booksellers, Price 9d', hereafter referred to as 'the Pratt edition'.

Its preamble set the scene for what was to prove a contentious and emotive trial: 'At an early hour, so intense were the feelings excited by this murder, unparalleled in the criminal history of this country [*sic*] for the violence, brutality and ferocity with which it had been perpetrated, that the Castle Gates were almost literally assailed by an immense number of persons of every rank and condition. When the gates were opened…a tremendous rush was made, and in an instant every part of the spacious Hall was crowded to suffocation.'

Dale looked surprisingly young as he stood in the dock. He had attained his 19th birthday while in prison, but, as the *Courant* observed, he was still 'more boyish in his appearance than such years would seem to indicate'.

An engraving of the defendant, printed in the Pratt edition, bears out the image of the fresh-faced adolescent, though in the set of the jaw and the pout of the lips the artist has brought a hint of petulance to his features.

Dale pleaded 'not guilty' to the murder charge, which, as it will assume greater significance later on, is given here shorn only of its more dispensable tautologies. The indictment, one of the few surviving papers in the official records, alleged that Dale, along with Platt and Taylor, 'on William Wood did make an assault…[and] with certain stones of no value…in their right hands…in and upon the back part of the head of…William Wood, did cast and throw…[which stones] did strike penetrate and wound…giving the said William Wood one mortal wound bruise fracture and contusion of the breadth of one inch and of the depth of half an inch, of which said mortal wound…William Wood…died…[and] that William Wood [they] did kill and murder'.

Chester's Attorney-General John Hill acknowledged that the evidence in this 'horrid affair', as he termed it, was entirely circumstantial. However, reciting what was almost the same speech he had made to the jury in the trial of Samuel Fallows four months earlier (see chapter 10), he pointed out that in cases of murder, it was seldom that any other kind of evidence could be obtained, such crimes being 'perpetrated with the utmost privacy and secrecy'. And he argued, 'When evidence, which is merely circumstantial, [is] throughout the whole chain unbroken in any of its links, it is strong and conclusive.'

By Dale's own admission, Mr Hill said, he and his two companions met Mr Wood on the road between Stockport and Disley, while the other links in the prosecution's chain

The scene at Longside where Mr Wood's body was found beside the highway, as portrayed in the pamphlet. (By permission of the British Library.)

of evidence would, he promised, prove that they were the three young men who were seen running away from the murder scene, that Dale was the one who purchased clothes and shoes at Macclesfield, and that he also bought a watch in the town with a £5 note Mr Wood was known to have had in his possession the previous day.

After hearing of the three shabbily-dressed youths seen following Mr Wood as he walked towards Whaley and of the discovery of the body by the passing carter, the members of the jury had their first sight of the bloodstained gritstones. Again the alleged murder weapons caused a genuine 'sensation in court'.

As the spectators crowded around the periphery of the court pressed forward for a better view, the grisly exhibits were lifted from a large box and placed one by one on a table in the well of the court. The first was 'much like a butcher's cleaver in shape', the edges sharp and the stone thick and heavy, while the others were lozenge-shaped and 'resembled large fragments of thick grave stones'. The two larger stones were heavily bloodstained and bore traces of human hair.

'The prisoner appeared to gaze on them without the slightest emotion,' the Pratt edition recorded, 'while everyone else was struck with horror at the appalling spectacle.'

Although the similarities in the various witness descriptions strongly supported the prosecution's case that the three young men who were following Mr Wood just before he was attacked were the same three who were seen fleeing from the area afterwards, in court none of those who could place them in the vicinity of the murder was able to identify Dale as one of the trio. However, the prosecution fared better with the Macclesfield witnesses.

Ellen Broadhurst, landlady of the Golden Lion, remembered two young men coming to her house between 9 and 10 o'clock on the morning of 17 July, followed a short time later by a third. The latter, she swore, was the man she now knew to be Joseph Dale. He was dressed in a blue coat. One of the others (Platt) had on 'a round jacket and trowsers of pillow fustian' and a pair of shoes but no stockings. Taylor was wearing a black coat but, she was surprised to see, neither shoes nor stockings (as the Macclesfield publican was the first to notice this rather conspicuous fact, we can only assume that, after subjecting it to some fairly-heavy punishment in the previous 24 hours, Taylor finally shed his worn-out footwear somewhere en route to the town).

Mrs Broadhurst said Dale went out of the house several times. When he returned for the last time he was carrying a parcel, after which she saw him change his stockings. Platt put on a new pair of 'quarter boots' and gave his old shoes to Taylor, who by this time had also acquired stockings. Dale and Platt asked to be allowed into one of the pub's upstairs rooms to change their clothes. In the event, she said, only Dale changed, coming down in a new blue coat and matching trousers.

That afternoon, after the men had left the pub, a pile of old clothes was found on a chair in the room, including a black coat, two pairs of trousers, a striped waistcoat and a muslin neck handkerchief. Dale's old blue coat was not among them, Mrs Broadhurst added. Constable Frost took charge of the abandoned clothing the next day when he called to inquire after the three free-spending strangers.

Shoemaker William Wainwright also picked out Dale as the young man who came into his Chestergate shop around breakfast time on the 17th and bought a pair of 'quarter boots'. When he returned soon afterwards to buy a second pair, Dale made some comment about 'giving these things to some poor person'. Wainwright assumed he meant his old shoes and stockings and suggested his customer gave them to an orphan boy he knew. The act of charity, however, would have to wait, for Dale's immediate response was that he was also in need of new clothes, whereupon Wainwright volunteered to accompany him to the tailor's shop of Thomas Burgess just up the street.

Shortly afterwards, having changed into his new clothes, Dale called at the shoemaker's again; he was carrying a bundle, which, he said, was for the orphan boy. Wainwright, in handing it to the lad (who just happened to be outside the shop at the time), saw that it contained shoes and clothing, but he said he did not take particular notice of it. It wasn't until a couple of hours later – 'when the rumour was afloat about the murder,' as the *Courant* put it – that Wainwright traced the boy and examined the bundle. In it was a blue coat. Wainwright told the court he thought it was Dale's from a rip in one of the elbows.

If the three young tearaways had set out to draw attention to themselves, they could not have tried harder. For Thomas Burgess testified that all three of them had been in his shop between 9am and noon, Dale no fewer than five times. In all Dale bought a blue suit, a yellow 'kerseymere' waistcoat and a greatcoat for himself, a coat, trousers and a waistcoat for Platt and a suit and a greatcoat for Taylor. Taylor even went back with him at one stage to change his new suit, complaining that it was too big.

Burgess could not say exactly how much Dale had spent, but it was at least £9 3s – nearly £700 in today's money.

Cross-examined by Mr David F. Jones, lead counsel for the defence, Burgess said he had not noticed any bloodstains on Dale's clothing. He commented, 'When he tried on the new [suit] coat he threw down the old one. If I had seen anything wrong about him, I would not have dealt with him. I saw nothing on it but dirt.'

After leaving Burgess's shop for the last time, Dale went with Taylor to Latham's the watchmakers. They both bought pocket watches: Taylor paid for his with a Macclesfield note and eight shillings in silver, but when Dale proffered a £5 note in payment for his two-guinea watch, the shop assistant, John Longstaff, had to go to the bank to get change for it.

While he was away, the two men remained in the shop with Mr Latham's housekeeper Elizabeth Tomlinson, who had been present when they made their purchases. Longstaff was gone some time and, said Mrs Tomlinson, the two men started to get agitated, as if they were in a hurry to be on their way.

Longstaff said he had not taken sufficient notice of the two men to be able to recognise them again, but the housekeeper had no doubt that it was Dale who had had the £5 note. It was another link in the prosecution chain; now, if the note could also be identified as one William Wood had had on him the day he was killed, it would be the strongest connection yet between Joseph Dale and the murder. The evidence was about to be presented to the court.

George Hankinson, the Macclesfield bank clerk who had given John Longstaff change for the note, deposed that, because it was of a large denomination (its equivalent value today would be almost £400), he had followed the bank's usual practice and made a detailed record of the transaction in his desk ledger. This included the number of the note (721) and another number (10671), which he had written on the back in red ink to show he had handled it.

Later that day, when word reached the town about a robbery and murder near Whaley, he put the note into an envelope and sealed it. It had been in his safekeeping ever since. He said he would also be able to recognise it by a small tear in one of its edges. When a Bank of England £5 note was handed to Hankinson, he confirmed it was the one.

It was the same £5 note that Mr Wood had received from Josiah Cheetham just a few hours before he was murdered.

Mr Cheetham, of Stockport, also a textile manufacturer, said it was part of a payment, totalling £48 7s 0d, that he had made to Wood, with whom he did regular business, in the afternoon of 16 July. Cheetham also exercised great care when dealing in paper money and kept detailed records of the higher-value notes that passed through his hands. His accounts for that day contained an entry relating to the payment made to William Wood and a reference to a certain £5 note. Its number was 721…and it had a piece torn out of it.

Thomas Bowcock, the waiter at The Greyhounds pub in Manchester, who surmised correctly that Platt, Taylor and Dale had been involved in a robbery, told the court how his suspicions had arisen. He said Platt and Taylor called at the pub on 15 July inquiring after Dale, only to learn that he had just left (they must have met up at some time that day, however, as all the evidence points to their planning their Derbyshire trip on the 15th). When Bowcock next saw them on the 17th, the day after William Wood's murder, they came into the taproom together. They were all wearing new clothes. He stated, 'I asked Dale where he had been to have a new suit of clothes. He said he had been amongst his friends. I challenged them all [about] having new clothes on. The other two gave no answer.'

After being taken into custody, Dale gave an unhelpfully short account of his involvement in the crime, first during a conversation he had with Stephen Lavender at Manchester Police Office, and then in a statement sworn before Whaley magistrate George Newton. As defendants in criminal trials were not allowed into the witness box to give evidence on oath at this time, these two brief submissions were all the jury heard of Dale's version of events.

He did provide a fuller explanation, but only after his trial. Supposedly based on a written statement he made in Chester Castle Gaol, it was among documents contained in a Home Office file on the case and will be set out in detail later.

In his written deposition to the Whaley JP (it was essentially the same story he had told Lavender), he claimed – and would continue to claim right to the end – that he was an unwitting accessory who had been forced to submit to the will of men who, though of similarly tender years, were physically stronger and more abandoned than himself. He stated:

'Platt, Taylor and me left Manchester on Wednesday the 16th of July, intending to go to my Aunt's at Castleton [in Derbyshire]. We were on the old road from Disley to Whaley where we met with an elderly [sic] person in a blue coat and light trowsers, and we got into conversation with him. He invited us into a public house to take some ale. Platt gave me sixpence, and told me to go on and wait for them at a public house half a mile off. I waited at the public house a considerable time. When they came up to me they were running, and I saw they were bloody. They said, "Come along". I ran with them a good way, and then said I would run no longer. Platt damned me, and they said, "Good bye." When I came near Buxton they were waiting for me, and they cursed me for keeping them so long. We had supper and slept together that night near Buxton. The next morning we went to Macclesfield, where they asked me to buy clothes for them, which I did.'

Significantly perhaps, there was no mention of the visit to the watchmaker's – where he was alleged to have spent the stolen fiver. And only once during these interviews did he refer directly to the crime, insisting to Lavender at one point that all he had had of the robbery money was '£3 and some silver'. Lavender stated in court, 'From the first to the last he denied having anything to do with the actual murder…He seemed to be a beginner in these things.'

Dale's claim that he was in a nearby pub at the time of the murder was easily exposed as a lie, however. Joseph Hadfield, one of the two Higher Disley neighbours who saw Mr Wood being followed by three young men along the old road to Whaley, lived about half a mile from the murder spot. And Thomas Etchells's observations about the 'running men' placed all three together about half a mile beyond it. As Attorney-General Hill pointed out, there was no public house in between.

William Wright, the Disley surgeon who conducted the postmortem on William Wood's body, said he counted 10 separate head wounds. Seven of them were on the back of the head, the most serious of which had resulted in a portion of the skull being driven into the brain. The other three were on his forehead.

With the prosecution case closed, Dale was asked if he had anything to say in his defence. He replied simply, 'I am innocent of both the robbery and murder.'

He called three witnesses, two former employers and a police officer, who all confirmed that he had been of previous good character. George Burgess, Constable of Bucklow, who, for eight years, was deputy constable of Chorlton Row, testified 'The prisoner lived near me a long time. He always attended the Sunday School. He was considered a good-tempered, well-behaved lad.'

It was 5.30pm when Chief Justice Warren began his summing up. Describing the murder as 'barbarous in the extreme', he told the jury, 'It is not a question for you to consider, whether the prisoner was the man who actually struck the fatal blow. It is sufficient that he was either present, or aiding, abetting and consenting to the perpetration of the crime. For, in point of law, he is equally as guilty as if he had inflicted the mortal wound.'

The account Dale had given was, said the judge, 'pregnant with suspicion'. His story about being in a public house waiting for his two companions at the time of the murder was 'an evident falsehood', while his claim of only receiving 'three pounds and some silver' was at odds with his extravagance in Macclesfield.

His Lordship declared, 'The money which has been traced to him [the £5 note] is clearly the money that belonged to Wood. He who was guilty of the robbery was also undoubtedly guilty of the murder. If he were present at the robbery then he is guilty of the murder.'

The members of the jury did not even bother to retire to consider their verdict. After a consultation lasting little more than two minutes, the foreman pronounced Dale guilty.

There is no doubt that, despite the enormity of the crime, Dale's situation had aroused much sympathy. His youth, his previous reputation as a decent, hard-working lad, the manifestly bad company into which he had fallen and the popular belief that he had been no more than a frightened bystander at the murder of William Wood, were extenuating circumstances that many people felt made him deserving of compassion – a view that would attract some eminent supporters in the months ahead.

The atmosphere in the lofty magnificence of Chester Castle's Shire Hall was more-than-usually sombre, therefore, as the court awaited the judge's inevitable response. The mandatory sentence for murder was death: the moment for that ritual black-capped declaration of doom had surely arrived. David Jones, however, was not ready to throw in the towel just yet.

Immediately after the jury foreman sat down, Mr Jones – a former recorder of Chester and an able lawyer much liked and respected in this the city of his birth – rose to his feet to make one last desperate attempt to save his young client's life. He formally moved a 'motion in arrest of judgement'. It meant the defence had identified errors in the written indictment that made it unsafe for the judge to proceed to sentence. The bloodstained gritstones – and, more specifically, the way they were described in that elaborately-framed murder charge – were about to become the focus of attention once again.

In stating the three grounds for his motion, Mr Jones first argued that a charge of murder required the 'instrument of death' to be described in such a manner as to show beyond doubt that it was the one that had inflicted the fatal wound. In this case, instead of the vague reference to 'certain stones of no value', the exact number of stones that were alleged to have caused Mr Wood's death should have been specified, as also should their values, for, under ancient law (in force until 1846), all 'instruments of death' were designated 'deodands' and technically the property of the Crown.

The second objection was that the indictment appeared to allege that all three men with several stones had inflicted the same wound – which, he said, was patently impossible – while the third was that the wording was ungrammatical, rendering it unintelligible. The latter point, Mr Jones explained, turned on the single word 'with'. One might say that a person 'did cast and throw stones', he said, but not 'cast and throw *with* stones'.

It may have been a clerical error, he accepted, but it meant the indictment did not conform to 'the strictest legal accuracy' on which 'the safety of us all depends'.

To those unversed in the complexities of criminal law, it must have sounded a rather feeble, if not frivolous, argument. The Attorney-General, in his response, submitted that the meaning of the words in the indictment was perfectly clear, the charges properly laid (and, he might have added, the verdict unhesitatingly given). Although an 'arrest of judgement' motion could, in certain circumstances, lead to a verdict being overturned and the convict pardoned, it was more likely to result in a redrafted indictment and a fresh trial. It seemed the defence move was merely postponing the inevitable.

The Stones that Cried Out 'Murder!'

However, Judge Warren ruled that the second objection was 'deserving of consideration', and he adjourned the hearing to seek clarification on the point. According to the Pratt edition, when the court reassembled two days later 'there was a general expectation that the judgement would be pronounced, consequently great numbers of respectable ladies and gentlemen attended'. However, Mr Justice Warren announced that as he and his fellow judge, Mr Justice Marshall, had differing opinions as to the validity of the defence claims, judgement would have to wait until the next assizes.

In the meantime, the matter of the disputed indictment would be reserved for the consideration of 'the 12 judges'. These were senior judges drawn from the three superior courts of common law (Common Pleas, King's Bench and Exchequer), with whom circuit judges consulted on particularly problematical issues. Sitting in camera at Westminster, they conferred informally, but their conclusions were always influential.

Dale's trial on a second capital charge of highway robbery – in which he, Platt and Taylor were alleged to have stolen from Mr Wood banknotes and other money totalling £110 – was also deferred (in the light of subsequent legal decisions it was eventually set aside).

Dale was returned to gaol, where his mental and physical condition deteriorated to the point where it looked as if he might not last out until the next assizes. But the machinery of justice could not be hurried, and it would be early February 1824 – almost six months later – before the 12 judges (11 actually: one was unable to attend due to illness) delivered their opinion. It was that the defence's objections were invalid and that the indictment was 'good and sufficient in law'. The guilty verdict would stand…Dale was to hang.

Now began some sustained and eloquently-orchestrated petitioning by the convict's growing army of supporters, some of whom were very well connected indeed. The Home Office file includes four petitions for clemency and three individual letters urging the King to exercise the royal prerogative and spare Dale's life. Men of mark from the church, the gentry, industry and commerce – even the police – were among the signatories.

As can be seen from this present-day view, the Wood murder spot has changed little in more than 180 years. (Photograph by the author.)

The file also revealed the existence of a more comprehensive statement Dale made about his role in the crime.

Its substance was reproduced in a nine-page personal appeal to the Home Secretary (Robert Peel) by the Revd Robert I. McGhee, of Eaton Road, Chester, who identified himself only as 'a Clergyman of the Established Church'. He seems to have been one of several clerics who visited the prisoner regularly in the Castle Gaol. His letter, dated 27 March 1824, referred to a 'paper' which Dale had written with the proviso that it was not made public until after his death. Its contents are published here for the first time.

Contradicting Thomas Bowcock's sworn testimony that on the day before the murder, the other two had called at The Greyhounds asking expressly for him, Dale stated in his 'paper' that he met Platt and a man he did not know (Taylor) 'by accident'. He was unemployed at the time, and when Platt said he could help him find work he agreed to go with them to Castleton in Derbyshire. The next day they set out and on the journey they fell in with 'a decent man' (Wood).

Revd McGhee's letter went on: 'Dale and he conversed together while Platt and Taylor dropped behind in consultation; and Dale, in a few moments, was thunderstruck to see Taylor come up behind the man and knock him down while Platt struck him with a stone and was lifting others.

'Dale cried out and besought them to stop. Platt cursed him that he would serve him in the same manner if he did not hold his tongue. When he saw he could not hinder them from beating the man, he ran off but, before he had gone forty or fifty yards, Platt overtook him and cursed him for his folly, [and] said they had only given the man a beating. He had a stain of blood on his coat and Dale saw it.'

When, following their stop-over in Buxton, they arrived in Macclesfield, Dale's companions 'abused [him] very much by cursing him', but they said that if he would go out and buy fresh clothes for them they would buy him a new suit.

'And here poor Dale's guilt actually commences', McGhee believed, 'for seduced by the promise of the clothes for himself, he...became implicated with these men, who evidently made a tool of him to screen themselves. But he knew nothing of the man's murder; his consciousness of the robbery made him afraid and he went to Liverpool and wanted to get employment and when, in about 10 days, he took up a newspaper and saw the account of the murder and a reward offered for himself, he fainted from surprise and terror.'

All four of the petitions were sent to the Home Department (as it was then known) but were addressed to the King, in the hope that he would intervene personally. But a terse note scribbled on the back of one of them summed up the official reaction to the mercy campaign. Alongside the date, 2 April 1824, Home Secretary Peel had written the single word 'Nil'. The seemingly curt rebuff (short for *nihil*, Latin for 'nothing') signified his decision was 'no action' and was the standard response to appeals the minister felt did not justify a recommendation for clemency. The law, the minister indicated, must 'take its course'.

As promised, Charles Warren announced the decision at Chester Assizes on the morning of Monday 19 April. It was a week since the start of the spring sessions and mounting anxiety was now having an additionally debilitating effect on Dale's fragile health. Following a restless night, he had to be helped to dress and only made it up the steps from the cell area of the castle to the courtroom with the assistance of two prison warders. He was allowed to kneel on a wooden ledge inside the dock to hear the judgement he had long been dreading.

The judge referred briefly to the crime – 'a more barbarous and inhuman transaction was scarcely ever known' he said – and the defendant's insistence that he had had nothing to do with it. He told Dale, 'You prevaricated, you told stories in accounting for your share of the transaction.' And he added, 'These, with other facts connected with the case, leave no doubt whatever of your guilt.'

In sepulchral tones he passed the sentence of death and, aided this time by the prison governor, the broken young man in the dock struggled to his feet and was taken below.

The *Courant* remarked that there had been 'a strong feeling of sympathy excited for the situation of this unfortunate, but interesting, young man throughout the crowded court'. However, the *Courant*'s rival, the *Chester Chronicle*, took a considerably more cynical view of Dale's apparent religious conversion…and of the activities of his apologists.

It was an unholy row that blew up when the *Chronicle*, in its edition of 23 April, declaimed intemperately about 'a set of young maudlin Philanthropists and Evangelical Damsels' who, the paper claimed, had been 'let loose' on Dale while in the Castle Gaol. It seemed to the *Chronicle* that this sort of thing was now happening with every criminal sentenced to death.

The paper thundered, 'The ATROCITY of the Crime for which conviction takes place, is never once contemplated in the struggle for saintly interference: the *Murderer* immediately becomes the object of pity and tender sentiment! – whilst the "sudden reckoning" which the unfortunate MURDERED had to make – the distress and probably the total ruin of his WIFE and HELPLESS CHILDREN, is never once contemplated. No, no, such immaterial things are never dreamt of in their philosophy. A Murderer is to expiate his crime with his life, and his death is to become the subject of undeserved commiseration.'

Urging the magistracy to allow only authorised clergymen access to condemned persons in future, the *Chronicle* commented, 'What could be more absurd, than in dressing up Dale in the way he appeared at the Bar to receive judgement? A young man, whose wishes for decent wearing apparel probably never went beyond a fustian jacket and trowsers, is brought up from a Common Gaol, and stuck at the Dock, at the most awful period of his existence, dressed in a fashionable cut coat, pantaloons, and silk stockings, thickly starched shirt collar as high as his ears – *all lent to him for the occasion* – and his hair turned back à la Brutus'…adding, in the following week's edition, that 'round his shirt neck [was] a quantity of muslin sufficient almost to suffocate an ordinary member of a common council'.

On 27 April the *Courant* responded to the *Chronicle* article – 'as impudent as it is uncandid, and as intolerant as it is untrue' – by first insisting that Dale's visitors were 'almost exclusively clergymen or members of the Established Church'. To the *Chronicle*'s references to Dale's appearance in court, the *Courant* countered, 'Of his thickly starched collar, and his turned up hair, we say nothing more than, when present with him in the dock, we observed nothing remarkable in either. Upon diligent inquiry, and satisfactory evidence, we assert [that] his *fashionable cut coat* and *pantaloons* were cast-off articles, *given* to him.' And the silk stockings were 'no other than a pair of *common woollen hose*!'

For the record, in the portrait in the Pratt pamphlet Dale *does* appear rather fashionably dressed and well groomed. And the *Courant*'s own report of his final court appearance contains this description: 'He was neatly dressed in a black coat, buff striped waistcoat, drab kerseymere pantaloons, and a clean cravat.'

Joseph Dale was hanged on Wednesday 21 April 1824, eight months after his conviction and still four months short of his 20th birthday. His short cart ride to the City Gaol was watched by a crowd estimated at 3,000. There were, however, far fewer at the actual execution than usual. Dale himself saw to that.

After all the delays on his journey to the gallows, he was in such a hurry to get it over with, apparently, that as the time for the execution approached he became more and more anxious, almost impatient for the arrival of the city sheriffs, and as soon as they appeared, on the stroke of noon, he begged them to begin at once. His dying wish was granted.

'The drop fell at four minutes past 12 o'clock, nearly an hour earlier than the usual time of executions taking place', the *Chronicle* recorded. 'When the drop fell there were not 300 persons in the area in front of the gaol; but by a quarter before one there were some thousands.'

The next day, in compliance with the judge's order under the 1752 Murder Act, the body of Joseph Dale was publicly dissected in a basement room directly below the Turnkey's Lodge at the castle.

In the aftermath of the execution most of the local and regional papers alluded to the statement quoted in Robert McGhee's letter to the Home Secretary. Much was made of Dale's rehabilitation as a born-again Christian – the *Chester Courant*'s coverage straying further than most into the realms of unbridled sentimentality – and the press consensus was that Dale was the unfortunate victim of events beyond his control, a young man without criminal habits or inclinations who, in the words of the *Manchester Gazette*'s story, had been 'brought to the gallows through a brief and casual association with persons of an opposite description'.

In short, he had simply been in the wrong place at the wrong time – just like poor William Wood.

* * *

The Wood case was the most piercing alarm among the warning blare of violent robberies and burglaries that shook Cheshire in the 1820s. Eventually, the county's Quarter Sessions recognised that this worrying crimewave called for a radical new approach to law enforcement. And so it was that, on 1 June 1829, the county's first professional police force came into being. In the beginning, they did not operate everywhere in the county, but in January 1831, in the cotton-manufacturing district of Stockport, the 'new police' – dressed in frock coats and top hats and issued with cutlasses, staffs and handcuffs – went into action to tackle their first major murder investigation...

Chapter Twelve

Whose Finger on the Trigger?

L ying in his prison cell, the new inmate is haunted by a recurring vision. Through the misty veil of sleep he sees again the familiar image of the old dirt road. It is a winter's night, cold and black, and in the hedgerows three figures crouch among the shadows. Two of them carry guns. The men wait in silence, listening anxiously for the sound of footfalls. Suddenly, their unsuspecting quarry appears, only yards away from them. As he reaches their hiding place, the ambush is sprung. A shot rings out and the passer-by falls, a young man cut down in the prime of life, killed with a pistol fired at point blank range. The weapon does its job with such devastating effect that he is dead before he hits the ground, the attack so swift he has no chance of defending himself. When his body comes to rest, in the shallow ditch at the side of the lane, the hand he had stuffed inside his overcoat, snug against the evening's chill, is still in his pocket.

Then the picture fades...stirred from his fitful slumber, the prisoner is back in his cramped, cheerless cell. He is sweating and shaking. He has been tormented like this regularly over the past few weeks; now, as the prospect of another year and a half in gaol stretches out before him, the convicted thief realises there is only one way to exorcise the ghosts that stalk his dreams and startle him into feverish, fear-filled wakefulness...

This was the moment when, apparently tortured by guilt, James Garside decided to confess his terrible secret...to reveal that the stuff of his disturbing nightmares was all too real, his bedtime visitations replays of a horrendous crime that had baffled police – and disquieted the nation's leaders – for more than three years. In finally surrendering to the demons that had long been preying on his mind, he broke an oath of silence he and his two co-conspirators had taken at the point of a knife. Had he not done so, the murder of a young Cheshire mill boss in January 1831 may never have been solved.

To the law officers who had toiled in vain to crack the case, it was the break for which they were desperately hoping. It did not turn out so lucky for Garside.

While here was a man clearly troubled by his past, in volunteering to make a statement about the crime, and his part in it, Garside had not been swayed solely by feelings of remorse and the need for redemption. He was also seeking a more practical salvation. As well as his release from the prison sentence he had just begun, his main objective was the royal pardon promised to any of the principles in the murder – 'except the person who actually fired the shot' – prepared to turn King's evidence. There was also the not-inconsiderable incentive of a £1,500 reward.

But he was in for a nasty surprise. After the leads he had so helpfully supplied had been investigated, it was Garside who found himself in the dock and one of his two accomplices who was allowed to save his neck by appearing as chief witness for the prosecution. For the new evidence, far from portraying him as the unarmed spectator he was claiming to be, showed that he might, indeed, have been the person who fired the fatal shot.

A rare photograph, possibly dating from the late 19th century, of the spot in Apethorn Lane, Werneth, where cotton mill boss Thomas Ashton was shot in 1831 during a bitter strike by spinners. (By permission of Tameside Local Studies and Archives.)

A modern view of Apethorn Lane, showing the Ashton murder location. In the background are the remains of the old Swindells farm. (Photograph by the author.)

Whose Finger on the Trigger?

In England, the murder of 24-year-old factory manager Thomas Ashton at Werneth, near Hyde, during a tumultuous wage dispute between cotton spinners and their employers, was one of the great *causes célèbres* of the early 19th century. The shooting triggered a countrywide wave of revulsion and – as it appeared that the killing had been ordered and financed by the spinners' union – dealt a severe blow to the fledgling labour movement.

Locally – and of more relevance here – the case was to lead to a unique judicial crisis that brought the authorities in Cheshire into head-on collision with the Government of the day. The death sentences passed on the men eventually found guilty of the murder resurrected the thorny question of who should be responsible for executing criminals condemned at the assizes. Should it be the county's high sheriff (as was the situation everywhere else)? Or, following that ancient – and, of late, increasingly unpopular – tradition, the sheriffs of the city of Chester?

As the old arguments were dusted off for another airing, and the views of the two opposing camps became more and more entrenched, the amazing row rumbled on towards an unprecedented stand-off. The end result would be that, for the first and only time, the answer to the question was…neither.

The source of conflict that was occupying the public's attention at the beginning of 1831, however, was the industrial unrest in the cotton-producing towns of south-east Lancashire and north-east Cheshire, principally Ashton-under-Lyne, Stalybridge and Hyde. The industry was progressing apace, King Cotton reigned supreme, but expansion brought with it increased competition, and employers – still suffering the effects of the recent economic slump – were looking for ways of cutting their labour costs.

They were already investing heavily in new technology, installing machines that were bigger and more productive but which also carried the threat of unemployment. Now there were moves to reduce wage rates. It was little wonder the workers felt threatened, or that they turned to the recently-formed spinners' union to help them protect their jobs and pay packets. And with the union keen to exploit the mood of militancy, in its efforts to establish credibility and extend its influence, the atmosphere was charged with powder keg tensions.

There had been a full turnout in Hyde in 1824; in 1829 the spinners came out again in support of workers in Stockport and Manchester, where the employers were attempting to impose lower piecework rates. Further disputes occurred in Hyde, Ashton and Stalybridge in 1830. But the most serious confrontation in the region – and the biggest power struggle in the industry thus far – began to develop in November of that year, when the 'master spinners' (the mill owners) of Ashton, Stalybridge, Mossley and Dukinfield joined forces in a concerted bid to lower wage rates at all their mills and, at the same time, break the union.

Establishing uniform levels of pay had been one of their key aims when activists formed the Grand General Union of All the Operative Spinners of the United Kingdom, the first effective federation of local worker societies, in Manchester in September 1829. But this was not what they had in mind. The union was equally determined, therefore, to put on a show of strength in this, its toughest test to date. The scene was set for an angry and – as attitudes on both sides hardened – sporadically violent struggle.

By the middle of December 1830 the dispute had escalated into a full-scale strike, involving some 2,000 spinners from 52 factories in and around Ashton, the area that was said to be producing one-eighth of the cotton spun in England at that time. A further 18,000 were laid off as a result of the action. The strikers were demanding the equalisation of piecework rates at 4s 2d per 'thousand hanks of No. 40s'. This was the basic formula for wage calculation purposes, 40 being the number of hanks of standard thread that could be spun from a pound of cotton (the higher the number, the finer the thread). The employers were offering 3s 9d.

As union-organised meetings and marches in the towns affected by the strike began to degenerate into riots, vandalism and intimidation, the authorities became increasingly alarmed. The Government, uncomfortably conscious of the revolution that summer in France that had ended in the overthrow of Charles X, also viewed this apparent emergence of worker-power with some concern. With Home Office encouragement, troop reinforcements were drafted into the area and scores of special constables were sworn in. Day and night-time patrols were set up in order to safeguard the mills and deter troublemakers.

Even in this climate of resentment and hostility, however, the shooting of textile baron Samuel Ashton's eldest son at Werneth came as a crashing bolt from the blue. It brought both sides together in common condemnation, but, contrarily, it also ensured there could be no possibility of a compromise settlement to the dispute.

To the employers, who put up £500 towards the reward money offered for the capture of the culprits, it was seen as a sinister change of tactics by the strikers, a random act of revenge intended to frighten them into submission. In fact, it had the opposite effect, strengthening their resolve to resist the workers' demands.

For the strike leaders, who roundly rejected all allegations of union involvement in the murder plot, it was a huge setback, not only to their particular fight for factory-floor recognition but to the advancement of trade unionism generally. When, soon afterwards, the strike collapsed, so too did the Grand General Union of Spinners, which was forced to disband through lack of support.

While it was probably true that the Grand Union was not behind the murder – officially and collectively, at any rate – there were by this time many disgruntled strikers who believed they would not succeed while their leaders continued to advocate calmness and restraint. So did a small group of extremists from within the local spinners' federation decide to pursue a more menacing agenda and crank up the pressure on the mill masters by having a member of one of the area's best-known cotton-producing families assassinated? Most of the evidence in the Ashton case archive points unerringly in that direction.

Two of the alleged 'hit men', whose soul-baring finally lifted the lid on the mystery, certainly claimed so; though, if they were acting on the instructions of their union paymasters, their judgement was seen to be unreliable in at least one important aspect...they got the wrong man.

When, on the evening of Monday 3 January 1831, in Apethorn Lane, Werneth, three men sprang from the hedgerows and snuffed out his life with a single pistol shot, Thomas Ashton should have been on his way to a 21st birthday party three miles away in

Whose Finger on the Trigger?

Pole Bank Hall, the home of cotton magnate Samuel Ashton, as it would have looked in 1831 when son Thomas was gunned down as he walked from the house to the nearby Apethorn Mill. (By permission of Tameside Local Studies and Archives.)

Bredbury. At this time his father Samuel, head of one of the largest manufacturing families in the north of England, had two cotton mills: one in Apethorn Lane and another at Woodley.

Thomas was manager of the latter and a younger brother, James, was in charge of the Werneth mill. But on this particular night, James had gone early to the birthday party – it was being held in honour of his fiancée's brother – and Thomas agreed to go in his place to make the usual evening call at Apethorn and to collect some papers for his father. He planned to join the rest of the family at the coming-of-age celebrations later.

With clockwork regularity, at about 7pm, half-an-hour before most of the mill workers were due to knock off for the day, James Ashton would walk the half-mile from his home at Pole Bank Hall to check that everything was in order at the mill (there had been no trouble there or at Woodley because the Ashtons forbade union membership on pain of dismissal). From the hall – it continues to occupy a prominent spot on the western slope of Werneth Low, though it is now a local authority care home – he would take the private path that led across farm fields to Apethorn Lane, where it terminated in a little wooden 'clap-gate' (so called, apparently, because of the sound it made when it swung to). From there he had only a few hundred yards further to go to reach the mill, which was situated on the east bank of the Peak Forest Canal.

It had been an unchanging routine for months, and one that was obviously known to the three men hiding in the darkness of the narrow cart road that night. Although Thomas Ashton was as much a symbol of the power of the mill-owning plutocracy as his brother – and the company's non-union policy was strictly enforced at both its mills – James had recently sacked some of the Apethorn mill-hands for joining the spinners' union. He was undoubtedly the intended target of the waiting gunmen. They, however, were unaware of the late change of plan as Thomas Ashton, whistling softly and with his right hand shoved inside his topcoat pocket, strode obliviously into their trap.

A little after 7 o'clock, at a spot 30-yards beyond the clap-gate and some 300 yards from the mill, his killers struck. Leaping from the cover of the hedgerows, they were upon him in an instant and, before he could properly take in what was happening, one of them stuck a long-barrelled horse-pistol in his ribs and pulled the trigger. It was a single shot but the flintlock (also known as a 'holster-pistol') had been primed with extra

A horse pistol like the one used in the shooting of Thomas Ashton. (Photograph courtesy of Paulus Manders, gunsmith of Christchurch, New Zealand.)

powder to deliver two balls. The gun, which would typically have had an overall length of about 16 inches and a five-eighths-of-an-inch diameter bore, was fired at such close range that the lead balls ripped into his body through the same entrance wound. Then, after puncturing his heart and lungs, they struck his breastbone and were deflected upwards in different directions, exiting by two smaller holes in his left shoulder. He died instantaneously.

As quickly as they had pounced, the three assailants disappeared into the night and – for some considerable time afterwards – the bolt-hole of obscurity.

Thomas Ashton's body was found at around 7.15pm by William Taylor and George Wagstaffe. Taylor, a joiner from Werneth, and Wagstaffe, a mechanic from Gee Cross, had just finished work at Apethorn Mill and were walking home together. Taylor would later inform the inquest jury that Mr Ashton was lying on his back 'partly across the road with his head in the ditch'. There were low banks on either side of the lane at this point, topped by hedges, and the ditch was on the side opposite the clap-gate. The two men at first thought they had stumbled upon a drunk and because the blood that had flowed from his nose and mouth obscured his features, they were unable to recognise the deceased.

They ran about 60 yards back down the lane to Swindells Farm (the only dwelling close by at the time) to borrow a lantern, but still they could not be sure who the dead man was. It was only after local surgeon William Tinker had been called to examine the body at the scene that the victim's identity became apparent.

Taylor dashed to Pole Bank to relay the awful news. Finding none of the family in, he returned with two women servants and an armchair, in which to carry the body back to the hall. In the meantime, the Ashtons' carriage was making its way earlier than expected back to Bredbury to collect the party-goers. During the day the mood at the hall had been one of gaiety and promise, yet when a local minister-friend visited the family soon after their return he was reported to have found them 'overwhelmed with affliction' and young James badly shaken and distraught, convinced that the pistol balls had been meant for him.

The murder was sensational news, of course. The implication of trade union involvement, which was a feature from the start, gave it a uniquely interesting new angle. And, although the press's treatment of the latter subject raised an almighty stink, the strong whiff of conspiracy lingers to this day.

Below a headline that exclaimed 'COLD-BLOODED ASSASSINATION', the *Macclesfield Courier* described it as a 'most cruel and sanguinary' murder that had 'excited sensations of horror, as well as alarm, in the bosoms of all classes of society'. The victim, said the paper on Saturday 8 January, was a young man who had 'always been remarkable for his kind and conciliatory disposition'.

The *Courier* commented, 'Had the melancholy occurrence taken place at Ashton, where the journeymen spinners are at variance with their masters, it would at once [have] been attributed to the former; but the assassination occurred at a place where there is no dispute about wages. It is said, however, by those who attribute it to the turn-outs, that as the Ashton masters justify their reduction in wages by the fact that the Hyde masters pay a great deal less than they, the irritation of the men is greater against the Hyde masters than against their own.'

Whose Finger on the Trigger?

On the same day, the *Manchester Guardian* revealed for the first time that one of four Apethorn Mill employees who had been discharged on the personal orders of Mr James Ashton had been a man called 'Stansfield'. This subsequently mutated into the alternative 'Stansfield or Schofield', but it later became apparent that these were the names of two different people which had become confused, and it was the latter – a certain Samuel Schofield – who would become more significantly linked with Thomas Ashton's murder.

Allegedly one of the union militants who put out the 'contract' on the younger Ashton brother, this mysterious individual hovered around the penumbral outer edges of the case like a cautious moth, repeatedly drawn to the flame but never quite getting close enough to be burned. He was eventually tracked down and arrested, accused of incitement to murder. But, at the 11th hour, the charge was dropped.

There were, said the *Guardian*, various theories in circulation. 'But a very general opinion…prevails (how correctly we cannot undertake to say) that the murder of Mr Ashton has been resorted to with the view to terrifying them [the Hyde master spinners] into a compliance with the wishes of the workmen; and it is supposed that Mr Ashton's family were selected as objects of vengeance…because the relative situations of the house and the mill offered greater facilities for assassination than were presented by those of any other spinner at Hyde.'

It was true that the local topography provided good cover for a night-time ambush and several escape routes, but there were still plenty of potential witnesses abroad in Apethorn Lane at this time in the evening…as was evidenced at the inquest into Thomas Ashton's death. It was held on Wednesday 5 January at the Boy and Barrel pub in Gee Cross before Cheshire coroner John Hollins.

It was from the press coverage of the proceedings that an eager public devoured the full details of Monday evening's outrage and learned of the possible murder plot, with all its alarming implications.

Only minutes before the murder, the suspects were seen in Apethorn Lane by three separate witnesses in quick succession, the inquest jury heard. Martha Percival, who, though only nine years of age, worked at the Werneth mill, was returning alone to her parents' house in Gerrard's Hollow at around 7 o'clock when she came upon the three men near the gate leading to the Ashtons' private road.

As she walked towards them, one of the men moved to the other side of the lane so that she had to pass between him and his two companions. She thought he was trying to conceal something he was holding against his right thigh. So, a few yards further on, the youngster, though obviously frightened by her experience, was sufficiently curious to look back over her shoulder, and she 'plainly saw' what he was carrying. It was a gun.

Moments later, 14-year-old Joseph Collier saw the men walking in single file in the direction of the mill. The last man, he said, 'carried something in his right hand, down by his side'. Collier had a lantern, but he did not get a clear sight of the object and could only say that it 'seemed bright'. Soon afterwards he heard 'the report of firearms' [*sic*].

Thomas Wood, a blacksmith from Werneth who also worked at the mill, was the third person to see three men loitering suspiciously in Apethorn Lane that evening. Wood said he met them at a point between Swindells Farm and the murder spot. They did not speak, but one of them 'looked at him closely under his hat'. A man, who he learned later was

Thomas Ashton, came through the clap-gate as he passed it. Several minutes later he heard what he, too, described as 'the report of firearms' (both he and young Collier presumably mistook the pistol's echo for a second shot). Wood was on his own. It was dark. He did not stop to investigate.

The postmortem had revealed fragments of a coarse blue paper, part of the wadding used in the murder weapon, embedded in the deceased's sternum just under the entry wound. It was an unexpected clue, which, it was thought, might help identify the gunman. But, like many promising leads, the paper chase ran into a dead end.

The jury returned its inevitable verdict of 'wilful murder by three persons at present unknown'. Now the hunt was on to catch the killers.

An impressive team was assembled to lead the investigation, which was to provide the first real test of Cheshire's 'new police', the county's first professional force created by an Act of Parliament in 1829. In overall charge was William Birch, the chief constable of the Macclesfield Hundred, who was one of the first appointments under the pioneering law enforcement initiative, which actually pre-dated the establishment of the Metropolitan Police by 18 days. Stockport's diligent deputy constable John Stapeley Barratt was his No.2. Manchester police chief Stephen Lavender sent some of his best officers to assist, and, following a petition to the Home Secretary (Viscount Melbourne) by the master spinners of Manchester, Hyde and Ashton, two officers from 'the Met', were also seconded to the inquiry.

Finally, in a move that was the 19th-century equivalent of 'sending for Scotland Yard,' Birch called in one of the celebrated Bow Street Runners, the experienced (if controversial) Daniel Bishop. Known as the 'indefatigable Bishop,' because of his doggedness in pursuit of criminals, he was the man who, in February 1820, had arrested the leader of the Cato Street Conspiracy gang.

In the Ashton murder inquiry, however, the 'ace detective' failed to turn up trumps, and it would appear that his most significant impact was on the cost of the investigation. For, while the veteran Runner earned a basic salary of only 1s 6d a week on his regular London 'beat', for his outside assignments he charged a fee of one guinea (21 shillings) plus 14s expenses *per day*.

Although he was involved in several early arrests, they all failed to produce a likely suspect and the *Macclesfield Courier* of 15 January commented disconsolately that the only hope now was that the offer of a pardon and the reward money would tempt one of the villains to confess. It did...but it was a long time coming.

By this point, with Samuel Ashton contributing £500 and his relatives a similar amount, the reward total had reached £1,500 (some £98,000 at today's values). It had been publicised in a 'Royal Proclamation' issued on 6 January 1831. The notice, as it appeared in the *Stockport Advertiser*, referred to the commission of the murder 'by some evil disposed person unknown' and then announced, 'His Majesty [William IV], for the better apprehending and bringing to justice [of] the persons concerned in the felony before mentioned, is hereby pleased to promise HIS MOST GRACIOUS PARDON to any one of them, except the person who actually fired the said shot, who shall discover his accomplices therein, so that he, she or they, may be apprehended and convicted thereof.'

That the murder was the tragic result of the current dispute was such an obvious conclusion that it was now being mentioned routinely in most of the papers. Spinners' union officials were incensed and singled out the *Manchester Guardian* for special criticism. In its defence, the *Guardian* (which *was* one of the more outspoken of the press opponents of the stoppage) pointed out that in repeating the generally-accepted view, it had expressed the hope that it would eventually be proved that the murder was 'totally unconnected with the union'.

Events in the days immediately after the shooting, however, did nothing to dispel fears that the strike had engendered a dangerous new mood of anarchy among its supporters.

Five workers from the Werneth mill were reported to have been fired at by a striking spinner at Newton Moor, near Hyde; a mob of five or six hundred 'flying pickets' swooped on a mill in Longdendale, dragged out a number of spinners who had returned to work, turned their coats inside out, tied them together with cord and drove them along the road as far as Stalybridge. At another mill at Tintwistle, where all the hands had been sent home, the mob warned the mill owner that if any spinners returned to work at the lower rate they would 'come again and kill them and destroy the machinery'.

Like Thomas Ashton appeared to have been, other master spinners became targets for the hot-heads. The proprietor of a mill at Spring Grove, Stalybridge, had a narrow escape when he was shot at through the window of his counting house. A mill owner from Mossley was at home when a blunderbuss blasted his sitting room window, showering him with glass and shot. Eleven 'bullets' were recovered; fortunately, not a single one hit its mark.

Gradually, however, support for the strike crumbled and the turnouts drifted back to work, forced through financial hardship to return cap-in-hand to their employers and disillusioned by the union's failure to honour promises of strike pay. By the middle of February 1831 it was all over: the mill wheels were all turning productively once more, the master spinners were paying their employees at the lower rate and the striking workers had gained nothing by their action. Indeed, they had lost a significant amount of money, up to 10 weeks' pay in many cases. Spinners at this time earned an average of £1 7s 9d a week (a little over £85 at present values) and the *Manchester Guardian* reckoned some of them would have been out of pocket by as much as £15 (approaching £1,000 today) – 'no trifling loss to a working man'.

Meanwhile, the Apethorn Lane mystery was nowhere near resolution. It was not until April 1834, three years and three months after Thomas Ashton was gunned down on his way to his father's cotton mill, that the impenetrable weave of the murder plot finally began to unravel. The investigation had long since disappeared from the pages of the newspapers that once followed the story so avidly, but now press, and public, interest was about to be rudely reawakened...by a sleep-deprived convict and a nagging nightmare.

Since 8 February 1834 James Garside, from Marple, had been in Derby Gaol. He had been convicted at the Derbyshire Lent Assizes of stealing 'a brass spindle-box' from his employers. He was sentenced to 18 months' imprisonment with hard labour. In the first week in April, he sent word to the prison governor that he had some information about an unsolved murder; a local magistrate was summoned and Garside made the first of several statements about the shooting of Thomas Ashton.

He identified his two fellow conspirators as Joseph Mosley, aged 34, and his brother William (33). The 25-year-old Garside would claim later that he and the Mosleys – who, according to the *Derbyshire Courier*, were 'well-known desperadoes in the neighbourhood of Marple' – had recently formed a gang. They had committed one robbery and were disturbed while attempting a second, but, undaunted, they had agreed to take part together in other similar 'jobs'.

Joseph Mosley had recently taken up fortune-telling and was, apparently, beginning to gain quite a reputation for predicting future events at the time of his arrest. He obviously didn't see that one coming.

Press interest intensified, and on 19 April the *Manchester Guardian* said it had been reliably informed that the three suspects were 'men having no personal enmity against any member of Mr Ashton's family' and that 'the motive for the murder, if it was committed by them, must have been of a different description'. Then, in an appetising foretaste of the revelations to come, it added, 'Indeed, if the statements we have heard on the subject should be proved in evidence, the case will throw a light on the working of the trades' unions which will be as startling as, at the present moment, it is opportune.'

A week later, from the same source, presumably, the *Guardian* had learned of the conscience-stricken moments in Derby Gaol that led to James Garside breaking his three-year silence and letting the world in on his burdensome secret. The paper's enterprising correspondent wrote, 'We understand that, from the time of his first commitment to gaol, he has been very uneasy in mind, and frequently started up from his sleep in a state of apparent horror and alarm. When questioned as to the cause, he at first gave evasive and mysterious answers; but, very shortly, [he]…made the deposition that forms the basis of the present inquiry.'

When James Garside's claims were examined, however, the direction of the case suddenly changed, and it was the deposition made by William Mosley that became the basis of the inquiry…and the prosecution's preparations for the trial. In committing to writing the information that finally solved the three-year-old riddle of Thomas Ashton's murder, Garside was to be the author of his own demise.

Crown lawyers switched tack some time after 7 May, when the three suspected murderers were transferred from Stockport's New Bailey prison to Chester Castle. It was at the County Gaol that William Mosley abandoned his protestations of innocence and, in the statement that would convince the prosecutors they were on safer ground admitting him as King's evidence rather than Garside, he confessed to his involvement in the murder plot. In the statement he, like Garside, denied firing the fatal shot. But while Garside had accused Joseph Mosley of being the gunman, William Mosley now put the blame on Garside.

On one essential issue, however, their stories tallied: the all-important question of who ordered the killing. The prospect of hearing the answer to that one – and of discovering the truth about Cheshire's most famous unsolved murder at last – lent extra frisson to the public's expectations of a trial that was about to become a landmark in Cheshire's judicial history…both in and out of court.

It opened at Cheshire's Summer Assizes on Wednesday 6 August 1834. As the prisoners entered the dock, the *Manchester Guardian* reporter noted, 'Both…were men of low stature, and of ordinary appearance, and were dressed as labourers. Garside was a little taller than Mosley, and had much lighter hair and eyes.'

Garside, who lived latterly with his father in Barnsfold, Marple, but who had been brought up in the Bull's Row area of the town, was working at a 'cotton-band' manufacturers in New Mills when he committed the theft that landed him in Derby Gaol. Joseph Mosley, whose parents lived in Romiley, had been an apprentice calico-printer with a company in Strines, but in 1829 he, too, was dismissed for stealing from his employers. After some irregular employment as a handloom weaver, he moved to Marple Bridge and tried his luck as a travelling fortune-teller, a career move, apparently, that brought him a certain local celebrity and no little income. William Mosley had been an apprentice shoemaker but gave it up before he had served his time. From then on he worked as a canal boatman.

It was important that the jury knew from the outset that none of the men alleged to have conspired to murder Thomas Ashton were spinners or had any connection with the union or the industry. In setting out the motive for the crime, the prosecution made it clear that the three had not acted out of any personal animosity towards the deceased or his family. Nor were they striking a blow for the downtrodden cotton workers in their struggle against their autocratic employers.

They had, quite simply, agreed to carry out the 'horrible transaction' for money, the county's Attorney-General, Mr John Hill, explained in his opening speech. They had been hired, he said, by a representative of the spinners' union and paid out of the union's funds. The price on Thomas Ashton's head was just £10. The amount of blood money each of his killers was to receive was little more than £3.

The evidence to support the prosecutor's astonishing allegations, the court heard, was obtained entirely from the confessions of Garside and William Mosley (the seemingly uncommunicative Joseph Mosley insisted he had had no involvement in the murder and therefore had nothing to say on the subject). And it is from those two statements, the only

Derby Gaol as it looked in 1833, when James Garside made his sensational statement about the Ashton murder while serving time for a minor theft. From the Revd R. Simpson's *History of Derby*. (By permission of Derby Local Studies and *www.picturethepast.org.uk*.)

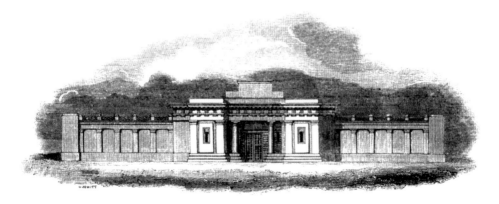

original documents remaining in the official file on the case, that the following passages have been transcribed.

First, the 'voluntary confession' that James Garside made in Derby Gaol, which brought the Ashton murder investigation to its explosive conclusion. The statement was dated 30 April 1834 and seems to have been compiled by Derbyshire JP William Lockett, from the notes he made over the course of several meetings with the prisoner.

On the morning of the murder, Garside began, he had set out to visit a friend in Hyde, but the friend was out. On his return journey he met Joseph Mosley on Werneth Low. Mosley told him he was on his way 'over the hill' and that he 'had a bit of a job to do' that night. It was a fortune-telling job, and he asked Garside if he fancied going with him – he was 'not going above a mile'. Garside agreed. A short distance along the road between Greave and Werneth (now Werneth Low Road), Mosley announced that he had arranged to meet his brother William. They stopped and waited for him by a gravel pit close to what was then known as Lousy Thorn Farm. Ten minutes later William arrived.

Reaching the top of Werneth Low, they stopped for a rest 'in a plantation'. It was here, Garside claimed, that the two brothers coolly announced that they were going to kill one of the Ashtons. 'What for?' He asked. 'For money', came the reply.

Garside went on: 'I said I would have nothing to do with it. Joseph Mosley replied: "Oh, aye, thou mun come and go with us. Thou needst do nothing but watch. I shall do the job." He then pulled out of his pocket a horse-pistol, which he said was loaded. He drew the ramrod out, which was on a swivel, and turned it into the barrel to show us that it was loaded. It was nearly half-full.'

It was the first of several inconsistencies that helped convince the Crown lawyers that Garside had played a more active part in the murder than he was admitting. For someone who claimed not to have handled the murder weapon, he seemed unusually familiar with its type and operation.

Eventually, Garside was persuaded to tag along and the three left the plantation and headed for Apethorn Lane. On the way Garside asked about the money they were to get for killing Mr Ashton. Was he to be robbed of it, he wanted to know. 'Joseph told me he was employed by the Spinners' Union at Ashton and he was to have 10 pounds. He said he and a union man had been over the ground the day before and had settled on how we were to proceed.'

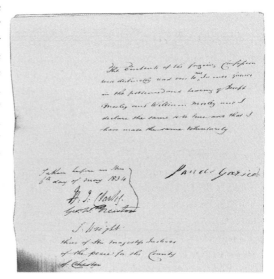

The last page of the 'confession' that finally solved the murder of Thomas Ashton, as signed by James Garside. (By permission of the National Archives.)

Whose Finger on the Trigger?

As they walked down Apethorn Lane, said Garside, the Mosleys were together on one side of the track and he was on the other side – the exact situation with which mill girl Martha Percival was confronted as she approached the three men on the night of the murder. And she had said at the inquest that the man who stood apart from his companions was the one carrying the horse-pistol. Had Garside, in making a seemingly innocuous remark, inadvertently nominated himself as the killer? It was another niggling suspicion that cast doubt on the veracity of his story.

Having located the spot in which they were to lie in wait for young Mr Ashton, Garside stayed on his own and hid himself behind the hedge on one side of the lane, while Joseph and William Mosley went behind the hedge on the opposite side – the side nearest the clap-gate and the best place from which to observe anyone approaching on the footpath from Pole Bank Hall. As they waited, a man (blacksmith Thomas Wood) came by.

'After he had passed me,' Garside's deposition continued, 'I became impatient and went on a little below the gate, when I heard somebody coming along the road whistling. I sat down under the hedge till this man (who was one of the Mr Ashtons, though I did not then know it) came opposite to me. I then heard Joseph Mosley get over the hedge. I got up and saw Joseph meet Mr Ashton…Mr Ashton stepped aside and stood with his back towards me. Joseph got between him and the hedge and discharged the pistol into his body. He fell on his back across the road…I run off.'

He caught up with the others at the canal bridge just below Apethorn Mill. 'Joseph Mosley said we should swear to secrecy,' Garside recounted, 'and we all on our knees took an oath and prayed God to strike us dead if we told of what had been done…[On] the towing path, we considered whether William or Joseph Mosley should go to Ashton to inform the unions [sic] that the job was done and to draw the money. It was determined that William should go. Joseph wanted to get home, having a wife and family and one of his children being ill.'

Garside said he met Joseph Mosley the next morning, Tuesday, at Hollingsworth Bridge. 'Joseph said William had brought him the money for the job from the Spinners' Union, and we were to meet the next Monday night at Dan Bank [on the western outskirts of Marple] to divide it. He swore that if I told, they would bring me into it, and that if I got off, the unions would put an end to my life. I asked him if he did not after[wards] think what he had done. He said he did not; that he would shoot all the Ashtons, if the unions would give him 10 pounds apiece.

'On the Monday [10 January] Joseph and William Mosley and a union man and I met at Dan Bank Wood. I did not know the union man. He did not speak. Joseph took me on one side…he said I need not be afraid; he was one of the union men. He [Joseph] offered me three pounds, but I refused to take it. He said he believed he had shot the wrong man. He offered money to me several times, but I…would not take it. I thought that our folks [his family?] would know I had got money and that it might betray me.'

Finally, he spoke of his feelings about the murder that had led him to turn informer: 'I have had no peace of mind since the job. I have been cast down and wished to have told, but I durst not speak from fear of getting into trouble.'

In his deposition, William Mosley recalled that a few days before 3 January 1831 he had met his brother Joseph and James Garside at the Stag's Head pub in Marple Bridge.

He mentioned that he was going to Macclesfield to look for work. 'They said I had better stop a day or two on that side [of the River Goyt, presumably] as they could find me a job as good as I can get and told me I must come down and meet them at Marple Bridge the Sunday following.'

This he did, and it was after the other two announced that they 'had to meet two men on Compstall Brow and wished me to go with them' that he learned what the 'good job' was to be.

William Mosley then made the first of several references to the shady character who was alleged to have been the spinners' union paymaster. '[On Compstall Brow] the two men spoke to Garside and my brother. One they said was "Schofield" or "Stansfield", who lived towards Hyde or Ashton, a joiner. I knew the other man by sight but not by name. He was a unionist and lived towards Hyde. My brother bid me stand a little way off as they began talking. I don't know what was said but I heard the union mentioned. After the two men left, my brother and Garside told me that they had agreed to shoot one of the Ashtons at Apethorn for the union and that Schofield was to bring them 10 pounds for it from the union. I asked them what they were to shoot him for and they said it was on account of the turn-out.'

After some hesitation, William Mosley agreed to 'go with them and do it'. The next day the three men met up again near the gravel pit at Lousy Thorn. His deposition went on: 'They showed me two pistols, a large one and a small one, which they had in their side pockets and which they said were loaded. Garside had the large one, which they said must be fired [presumably because it had been specially prepared with the double charge]. It was like a horse-pistol. My brother had the smaller one. It was a bright one and was to be kept ready if anything happened.'

Coming to the events in Apethorn Lane, Mosley said, 'Our Joseph and Garside then went over the hedge on the left-hand side of the lane going down and I went over on the right [like Garside, he seemed to be placing himself as far away as possible from the clap-gate and the spot where Thomas Ashton was gunned down]. Joseph and Garside came over the hedge again into the road, crossed the road towards where I was and reared themselves up against the hedge backing [the bank on top of which the hedge was laid].

'Directly after this, a man (whom I afterwards learnt to be one of the Mr Ashtons) came down the road on the same side as the clap-gate and Garside got up from the hedge backing, stepped towards him and...discharged his pistol at him and he fell on his back across the road with his head towards me. My brother stood about a yard off with the small pistol, but it was not fired.'

When he reached the canal bridge, said Mosley, he 'found Joe and Garside standing there, Garside with his piece in his hand'. He said to Garside, 'Hast shot him?' Garside replied, 'Aye, dead enough. I never saw him lift a limb after he fell.'

Mosley claimed that a little while later, when he asked which of the Ashtons had been shot, he thought it was his brother Joe who replied that he did not know, but – words to the effect that – it didn't matter to him which one it was. He was told that Schofield would bring the money from the union on Wednesday (5 January) and he was to meet them at 1 o'clock at Marple locks for the share-out.

Whose Finger on the Trigger?

He went to the rendezvous ('the seventh lock coming up from Marple') and he found his brother and Garside with Schofield. They left the towpath and went down a footpath to the edge of a plantation. 'Schofield', said Mosley, 'said he had settled with Garside and my brother for the job we had done. He then said to me, "I shall settle with thee now" and pulled out three sovereigns and offered them to me. I said I would as lief [willingly] have none and he said I must have something. He asked me what I would have. I said I would take two sovereigns.'

According to Mosley, it was then, not immediately after the murder (as Garside had stated), that the men took their vow of silence. It was Schofield's idea. Mosley continued, '[We] all four went down on our knees and wished God might strike us dead if we told what had been done; and while each took the oath one of us in turn held over him who took it an open knife and threatened to stab him if he did not use the words.'

Finally, as if to put their deadly transaction on a strictly business footing, Schofield produced a little red book, which he got the three assassins to 'receipt' (the younger Mosley made his mark), and they all 'shook hands and parted'.

In court, William Mosley expanded slightly on his written statement. The *Manchester Guardian* seems to have carried the most extensive coverage of the case, and, except where indicated, it is from that source that the trial quotations are taken. The *Guardian* (9 August) claimed Mosley had only admitted being involved in the murder plot 'to save myself from being hanged'. He was said to have commented, 'From January 1831, to May 1834, I kept this secret. I did not know what to do. I thought of telling it when I was at Stockport on 1 May [the day originally fixed for his committal hearing, though it did not, in fact, take place until the 6th]. I never thought of telling it before.'

When Garside's defence counsel, Mr James Dunn, suggested he had agreed to kill a man he had never seen before for £10, Mosley replied, 'I agreed to go with them. I would not shoot any man for £10...I would not take £1,000 to shoot a man...They both said I must go with them, and I must have a share. I didn't consent all at once. I took time to consider it. I thought it was an easy way of getting money.'

Joseph Mosley's response, when asked if he had anything to say in reply to the murder charge, was to hand the clerk of the court a statement he had written.

In it he pleaded with the jury, 'I pray you, gentlemen, take it into your consideration whether it is likely I should commit such an outrage on a person I never knew or saw in my life.' The allegation that the spinners' union had been behind the 'horrid crime' did not surprise him, for, he wrote, 'I always thought their intentions were bad.' However, he did not believe the union would have employed non-unionists 'in such a case as this'.

Of his two alleged accomplices, he stated, '[They] are united on this occasion and they are both bad characters.' Garside, he claimed, had avoided punishment for a number of thefts only because his parents had paid compensation to the victims. And of his own brother, he declared that William Mosley was a convicted thief who was 'a very loose, drunken character [who] would sell me or anyone else, and even himself, for the sake of drink'.

Garside complained to the judge (Mr Baron Parke) that he had only agreed to confess after being promised 'his liberty' – the chance of turning King's evidence and, consequently, of being granted a pardon – by a Dr Forrester, the first magistrate he spoke to in Derby Gaol. Forrester was not called to give evidence. 'They've kept him back for fear he should tell the truth,' Garside protested.

William Lockett, the Derbyshire JP who interviewed Garside later and produced his 'compilation statement', pointed out, however, that, at one meeting on 14 April, he told Garside it was his opinion that he would *not* be admitted a witness for the Crown. 'I told him I was quite confident he knew more of the transaction than he had disclosed…I also told him my apprehension was that he was the person who had fired the shot.'

In his summing up Baron Parke advised the jury that they did not have to determine which of the accused had fired the fatal shot. 'If both were present, going on a joint enterprise, intending to support each other, and one of them fired a deadly weapon, that would make the act of one the act of both,' he said. As far as Garside was concerned, his confession alone was enough to convict him, said the judge.

He described William Mosley as 'a very atrocious character'; there was little doubt, he said, that a man who could commit murder would not balk at perjury – 'if he thought it [was in] his interest'. But if the jurors believed him they would have to find both the accused guilty.

After conferring together for about seven minutes (they did not retire), the jury returned guilty verdicts against both men, who promptly fainted and collapsed to the floor of the dock.

Although the jurors had not been called upon to decide who fired the fatal shot, the question was a matter of considerable interest to a lot of people – not least the Crown lawyers who had based their case on the premise that the culprit was not William Mosley. The judge, too, was anxious that the issue was not left unresolved, and he took the unusual step of asking the foreman for the jury's opinion. When the foreman replied that the question 'appears so very intricate' and requested an adjournment, the jurors were given a candle – it was by this time about 10.30pm – and closeted in the Grand Jury Room (without refreshment) to deliberate further. They were soon back in court, however, and the foreman informed the judge that they all agreed that the killer 'must have been James Garside'.

To the two convicted murderers, Baron Parke said, 'There cannot be a single doubt…that you are the men who perpetrated the deed. Your conduct in the commission of it was most dastardly. And what stamps your conduct with greater infamy is that you did it from the basest of motives – for money.'

He told the pair there could be no hope of a reprieve: they would be hanged in less than 48 hours. For once, however, the learned judge did not have a full grasp of the facts. This case – a long stuttering journey of blind alleys, disappearing trails and surprise turnings – had not yet run its course. Justice, already forestalled for more than three-and-a-half years, would have to wait a little while longer.

Unbeknown to Baron Parke, Chester's civic leaders were planning an unparalleled act of civil disobedience in a provocative new bid to unburden the city sheriffs of their age-old responsibility for executing criminals condemned at the assizes. The mayor and corporation, in a move endorsed by the grand jury of the city's Quarter Sessions, had decided to force the issue by refusing to execute Garside and Mosley.

Whose Finger on the Trigger?

Cheshire magistrates, backed by the grand jury of their Quarter Sessions – and at least 500 years of tradition – pointed out that hanging was no business of theirs and resolved to fight any move to make it so. Neither side would budge – even when served with writs by the Government's Attorney-General – and the situation reached impasse.

With the sentences against Garside and Mosley on hold, the press had more time in which to root out background material on the two convicted men. The *Stockport Advertiser* was especially active in this regard.

Garside, the newspaper discovered, had had 'a tolerable education', but from petty pilfering he had developed into a confirmed thief and was associated with 'consummate robbers and hardened villains' in a series of robberies and property break-ins.

Joseph Mosley, said the *Advertiser*, was one of four brothers, all of whom 'gave their parents problems'. The same year he and William were involved in the Werneth murder another brother, Thomas, was transported for house-breaking. Joseph was apprenticed at 13 but 'constantly stole from his employers'. He became a hand-loom weaver, but 'he [only] worked when he felt like it'.

After taking up the 'profession of wizard', he travelled the country and 'for some time he continued to practice his deceptive arts with considerable profit'. The newspaper claimed that he was assisted by Samuel Schofield on some of these fortune-telling expeditions.

The most sensational revelation since the end of the trial, however, appeared first in the *Manchester Guardian* of Saturday 11 October, when it was reported that the deputy constable of Oldham had received a tip-off that a man in the Half Green area of the town was in possession of the horse-pistol that had killed Thomas Ashton. When questioned, the man, named simply as 'Jones' and aged about 20, was at first evasive; but, after some prompting, he admitted he had had the gun 'since Garside returned it'.

Garside had told him he wanted to borrow it 'for a lad named Tallent to shoot with' (Tallent was his wife's maiden name). At that time the mainspring of the flintlock was broken off, and when Garside brought it back 'shortly after the murder' he said it had not been used because of the defect. However, Heywood, the deputy constable, learned that Garside had taken the pistol to a local gunsmith to be repaired. The gunsmith recognised the weapon and told the constable he remembered replacing the mainspring. Garside, he believed, had called for the gun on the Thursday night before the murder. Two other men waited for him at the door, but he could not identify them.

Meanwhile, the legal wrangling over the executions of the two convicts continued. Further respites followed until, on Thursday 6 November 1834, the matter was finally settled in the Court of King's Bench when Lord Denham, the Lord Chief Justice, granted the court jurisdiction over the two convicted men. Garside's counsel, James Dunn, was also given leave to seek a pardon for his client on the grounds that he had supplied the information that led to the solution of the murder.

There were those who believed Garside had good reason to feel hard done by. In a well-argued editorial in its edition of 22 August, two weeks after the assize court's verdict, the *Chester Chronicle* had expressed its unease at his treatment. The paper commented, '[The] whole tenor of Garside's conduct in Derby gaol...proves if no actual or implied promise of pardon was held out to him, that, at all events, he made the confession "in the hope and with the expectation" of obtaining one. In the opinion of many gentlemen learned in the law, a confession made under these circumstances…is sufficient to bring a prisoner within the [royal pardon] proclamation, unless he be the actual murderer; and that Garside was the actual murderer in this case rests upon no better evidence than the unsupported declaration of William Mosley, the accomplice.'

On 22 November, however, Garside's petition for clemency was rejected by the Duke of Wellington, the Home Secretary. He and Joseph Mosley were hanged three days later at Horsemonger Lane Gaol, the county prison of Surrey.

By a strange twist of fate, the two men, whom both the city and the county had refused to execute, were eventually hanged in the presence of 'Chester' and 'Cheshire'. The former was the name of the deputy marshall of the King's Bench and the latter was Thomas Cheshire, the executioner.

For providing the testimony that sent Garside and Joseph Mosely to the gallows, William Mosley, the third partner in the crime, was duly discharged and pardoned (and, presumably, collected at least some of the £1,500 reward money). A year later he was back in gaol on suspicion of burglary at Whaley Bridge, but the evidence against him was inconclusive and he was released.

It was generally believed that he went to America immediately after the trial, but, as the *Chronicle* revealed on 7 August 1835, 'from his own account he has been working on the Peak Forest Canal ever since as a coal-heaver'.

Mosley did eventually emigrate to America, apparently hoping to get a job as a navvy. But at some point he returned to England, to Cheshire and to Hyde. It was from there that, on 7 April 1868, penniless and in poor health, he was admitted to the Stockport Workhouse, where he died

A broadside detailing the 'trial and awful execution' of Garside and Mosley for Thomas Ashton's murder. It was three years before they were brought to court. (By permission of CCALS.)

on 29 April at the age of 67. The workhouse registers record that he was buried in the borough cemetery, a humble ending for a self-confessed accessory to murder who won his freedom but could never escape his past.

The elusive Samuel Schofield, whose arraignment might have yielded the evidence that would have proved once and for all whether Garside and Mosley *were* part of a union-backed murder conspiracy, didn't even have his day in court. After being committed for trial, the 24-year-old joiner and father of two from Hyde was due to appear at the Cheshire Spring Assizes at the end of March 1835, charged with 'having feloniously and with his malice aforethought counselled, procured and hired Joseph Mosley, James Garside and William Mosley to shoot and kill one Thomas Ashton'. But, on the advice of the Judge, Mr Baron Bolland, the members of the grand jury decided it would be prudent to drop the case.

In his customary address at the start of the sessions, Baron Bolland had pointed out that for there to be a realistic chance of a conviction it was essential that 'the testimony of the accomplice William Mosley should be corroborated in some material particulars'. They should consider, therefore, whether it might be 'more conducive to the ends of justice' not to proceed with the case at this time. For, as he explained, 'were he [Schofield] once put upon his trial and acquitted, no disclosures, however important, that might hereafter take place, could affect him'.

There were, however, no important disclosures that led to Samuel Schofield being tried on this or any other charge relating to the Werneth Murder case, nor was any additional evidence forthcoming to show, one way or the other, whether the plot to shoot Thomas Ashton was hatched by the spinners' union in a bid to step up their wages war with the mill owners.

From the evidence so far uncovered, there can be no doubt that the murder *was* bound up with the strike action and that if the leaders of the spinners' union were not involved rogue elements within the membership were. In the greater part of two centuries no other rational theory has ever been advanced.

So was it Garside or Joseph Mosley whose finger was on the trigger that bleak winter's night in 1831? History records that it was Garside. The trial jury, when pressed, felt that 'it must have been' him, and the judge concurred. And the circumstances surrounding the subsequent discovery of the alleged murder weapon in Oldham lends powerful support to the proposition that if Garside had acquired the gun and gone to the trouble of getting it repaired ready for action, he was the more familiar with its operation and, therefore, the one most likely to have fired it.

One final piece of corroborating evidence comes from the pages of *Annals of Hyde and District* by Thomas Middleton, first published in 1899. In the book the author reproduced a letter purporting to have been written to a relative of his by the relieving officer who admitted William Mosley to Stockport Workhouse in 1868. The official recalled how he had asked the new arrival whether he was 'the William Mosley who shot Mr Thomas Ashton?' Mosley, who probably knew by then that he had not long to live, replied, 'I was with Garside when Thomas Ashton was shot. I did not shoot him. We tossed up, and it fell to my lot, but Garside took the pistol out of my hands, and he shot him.'

A rather timeworn copy of an unusually-pictorial broadside relating to the Ashton murder case, complete with illustrations of the principal events. (By permission of Stockport Heritage Library.)

* * *

Despite the successful stand over the Garside-Mosley executions, Chester Corporation's victory was short-lived. In March 1835 Parliament enacted new legislation that continued the city sheriffs' ancient hanging duty 'for the time being'. The time, in this case, being 32 years, for it was not until July 1867 that the Act of Parliament that finally relieved them of the responsibility came into force. The last hanging at which they officiated was a doubly-historic occasion…

Chapter Thirteen

Evil Afoot in the Christian Field

Contagion was all around. It had come upon the land like some vengeance-wreaking biblical pestilence and few places escaped its deadly wrath. 'Cattle plague' – a name straight from the pages of the Old Testament – was stampeding through the country, leaving behind a trail of devastation. And in an age when religious teaching was still strong on hell-fire and damnation, most people, reminded of the words of the Book of Exodus and the 'very grievous murrain' inflicted by God on the Egyptians, were quite prepared to believe it was divine punishment for society's sins.

It had begun in the summer of 1865. The following January the Archbishop of Canterbury called for a national 'Day of Humiliation', and a month later, at church services up and down the country, congregations said a special prayer seeking the Lord's forgiveness for their 'transgressions' and beseeching him – 'in humble penitence' – to 'stay His chastisement' and bring an end to the suffering.

The supplications went unanswered. The outbreak rapidly acquired the status of 'The *Great* Cattle Plague' and a place in history as one of the worst epidemics of animal disease ever seen in Britain. It raged until September 1867 and decimated British herds...and the predominantly-dairy county of Cheshire was its most serious casualty.

At its height, Cheshire losses accounted for a quarter of all the cattle that either died or were slaughtered as a result of the outbreak nationally. When it ended, the county's death toll had exceeded 70,000 – about two-thirds of its entire stock.

By early 1866 most Cheshire farm workers had become all too familiar with its distressing consequences, especially the demoralising drudgery of burying the dead animals. Mass graves pock-marked the landscape as stringent measures were taken to limit the spread of the highly-infectious, high-mortality disease. Carcasses were not routinely burned (as in the case of foot and mouth), but a dark pall of death hung over the countryside nonetheless.

The Cattle Disease Prevention Act, the law rushed through Parliament to add teeth to the Government's emergency plans, had been in force only a matter of days when, in the late afternoon of Monday 26 February, farmer John Lightfoot received word that some of his heifers had strayed on to a neighbour's land. Farmhand Samuel Joynson was sent urgently to round them up and 'quarantine' them in a shed for the night. Joynson, 44, had already seen more than enough bloody slaughter, but nothing could have prepared him for the heart-stopping sight that greeted him as, his task accomplished, he set off back to the farm in the sleepy Cheshire hamlet of Dunham-on-the-Hill.

He was walking across the meadows when something in a ditch, close to the footpath, caught his eye. The time was a little after 5.40pm, and in the dwindling daylight he took it for an old sack...until he went and took a proper look. Only then did he realise the full horror of what had taken place there that day. In a corner of the Christian Field (as it was known) he beheld a scene of unthinkable evil.

CHRONICLE MARCH 3, 1866.

DIABOLICAL MURDER OF A FARMER IN CHESHIRE.

APPREHENSION OF THE SUPPOSED MURDERER.

On Monday last the quiet and picturesque village of Dunham-on-the-hill, situate about six miles from Chester, was aroused from its monotonous slumbers by the alarm that a farmer had been murdered in one of the meadows adjoining. The news spread like wild-fire and the villagers came out of their houses and were very actively astir. The consternation was general, and all were anxious to know who were the victim and the author of the foul deed. Suspicion was general, and no time was lost in apprehending the person who is said to have committed the dread crime. So far as we have been able to glean the facts of this melancholy case, we may state that the deceased, Mr. Isaac Newport, a small farmer and large pig dealer, resided at Long Green, Barrow, about a mile and a half from Dunham. He was 65 years of age, much respected by those with whom he had to do business, as well as others with whom he came in contact. It appears that he had sold three fat pigs to Mr. Lightfoot, a "higgler" who lives at Overton, who according to appointment met Mr. Newport at Mr. Richards', the Railway Inn, Dunham, on Monday morning, for the purpose of paying him the price of the same. The buyer and seller came together, and the amount handed over by the former to the latter was £15 7s. This transaction was witnessed by those who were in the room, the prisoner, Samuel Griffiths, a young man of 24 years of age (of whom we shall have to speak in more measured terms by and by) being amongst the company. The amount was handed over to the deceased at ten o'clock in the morning, and the prisoner was observed to glance eagerly at the coins as they passed from hand to hand; so much so that a person who was in the room remarked in an under tone to Mr. Lightfoot, "Do you see that young man?" "Yes." "Well, he would not scruple at knocking a man down and robbing him if he had the chance." Scarcely any notice was taken of this remark, and for a time all went on as usual. Drink was called in, and glass after glass was enjoyed in the most indulgent manner, for deceased with his usual generosity and hospitality "would stand treat," and in so doing he "kept pace" to such an extent that he at last got powerfully refreshed, although not incapable of walking. His limbs were not ungovernable, for he was able to get over "hedges

The introduction to the *Chester Chronicle* report of the slaying of Isaac Newport and the 'apprehension of the supposed murderer'. (By permission of CCALS.)

Evil Afoot in the Christian Field

Sprawled in the flood-filled ditch, like a broken and discarded mannequin, was a man's body. It was caught on the lower branches of a gorse bush growing out of the side of the bank, which had prevented it from being totally immersed. Only the head, which was crooked at an unnatural angle, and the right shoulder were clear of the water. The dead man had been battered severely about the head, and caked blood and heavy bruising made his face unrecognisable.

It was a cold day and a few scattered traces of the light snow that had fallen during the morning still speckled the ground. But when Joynson touched the body he found it was warm. It also showed no signs of rigor mortis. The man, seemingly, had not been dead long.

Once he had recovered from the shock, Joynson hurried off to raise the alarm. Dunham-on-the-Hill, as the *Chester Chronicle* would depict it on the following Saturday (3 March), was about to be 'aroused from its monotonous slumbers' with a startling jolt. For the inhabitants of this 'quiet and picturesque' village, it must have been like awakening to a terrible nightmare.

The *Chronicle* reported, 'The news spread like wild-fire, and all the villagers came out of their houses and were very actively astir. The consternation was general, and all were anxious to know who were the victim and the author of the foul deed...'

They didn't have long to wait: the victim was quickly identified as Isaac Newport, a 65-year-old farmer and pig dealer from Long Green in the neighbouring parish of Barrow. And the alleged 'author' of the crime was named shortly afterwards as Samuel Griffiths, aged 26, a casual labourer, petty villain and troublemaker, who lived in Dunham.

Still reeling from the shocking discovery in the meadows, Dunham's tight-knit farming community of 300-odd souls now learned with a deepening sense of unreality that the murder was linked to the day's big social event in the village, the wedding of a young local couple. Though there would have been no one in Dunham who did not know something about it by then, the improbable connection was confirmed in the *Chronicle* five days later.

It appeared that after the mid-morning ceremony the wedding guests had repaired to the Railway Inn, and towards noon the bridegroom temporarily abandoned his new bride and adjourned to the taproom to treat some of the pub regulars to a drink. Among them were Isaac Newport and Hatitia Lightfoot. By the early afternoon the ale had been flowing freely for several hours and, of the handful of men remaining in the smoky bar, Newport and Lightfoot had imbibed more freely than most, for that day they had another reason to celebrate.

Newport, described by the *Chronicle* as 'a small farmer and large pig-dealer', had just sold Lightfoot 'three fat pigs' and the pair had been toasting the deal since before 10am. 'Tie' Lightfoot, as he was known, was also a farmer and pig dealer and a small-time 'higgler' (a travelling pedlar), who lived in the Overton area of Frodsham.

Newport, said the *Chronicle*, was 'a hard-working man, generally sober and industrious', but, like Lightfoot, he had been happy to tarry a while longer at the pub when the just-married Henry Garner, a farm labourer from Dunham-on-the-Hill, began buying drinks for everyone.

Consequently, when the two farmers finally left the pub, they were both in hearty good spirits – though, with the cash from the livestock transaction making a comforting

The former Railway Inn, now much enlarged and renamed, where the Newport murder story began. On the right is Church Lane, where the murder victim was last seen alive. (Photograph by the author.)

bulge in his coat pocket, Newport had an extra glow of satisfaction on his ruddy, weather-beaten features.

He would have been in a rather less carefree mood, however, had he known that the gold and silver coins that were threatening to burst the seams of his home-made calico purse had excited the interest of one of his drinking companions. Samuel Griffiths, another early arrival at the pub, had also partaken in the traditional 'wedding glass' – in his case, several glasses. But even in this beer-befuddled state he was alert to the possibility of turning the farmer's pig trade into a money-making scheme of his own, and for some time had been monitoring Newport's advancing intoxication for an opportunity to get his hands on the old man's newly-acquired funds.

He discovered just how much cash was involved when, soon after the wedding party arrived, Newport and Lightfoot shook hands on their deal and the former received payment for the pigs – £14 in gold sovereigns and 27s in silver, a total of £15 7s 0d (the equivalent today of over £1,100).

Griffiths, a lowly-paid general labourer with a police record and a reputation as a nasty piece of work after drink, was standing only a couple of yards away warming himself by the taproom fire and was noticed staring fixedly at the money passing across the little round table at which the two farmers were sat. Then, over the bowl of the unbelievably small pipe on which he habitually sucked – it was, contemporary press reports insisted, no more than an inch long – he continued to watch the proceedings closely as Newport, not normally a heavy drinker, matched his friend shot-for-shot until (as the *Chronicle* so eloquently put it) he was 'powerfully refreshed'.

When he eventually left the warm conviviality of the inn – it is still there beside the Warrington-Chester road (A56), though now substantially enlarged and renamed the

Evil Afoot in the Christian Field

Dunham Arms – and tottered off into the chilly afternoon air, Newport crossed the road and headed up Church Lane. Minutes later Griffiths followed him out.

It was shortly after 2pm when Isaac Newport set out to walk the mile and a half to Long Green. He never arrived. He was last seen steering an unsteady course towards the familiar footpath route that should have taken him to within yards of his farmhouse home at Rose Cottage. The path, then a fairly well-used short cut to Barrow, began at a high stile beside a track described on early maps as 'The Old Lane', which runs from Village Road and down past the village green before losing itself in the farmland beyond. Newport had safely negotiated five fields, and had travelled about three-quarters of a mile from the pub, when his journey, and his life, were abruptly ended.

Griffiths was in custody within three hours of the body being found. The twice-married Newport, father of 13 children, had been a popular and well-respected man and everyone in the village was anxious to help catch the perpetrator of a crime whose horrific nature was unheard of in this tiny rural backwater. When local bobby William Marsh learned of the day's activities at the village pub – and that a quarrelsome Griffiths was at that very moment being 'persuaded' to leave the premises after returning for more ale – he immediately made tracks for the Railway.

PC Marsh found his suspect lying, dead drunk apparently, in the gutter outside the pub's front door. His face was smeared with blood – it looked as if he had been thrown out and landed heavily on the cobbled forecourt. As Marsh searched him, Griffiths started to come round and began lashing out, giving the policeman a bloody nose in the process. But he was eventually restrained and arrested when one of the two local men who had accompanied Marsh to the pub came to the officer's aid. Isaac Newport's calico purse, containing £13 15s, was found in the inside pocket of Griffiths's waistcoat. By late evening Griffiths was under lock and key at the police station in Frodsham, some four miles away.

Back in Dunham the village was a-buzz with talk of the murder, and in the public bars and around the household supper tables that night the story was that Griffiths, a much younger and fitter man, had trailed Newport and eventually caught up with him as he climbed the stile into the Christian Field, where he beat him to death, stole his purse full of money and heaved his body into the ditch. Which was correct...to a point.

However, Isaac Newport was not the victim of a sudden, surprise attack, nor did he die mercifully swiftly, as it was thought. His death followed a more sustained battery. And his killer added a final devilish 'refinement' to his *modus operandi* to ensure the old man did not survive the murderous assault. The details only emerged after Griffiths's trial and will be considered in context later.

Inquiries into Griffiths's background revealed that he was one of the few people who had actually benefitted from the cattle plague (also known by its German name of *rinderpest*). For him the continuing outbreak meant regular work. As the *Chronicle* explained, 'The cattle plague has lately been most prevalent in the village, and Griffiths was constantly employed to bury the cattle dying of the disease. Only a day or two ago, speaking of what he had seen when so engaged, he appeared to be much affected, and said it would produce pity in the breast of anyone who witnessed the sufferings the poor beasts endured.'

The corner of the Christian Field showing the original line of the ditch, the spot where Isaac Newport was found battered to death and (centre) the tree-shaded pit into which the watercourse then ran. (Photograph by the author.)

In the days pre-dating the law of *sub judice*, the papers were also able to report that the accused, a strongly-built man about 5ft 9ins tall, was well known to the police. At the age of 13 he was said to have burgled his uncle's house, and since then he had been in custody on various charges of assault, theft and poaching, for which he had served time in both Chester Castle Gaol and Knutsford's House of Correction. The *Chronicle* claimed, '[In] his drunken fits he was a complete terror to the neighbourhood.'

Griffiths, who was unmarried, was said to live with his parents in a cottage – long since demolished – opposite the Wheatsheaf Inn. He was also, it seems, better known locally as Samuel 'Malpas' – 'the cognomen [nickname] of the family for years back', according to the *Chronicle*. The tradition seems to have started with his grandfather, John Griffiths, a cowherd on one of the larger farms in Dunham, who came originally from Malpas. The farmer had another servant with the same name, so, to avoid confusion, he took to identifying them by their birthplaces. The habit stuck, and the next two generations of Griffithses also answered to the name of Malpas.

It was at the Wheatsheaf – this was the original thatch-roofed inn, which was on the roadside in front of where the present pub stands – that the inquest into Isaac Newport's death was opened on Wednesday 28 February. While the 'mutilated and disfigured' body of the deceased lay in an adjoining room of what was described in the *Chronicle* as 'the large clubhouse attached to the inn', his aged widow sat in the kitchen 'crying and bewailing her terrible loss'.

The proceedings lasted only a few minutes. The coroner, Henry Churton, told the jury – 'all of them most respectable farmers and landowners from the three adjoining townships of Dunham, Barrow and Helsby' – that the police were 'not quite ready with their witnesses'. As this was 'a case of so much importance', he felt it was essential that the police should be given sufficient time to gather together all the evidence. At his behest, the members of the jury, whose number included one 'Thomas Newport' (almost certainly a relative of the deceased), went with him to inspect the scene of the murder and, on their return to the inn, the hearing was adjourned.

When they all reconvened at the Wheatsheaf two days later (Friday 2 March), Griffiths was also present. The *Chronicle*, which covered the resumed inquest extensively in its editions of 3 March and 10 March, reported, 'The prisoner was brought into the room handcuffed, and appeared much dejected. He was in his shirt-sleeves, and presented a very ragged exterior. He evidently appeared to feel the solemn position in which he was

Evil Afoot in the Christian Field

Key locations in the case of murdered farmer Isaac Newport in 1866: 1, the Wheatsheaf Inn, where the inquest took place; 2, the cottage in which Samuel Griffiths was said to have lived; 3, the Railway Inn; 4, the high stile at the beginning of the footpath to Barrow; 5, the stile into the Christian Field; 6, the pit in the corner of the field; 7, the section of the ditch in which the body was found; 8, the farm from where George Duncan saw the 'running, stooping man' near the site of the murder; 9, Nixon's Farm, to where Griffiths went to collect his pick after killing Mr Newport. (Plan produced by the author.)

placed, for he looked on the floor, and seemed as [if] he dared not so much as lift up his eyes to those who were witnesses against him.'

The first of those witnesses was Mary Newport, who recalled waving her husband goodbye at around 9 o'clock on the Monday morning. She did not see him alive again. She deposed, 'He was quite well and hearty when he left home. The next thing I heard of him was between 7 and 8 o'clock on Monday night, when my sons came up to Dunham in consequence of what we heard. I also went there with my daughter. I went to the village and the policeman turned me back, for he would not let me go any further...It was not until [Wednesday] night that I saw the body of my husband.'

Newport, she told the coroner, was 'a steady, sober and hard-working man'. He occasionally had too much to drink, '[but] when he did, it was the exception to the rule'. The couple, who were tenants of Lord Henry Cholmondeley (younger son of the 3rd Marquis of Cholmondeley), had about an acre of land and kept two cows.

At the Railway Inn he and Lightfoot seem to have finalised the sale of the pigs fairly quickly, but, said Lightfoot, it was only after the newly-wed Henry Garner joined them in the pub taproom that he settled up with Newport. He confirmed that Griffiths was also present at the time.

As the inquest wore on it became apparent that the witnesses who had joined in the wedding celebrations at the pub that day were a little uncertain about timings and somewhat conservative when it came to estimating the amount of alcohol they had all consumed. That the two things may not have been entirely unconnected seems to have occurred to the coroner, who, at one point, after hearing for the umpteenth time that only Griffiths was the worse for drink, commented sarcastically, 'Then I suppose they sell sober stuff at the Railway Inn.' The price of a pint at this time was three pence (3d).

Lightfoot, for instance, thought he had left the pub at 1pm, at which time he said, 'Newport was sober...I was quite sober...[but] Griffiths had had too much drink.'

James Richards, the landlord of the Railway, said he personally had only served Newport with two pints; he also drew two pints for the prisoner, which he allowed him to have 'on the slate'. Griffiths, obviously short of cash in the morning, would pay off his 6d debt when he returned to the pub some time after Isaac Newport was robbed and murdered.

The most reliable witness as to the time of Newport's departure was Joseph Barton, a 42-year-old self-employed bricklayer from Dunham, for whom Griffiths did some occasional work. He said he called at the Railway at about 2 o'clock. He was sure of the time because he had been in Mickle Trafford earlier and knew it was getting on for 1 o'clock when he set out to walk the three miles to Dunham. The journey usually took him about an hour. Newport was just leaving as he entered the pub.

Henry Garner testified that Griffiths was the only other person in the taproom when Lightfoot handed over the cash to Newport. Garner next saw the prisoner at around 3pm at the village smithy. Griffiths was having a pick sharpened and told Garner he was 'going to kill a cow for Joseph Lightfoot' (another Dunham farmer). The animal had been stricken with the cattle plague and the pick was needed to dig the animal's grave. Griffiths offered to buy him a pint if he would return with him to the Railway. Garner agreed and the two of them went to the pub for what turned into a further lengthy drinking session.

In contrast to the morning's jollity, Griffiths seemed to be out of sorts and, said Garner, 'was lying on the bench [in the pub] some portion of the afternoon'. He became maudlin and, out of the blue, he babbled, 'I look very rough and ragged. I have a good mind to drown myself.' Later, also for no apparent reason, he said to Garner, 'I will give thee half-a-crown [2s 6d].' Garner said he replied, 'No, Samuel, I dinna want it. Keep it thesel [yourself].'

Samuel Joynson told the inquest of the blood-chilling moment in the snow-dusted Christian Field when he came upon the body in the ditch. He recounted, 'He was lying on the left side. The feet and legs were in the water, as well as the left shoulder and the left arm. The head lay on the left shoulder, being raised and resting on a gorse bush. The head and face were covered with blood.' Though he knew Newport well, he said he did not recognise him at first, as he was 'so disfigured with the bruises and blood about the face'.

He went on: 'His head was quite loose and his body warm. I felt as if I should faint and fall upon him, so I stood on the bank to recover myself.' Then he dragged Mr Newport out of the ditch and also retrieved the pig farmer's hat from the water. It bore two distinct indentations, he said.

Christian Field, a name by which older locals still know it today – and which, it is thought, may derive from some bygone baptismal association – is the third field south from Manley Road. On a sketch plan prepared for the trial, the murder location was pinpointed as being exactly 34 yards from the field stile and eight yards from the footpath. From this and examination of 19th-century maps of the area, it is clear that the field pattern has changed slightly since then: there is evidence that at some time the field boundary has been straightened and the section of ditch in which Isaac Newport's body was found has been filled in. The nearby pit, in which – according to the *Chester Record*'s description – the ditch terminated, can still be seen, however, in the north-east corner of the field, and the old pathway, its course virtually unchanged in almost 150 years,

Evil Afoot in the Christian Field

continues to provide an alternative walking route between Dunham and Barrow, though less well-trodden now than it was then.

About 12 yards away Joynson found a hefty wooden pole; he made nothing of it at the time and stuck it in the hedge, thinking it might come in useful as fencing material. It was described in the *Chronicle* as 'a thick wooden rail, about 8 or 10 feet in length'; yet, despite its sheer size and weight, the paper declared confidently that 'as the edge corresponds with the indentations in his hat, there is no doubt but the murderer used this weapon in his attack on the old man'.

The reporter from the *Chester Record* – who boasted of having interviewed 'all the witnesses' and cross-checked his information with the police – also appeared to believe that the piece of railing had caused at least one of Isaac Newport's head injuries. He observed that 'there were finger marks on one end of the rail and the other was sharp and fitted exactly into a cut made in the hat of the deceased'. The other indentation in the hat, however, looked to have been caused 'as if by kicking'.

The relevance of the rail was far from cut and dried, however. At least one expert witness at the inquest expressed serious misgivings about its potential as a murder weapon; by the time the case reached trial even the prosecution would appear to have had second thoughts, while Griffiths himself always denied using any weapon at all. Nevertheless, the *Chronicle* reporter noticed that when the exhibit was produced 'the prisoner's countenance changed and he seemed much affected'.

When he had finally recovered from his unnerving experience, Samuel Joynson hurried back up the hillside to the village to alert the police. Bill Marsh, however, was not immediately available (he was out gathering cattle-disease statistics, apparently), and it was not until about 7.30pm that he first heard about the murder.

When he went in search of Griffiths, the constable said, he 'found him lying in the gutter, near the Railway Inn'. He appeared drunk and Marsh tried to lift him but couldn't. When he asked him – a little unnecessarily, one might think – what he was doing there, the prisoner made no reply.

Griffiths remained motionless while the officer searched the outside pockets of his coat and waistcoat, but when Marsh attempted to check the inside pocket of the waistcoat he said Griffiths suddenly revived and struck him 'a very severe blow on the nose'.

He went on: 'A struggle took place and I was obliged to call for assistance, when I continued the search. In the inside waistcoat pocket I found a purse containing gold and silver. I then took the prisoner into the Railway Inn and emptied the money on a table, which consisted of 12 sovereigns, two half-sovereigns, two half-crowns, four florins [two-shilling pieces] and two shillings, amounting in all to £13 15s.

'I asked the prisoner where he had got the money. He said, "Barton paid it me on Saturday night." I then asked him where he got the purse. He said, "That's mine." I cautioned him…and charged him with the wilful murder of Isaac Newport and the robbery of the money found on him. In answer to the charge of murder, prisoner said, "It's a damned lie." I got assistance and conveyed him to Frodsham lock-ups.'

As the inquest continued into the evening, John Davies Weaver, the Chester surgeon who carried out the postmortem examination, reported that the most obvious external injuries were abrasions and heavy bruising on Newport's right cheek and temple, which had caused severe bleeding in the underlying muscles. But it was when the surgeon removed the deceased's skullcap that the real damage became apparent. The skull was not fractured, but Mr Weaver said he found 'considerable congestion between the membranes and the substance of the brain'.

It was his opinion that 'death was produced by concussion of the brain, arising from [an] external injury'. He did not think such an extensive injury – it was about four or five inches long – could have resulted from a fall, unless it had been from a considerable height. He thought it had been caused by 'some dull, round instrument'. He agreed that a blow from the railing found near the body would produce that kind of an injury – but he was in some doubt as to the practicability of using such an unwieldy object as a weapon.

The surgeon also revealed one other piece of information that bore upon the manner of Isaac Newport's death…though its relevance would not be fully understood until after Samuel Griffiths's trial. Newport's skull, said Mr Weaver, was the thickest he had ever seen.

Important evidence relating to the time immediately before and after the murder was given by Francis Richmond Robinson, a Dunham cattle dealer who twice encountered Griffiths during that crucial afternoon period. He said that shortly after 2 o'clock he was at the bottom of Church Lane, and within sight of the Railway Inn, when Griffiths came up to him and asked whether he had seen 'old Newport' from Long Green. Robinson said he had not. Griffiths then inquired as to whether Robinson had just come down from his home at the top of Church Lane, and, when the latter said he had, Griffiths was obviously mystified as to how he could have missed the old man, who had been seen walking up Church Lane only minutes before (the explanation for that would have to await Griffiths's trial).

As if seeking to explain his apparent concern for Newport's welfare, Griffiths said to Robinson, 'Tie Lightfoot has been paying him for some pigs and has made the old man drunk.'

The conversation over, Robinson went on his way, crossing over Warrington Road and into Hob Lane, which runs down by the side of the pub. He was going to the railway station, which was situated about 200 yards down the lane. The station was closed to passenger traffic in 1952 and was subsequently demolished.

Returning home at about 3.10pm, Robinson met Griffiths again, this time at the top of Church Lane. He said the prisoner, who was carrying a pick over his shoulder, asked him for some tobacco; he duly obliged (no great sacrifice considering the size of Griffiths's pipe) and the two parted company once more. This could only have been about half an hour after Griffiths had supposedly committed bloody murder, but Robinson said he noticed nothing unusual about his appearance or demeanour.

Some time earlier – 'between 2 and 3 o'clock' was as close as she could put it – Samuel Joynson's wife Emma, 41, said she saw Griffiths in the field opposite her house talking to his sister. The field in question was the one in which the footpath to Barrow began. It also led to the Christian Field 'where the deceased was found', Mrs Joynson was quick to point out. A few minutes later, Griffiths went off alone across the meadows.

He was seen next at the nearby farm of Mr John Nixon. Alfred Pritchard, a labourer employed by Mr Nixon at what is now Town Farm, was working in the farmyard when

Evil Afoot in the Christian Field

Griffiths appeared in the adjoining field. He asked Pritchard if he could borrow a pick 'to sink a grave for Joseph Lightfoot's cow'. Pritchard was also vague about the time, but it must have been approaching 3 o'clock, for that was the time village blacksmith Thomas Williams said that Griffiths, his request obviously granted, arrived at the smithy, some 200 yards up the main street, to have the tool sharpened.

For once the witness was quite specific; Williams, 42, also had no doubt that Griffiths was then 'in drink'. The smith said he noticed the prisoner's trousers were 'wet up to the knees', and he inquired as to how he had come to get them in such a state. Griffiths replied that he had 'fallen into a hole in Mr Nixon's yard'.

With the evidence concluded, the coroner asked Griffiths if he had anything to say. The prisoner's verbal statement was taken down and, along with the witness depositions, would have been forwarded to the Crown prosecutors to help them formulate their case against Griffiths at trial. Along with the depositions of seven of the inquest witnesses – the Joynsons, Marsh, Weaver, Robinson, Pritchard and Williams – Griffiths's statement, such as it is, can still be found in the assize court files in the National Archives. It is scanty and adds nothing to our understanding of the crime, but it does, at least, provide official authentication of what would be the only evidence he offered in his own defence at his trial.

It was as follows: 'As I was going up Church Lane on Monday afternoon, and about three parts up it, I found that purse on the road. I picked it up and looked what was in it. I saw there was some silver and gold in it. I then went across Nickson's [*sic*] croft. I had been digging holes and had left my pick. It was gone from there and I went to Nickson's house. I got over the wall and then slipped into the pit. I had had some drink. I asked Pritchard where the pick was and he gave it me and I took it to the smith and went again to the ale-house and stopped there until night.' The illiterate Griffiths 'signed' the document with a spidery cross.

Summarising the evidence, Coroner Churton referred to the cause of Isaac Newport's death (it was 'impossible to conceive that such injuries could have been occasioned by a fall,' he commented), to Griffiths's inquiring about the direction in which the farmer had gone after leaving the Railway, and to the 'very important feature' of the prisoner's absence between 2 and 3 o'clock – 'when doubtless the deed was done'. Added to the fact that Newport's purse was found in Griffiths's possession when he was arrested, these various pieces of circumstantial evidence convinced the coroner that a *prima facie* case had been made out against the prisoner.

The jurors agreed, though it took a 15-minute consultation to reach their murder verdict, and the coroner committed Griffiths for trial at the next county assizes.

At the close of the inquest, he was placed in the custody of a Detective Burgess and – handcuffed to two uniformed constables – he was taken to Dunham-on-the-Hill station to catch the 7.45pm train to Chester. At the station, the prisoner and his police escorts sat in the waiting room, Griffiths continuing to talk to his father, still puffing his little pipe.

Local people turned out in force to send him on his way, many of them not unsympathetic to his situation. The *Chronicle* reporter was there, too. He wrote (10 March), 'When the train arrived the prisoner, accompanied by Detective Burgess and a reporter, entered an empty compartment of a second-class carriage. As the train moved out of the station, "Good-bye, Sam" resounded from every side, and several arms were thrust in at the window at one time to shake the prisoner by the hand.'

When the train arrived in Chester, the paper went on, 'a large crowd had assembled on the platform and a rush was made to the carriage which contained him as soon as Detective Burgess was recognised'. It was with some difficulty that the officer managed to get his prisoner into the cab that was waiting to take him to the castle. When the driver whipped up the horse, however, 'the crowd were soon left in the distance'.

As the cab passed through the castle's grand entrance, Griffiths 'cast a glance up at the windows and said with a sigh, "I know them windows. I've seen 'em afore."' The *Chronicle* report went on: 'In a moment afterwards, bending earnestly forward and looking in the face of Burgess, he said "D'ye think they'll hang us [me]?" He was simply answered that he was not yet tried, and that little answer appeared to afford him some pleasure, and his countenance brightened up. He was safely lodged in the Castle at a quarter past 8 o'clock, where he has previously been for crimes less heinous than the one for which he now awaits his trial.'

There was another big turnout for Griffiths's court appearance. 'Such a sensation had this case created out of doors,' reported the *Chronicle* when the case began at the Cheshire Spring Assizes on 5 April, 'that long before the opening of the court, crowds of eager persons were waiting to gain admission…and soon after access to the hall had been granted, it became densely crowded in every part…the tide of human beings was such that only about one half of those who had come to hear the prisoner tried could be accommodated inside the vast building…The excitement in the hall was intense amongst all parties, not least with the ladies, who mustered in large numbers.'

Griffiths entered the dock to a flurry of excitement. The most detailed description of him was given by the *Chester Record* (also on 7 April). He was said to be 'of middle height [with a] swarthy complexion, black hair, [a] low and retreating forehead, nose indented in the middle, high cheek-bones, [and] no whiskers or beard'.

Mr Hardinge Giffard QC and Mr Horatio Lloyd appeared for the Crown, Mr Edmund Swetenham for the defence. Griffiths – 'in a loud and clear tone' – pleaded not guilty. The trial evidence is taken from the extensive coverage in the *Chronicle*, unless stated otherwise.

In his opening speech, Mr Giffard (a future solicitor general and lord chancellor, who would later become the 1st Earl of Halsbury) commented, 'Where a man is found having the property of a murdered man upon him, it is presumable that he has not only committed the robbery but also the murder – the presumption is not only according to law but sound practical common sense – unless the individual can give a reasonable and rational statement of how he became possessed of the murdered man's property. In this case the purse and money [the] deceased had upon him when he started home was found on the person of the prisoner, who failed to account for the possession of it; therefore the presumption is that the robbery and the murder must have been occasioned by his hand. No other inference can be fairly raised.'

The evidence was essentially the same as that heard at the inquest, though a number of witnesses supplied additional details that reinforced the case against Griffiths.

The only totally new testimony came from George Duncan of Barrow Lane Farm, which overlooked the meadows in which the murder took place. At about 2.50pm on 26 February he was in his garden, one field away from the Christian Field, when, he said, he 'saw a man about 10 or 15 yards from where the body was found'.

Evil Afoot in the Christian Field

A criminal trial in progress around 1837 in the grandiose Shire Hall at Chester Castle, now home to the Crown Court. During some of the more sensational murder trials of the 19th century the public areas were packed to overflowing. Engraving by Thomas Allom. (From the author's collection.)

Duncan related 'He was commencing to run, and ran towards the gate in a stooping position. I lost sight of him then because the road [footpath] sinks, and I took no more notice. The man was running the nearest way to Nixon's farm. I did not know [recognise] the man, but I noticed he had a dark coat on and lighter trousers and a cap or a very low hat. He was a middling-sized man.'

If the 'stooping man' was Sam Griffiths, it certainly fitted neatly into the murder chronology. The field gate, as Duncan rightly pointed out, would have taken him in the direction of John Nixon's farm, where, according to farm-hand Alfred Pritchard's inquest evidence, Griffiths turned up unexpectedly around about this time inquiring after his misplaced pick.

Duncan's description of the man he saw in the Christian Field coincided with Griffiths's appearance on the day of the murder, as recollected by key witness Francis Robinson. The Dunham cattle dealer said that on each of the two occasions on which he had met Griffiths that afternoon the defendant had been 'dressed in a dark coat [and] corduroy trousers and he had a cap on'.

Robinson's trial evidence was particularly informative. He first cleared up the mystery of how he had missed seeing Isaac Newport as he walked from his home in Church Lane to the railway station. It seems halfway down the lane – in linking Village Road with Warrington Road, it carves a deepening wedge out of the sandstone outcrop on which the village stands – he took a short cut across the field adjoining the road. As he did so, he heard someone walking up Church Lane, but because of the high hedge in between he could not tell who it was. It could only have been 'old Isaac'.

Robinson said when he arrived at the railway station, he checked the time by the station clock. It was not quite 2.30pm. About half an hour later he left the station to return home. When, at the top of Church Lane, he met Griffiths again, Henry Garner was with him (so this was obviously straight after the pair had been at the smithy and were on their way back to the Railway for more drinks). It was then 'a little after 3 o'clock'.

Bricklayer Joseph Barton was called to refute the defendant's claim that it was he who had given him the money found on him when he was arrested. Barton said he had paid the prisoner two shillings on the previous Saturday for some work he had done for him. But he declared, 'I have never paid him a sum of £14 or £15. The largest sum I ever paid him was 25 shillings.'

After Samuel Joynson had pulled the dead man from the ditch, two of his farmer friends, Thomas Jeffs and William Woodward, helped him transport the body to the Wheatsheaf. They, it was now revealed, had eventually found PC Marsh and informed him of the murder, and, having themselves just left the Railway, told him where he could find Griffiths.

In his trial testimony, Joynson had pointed out that for Newport to have reached the place where he was murdered he would have had to climb five stiles, the first of which, he said, was 'a very high one and not an easy one for a man in liquor to get over'. It was a point that the defence took up with John Weaver, when, late in the day, the surgeon took the stand.

Weaver agreed that 'a fall from some height on[to] hard ground' could have caused the murder victim's injuries, but he was unable to go along with Mr Swetenham's suggestion that the deceased could have injured himself falling from the first stile – which was 4ft 6ins high on the Old Lane side – and then staggered on for a further 600 yards before collapsing into the water-filled ditch.

'If the man had fallen from that stile it might have caused the appearances I saw, but I don't think a man could get up again after such a fall,' he said.

The surgeon was also invited to give his opinion on body temperature and its relevance in determining time of death. He commented, 'I think a body, under the circumstances described in this case, might keep warm for an hour or two.' Re-examined by the prosecution, Weaver agreed that 'a person injured as the deceased was, might remain four or five hours alive [but] quite insensible'. He added, 'I don't believe he could have stirred after receiving such injuries on his head and face as I saw.'

The statement Griffiths made at the inquest (by which he doggedly stood) was put in and read to the court at the close of the prosecution's case. The rules governing the conduct of the trial precluded Griffiths from making a statement under oath, though by now the law had been changed to allow defence counsel to address the jury and have 'the last word' on the case – a reform of 1836 that established the familiar adversarial system we see in action in criminal trials today.

In his closing speech, Mr Giffard argued that the discrepancies regarding the time Isaac Newport left the Railway Inn were irrelevant. The 'order of events' of that afternoon had been established 'without much doubt', he said. Newport, Lightfoot and Griffiths all left the pub at around the same time and from that moment until he was found in the Christian Field no one saw Newport alive.

Evil Afoot in the Christian Field

Francis Robinson, said Mr Giffard, had left Griffiths the first time a little before 2.30pm and met him again just after three. 'Therefore,' said prosecuting counsel, 'for three-quarters-of-an-hour the absence of the prisoner was unaccounted for.' It was the Crown's case, he said, that Griffiths had committed the murder and robbery during that 45-minute period: he had 'sufficient time' in which to do so.

Of the notion that Newport's death might have been an accident, Mr Giffard asked the jury to 'look with great care at the evidence of the medical man', which, he said, showed conclusively that he had been killed.

As to *how* Mr Newport might have died, it was with a certain lack of conviction, one feels, that he again introduced the 'wooden-rail theory'. That is certainly the impression given by the *Chronicle*'s report, which stated, 'Having *briefly commented* upon the rail found in the hedge a few yards from the body, and one end of it fitting in the indentations of [the] deceased's hat…[he said] that *it was a very likely weapon* [with which] to attack a man who might not hear the approach of footsteps behind him' (author's italics).

Quite how one could effect a surprise attack while struggling with a cumbersome eight to 10-foot pole, while obtaining the balance and leverage required to execute two perfectly-placed blows to the head of the victim, he did not demonstrate, apparently. But he seems to have hedged his bets, as it were, by suggesting – rather lamely, if the newspaper report is to be believed – that another murder weapon might have been employed, which the defendant had afterwards hidden away somewhere.

Mr Swetenham rose to address the jury on behalf of the prisoner 'amid breathless silence'. He immediately went on the offensive, castigating certain elements of the press for their prejudicial pre-trial reporting…and answered those who had questioned his motives for defending the accused murderer. His speech lasted for one hour and 11 minutes. It was a valiant effort against overwhelming odds.

Of his critics, he said, 'So excited is the feeling out of court against the prisoner, that it has been said "How is it possible that Mr Swetenham, after what he has read in the papers, can conscientiously stand up and defend the prisoner?" Is it to be supposed that he stands up to defend the foul crime of murder? Far be it from me to do so…I stand up here to say that the counsel for the prosecution has shown only probabilities, and that by those probabilities he has contended that the prisoner must be guilty of taking away the life of the man Newport. But there are many circumstances that have been brought forward consistent with [his] innocence.'

It was his intention, he said, to see that his client was 'not found guilty at the bar of the press, or at the bar of the public-house', but that he had 'a fair and honourable trial'.

Mr Swetenham said he could not deny that, when he was arrested, Griffiths had claimed that Barton had paid him the money found on him and that the purse was his. But he pointed out that when he made that statement he was in 'a beastly state of intoxication' and 'might not have been conscious of what he was saying'. At the inquest he was sober and told a very different story; that was the one, he said, that should carry the most weight with the jury.

In reminding the court that 'no mortal eye' saw Isaac Newport killed, counsel contended that the most fundamental question was whether the prisoner, in the period between his two meetings with Francis Robinson, had the time to commit the murder.

Mr Swetenham continued, 'If...Robinson heard Newport the other side of the hedge in Church Lane, he [Newport] must have had at least five-and-twenty minutes' start on the prisoner. The jury must bear in mind that Robinson again met the prisoner a few minutes after 3 o'clock, and in the interval the prisoner had been at the smithy to get his pick sharpened. In this brief interval he would have had to travel nearly a mile, murder a man, rob him and come back unblushing, with no trace of the crime in his face or demeanour.'

But the greatest flaw in the prosecution's case, Mr Swetenham insisted, lay in the statement of Samuel Joynson that Newport's body was still 'perfectly warm' when he found it a little before 6pm. That, he believed, was 'conclusive' proof that the farmer was not killed between 2 and 3 o'clock and that Griffiths was not the murderer. 'If the deceased was murdered before 3 o'clock, his body would have been cold by six,' he maintained. If the murder was committed after three, it could not have been committed by the prisoner – 'as he was elsewhere'.

It sounded a reasonable thesis: it was a cold winter's day and the body was almost fully submersed in very cold water. Though he was wearing heavy winter clothing and may, as Mr Weaver suggested, have remained alive for some time after being knocked unconscious (thus delaying the cooling process), could his body really have been warm to the touch three hours later?

The answer, it would appear, is yes, it could. The rate at which a dead body loses temperature has been described as 'the most useful single indicator of the time of death during the first 24 hours'. But it is subject to many variables: the size and weight of the body, the position in which it is lying, clothing, etc. In his book, *The Encyclopedia of Forensic Science*, criminologist and author Brian Lane writes that 'the heat-loss process for the body's surface generally takes from eight to 12 hours' and that *even immersed in water*, it can be between five and six hours before the body feels cold.

Ultimately, counsel said, he was led to wonder whether a murder had been committed at all. He speculated, 'He [Newport] might, in climbing over the first high stile, have fallen and severely injured himself and gone struggling on in his intoxicated state, falling still more heavily, until at length he reached the place where the body was found and fell into the ditch. The united influence of the falls, the cold and exposure might have caused his death.'

The judge, Mr Justice Blackburn, told the members of the jury that if they believed Isaac Newport's death had been caused by violence, all they had to say was whether the defendant's hand had inflicted the fatal blow. It did not matter whether the prisoner meant to do it or not.

On the all-important question of time, Judge Blackburn's opinion was that 'there was just time for the prisoner to commit the deed, and none to spare'.

At the end of a trial that had lasted almost seven-and-a-half hours, it must have come as a surprise to many people in court when the jury foreman signified that he and his colleagues wished to retire to consider their verdict. Mr Swetenham had put up as good a defence as the circumstances would allow, and, in so doing, had fulfilled his stated aim of ensuring Griffiths got 'a fair and honourable trial'. But had he done enough to undermine the prosecution's case in the minds of the jurors? Judging by the fact that they

Evil Afoot in the Christian Field

were out for over an hour and a half, he had certainly made them think. What may have seemed unquestionable only a little while earlier had, in the end, demanded a more searching examination.

When the jury returned, the foreman announced that their verdict was 'Guilty', but with a strong recommendation to mercy. It was the cue for an astonishing exchange across the court. The judge, with what sounded a bit like impatience, asked, 'Upon what grounds?'

According to the *Chronicle* report, the foreman paused and 'seemed at a loss to answer', whereupon the judge demanded, 'I must know upon what grounds you recommend him to mercy, as it is usual for the grounds of the recommendation to be stated.'

Considering they had just found Griffiths guilty, the foreman's reply was surprising to say the least. 'Well, the jurymen think that the evidence is a little weak against the prisoner,' he said.

Judge: 'But that is no ground. I suppose you thought the evidence strong enough to convict, as you have already shown by your verdict. Is there any other reason why you recommend the prisoner to mercy?'

Here one of the jurors spoke up: 'We think that the time is very short for him to have committed the murder.'

Judge (his exasperation showing): 'That is no ground. I suppose you must have thought he had sufficient time to have committed the murder, or you would not have found him guilty. I suppose you are satisfied he did commit the murder?'

Foreman: 'Yes, my Lord.'

Judge: 'Then what is the ground on which you recommend him to mercy?'

Foreman: 'That he was drunk at the time he committed the offence, and probably had no intention of killing the man.'

Judge (relieved): 'Yes, that is certainly a ground on which you can recommend him to mercy, and I will take care that the recommendation is forwarded to the Secretary of State [at the Home Office].'

Sentencing him to death, Mr Justice Blackburn said Griffiths had been convicted on evidence 'which was entirely sufficient to convince me at least that you are really guilty of the crime'. He did not, however, believe that it was a premeditated act. He told Griffiths, 'Your chief object, no doubt, was to rob the poor man and to enable you the more readily to accomplish your design, you struck him down to prevent resistance on his part and the violence you used was the cause of the man's death. Therefore, in the eyes of the law it was wilful murder.'

He noted the jury's recommendation, but he warned the prisoner in the dock, 'I can hold out no hope that it will avail you anything.'

Griffiths did not expect his life to be spared. In prison later, he appeared to be 'fully resigned to his awful fate', the *Chronicle* reported. In his interviews with the Revd William Rowe, a minister of the Primitive Methodist Church in Chester, whose spiritual guidance Griffiths had requested, he was said to have revealed that, up until seven years ago, he had been a member of the Wesleyan Chapel in Dunham and at one stage had been completely teetotal for nine months. However, said the *Chronicle*, 'he fell away from these paths of virtue, and being overcome by drink he acquired fearful habits of immorality, which he now deeply deplores'.

On the morning after his trial, Griffiths had something rather more sensational to confide to the ministering clergyman, however. It was a confession: not one that merely acknowledged his guilt, but which exposed him as an even more callous murderer than had been made out. The confession, carried in virtually identical form in several papers, was reported as follows:

'He said that when he saw the money paid by Lightfoot to Mr Newport, he felt a desire to possess it. Yielding to this feeling, he followed the old man with the full determination of robbing him. Sighting his victim going across the fields, he hurried after and soon caught him. When he came up he dealt Newport a heavy blow on the face, the force of which knocked him down. While on the ground he took his purse and his money from him…The old man got up and asked the prisoner to give him £5 back and begged him to spare his life. Griffiths refused to give him any portion of the money. At this time, he says, he had no idea of murdering Newport. They walked on in company together, and crossed over the stile into the Christian field. Here it was that prisoner thought that he would kill the deceased, as otherwise he might inform of his robbing him and he would perhaps be transported. Determined to get rid of Newport, he struck him several violent blows over the head and face and knocked him into the ditch, where the body was found. Again the old man fervently begged of him to spare his life, and asked for £5 of his money. Griffiths said: "No, if I do you will tell of me and I shall be transported", and he determined to kill his victim in order that he might not tell of him. Finding that the blows he inflicted on Newport's head and face did not produce death, the prisoner held the body under the water (there being a large quantity in the ditch at the time) and life was extinct "in about a minute", which Griffiths accounts for from the fact that [the] deceased was very drunk at the time. He says that he knows nothing about the rail that was produced at the trial, nor the indentations in the hat. He did not strike Newport with anything but his fists, and did not deal more than three or four blows.'

Even now, it makes chilling reading, laying bare as it does the pitiless determination with which Griffiths took the life of the vulnerable old man and how much Newport must have suffered during the final moments of his footpath terror.

It also bears out one of the autopsy findings of surgeon John Weaver. For the 'thickest skull' he had ever seen was without doubt the reason why Isaac Newport was able to withstand so many blows to the head without losing consciousness, forcing Griffiths into his final act of cruel desperation in the water-filled ditch.

Griffiths's confession was the kind of eve-of-execution 'sinner's lament' usually received with almost self-righteous satisfaction by the press, but on this occasion several of the local papers responded with a vituperative attack on his lawyer.

Though he had fulfilled one of the essential duties of the defence in challenging the prosecution to prove its case 'beyond all reasonable doubt', the *Chronicle* savaged Mr Swetenham's tenacious advocacy. 'The confession of the wretched prisoner,' it began,

Evil Afoot in the Christian Field

'shows that a plausible defence may be made out of the most flimsy and worthless materials by a special pleader well up to his work.'

Griffiths's guilt, argued the *Chronicle*, had been proved by 'circumstantial evidence of as conclusive a kind as any ever given in a court of justice'. Yet the counsel for the defence had succeeded in 'confusing and bewildering the minds of the jurymen' to such an extent that it took them nearly two hours to 'recover themselves and venture upon a verdict'.

Others in the court had also thought they saw some plausibility in Mr Swetenham's reasoning. 'But' the paper concluded, 'the words of the now penitent culprit will be sufficient to satisfy the most sceptical. He says plainly that he did the deed, though "not in the way conjectured"...In spite of the old man's supplications, he struck him again and again, but to complete the tragedy, he held his head under water until the breath of life was gone. All will admit that his sentence, dreadful though it be, is just.'

After his conviction, Griffiths was so overcome with guilt, apparently, that he asked Revd Rowe to go and see 'the poor widow of the victim' to beg her to forgive him. Mrs Newport was not in a conciliatory mood, however, and told the minister she considered her husband's killer to be 'a vagabond and a vile wretch'.

Samuel Griffiths was hanged on Monday 23 April 1866. Despite the huge interest the case had generated, his last earthly journey, from the County Gaol to Chester City Gaol, was not attended by the usual raucous crowd of onlookers. This was because – against recent tradition and unannounced – the transfer took place at 4.30am on the Saturday before rather than at 5am on the day of the execution. Griffiths was put into a waiting hansom cab and, according to the *Chronicle*, was escorted across the city in 'so private and unexpected' a manner that only two people were sighted along the entire route.

The executioner was George Smith of Dudley in Staffordshire, long-time assistant to the notorious William 'Strangler' Calcraft. Griffiths's resigned and submissive manner was said to have moved several officials to tears, and the mood of the spectators was less boisterous than usual. 'The most decent order was preserved,' reported the *Chronicle*.

At exactly two minutes to eight, the prisoner appeared at the door leading to the scaffold; he was wearing his normal working clothes – an old long-tailed blue coat, with brass buttons and corduroy trousers. The rope was adjusted around his neck, the white cap was drawn over his head and the bolt 'which stood between the doomed man and eternity' was drawn back. Then, said the *Chronicle*, '[He] fell to the length of the rope, while the crowd was suddenly hushed to a perfect and appalling silence...His struggles were hard, but a hanged man has no chance with his fate. His body writhed, and his arms and legs were violently jerked as he twirled round with the rope, but in about two minutes all was over.'

An hour later the body was cut down and buried within the precincts of the City Gaol. Enclosed in a roughly-made shell, the corpse was placed in a deep grave beneath the cobbled passageway that ran alongside the south wall of the prison. Until the building was demolished in 1879 (the Queen's School for Girls occupies the site today), a small headstone let into the wall, and bearing the legend 'S. G. April 1866', marked the spot.

Samuel Griffiths was destined to be the last to be hanged at the prison, his death the closing paragraph in a unique chapter in the history of capital punishment. Chester's

Engraving of Chester Castle and the County Gaol in the 1830s, by artist Thomas Allom. Although the county prisoners were locked up here to await trial, between 1809 and 1866 all hangings in Chester were conducted at the nearby City Gaol. (From the author's collection.)

sheriffs, it would soon be confirmed, had carried out their age-old execution chore for the final time.

Following the personal intervention of Cheshire South MP John Tollemache, the county Quarter Sessions, at a meeting on 2 July, agreed unanimously to petition Parliament for a change of law to bring Cheshire into line with other counties in England and Wales.

In a forthright letter to the chairman of the Quarter Sessions (Major L.P. Townshend), Mr Tollemache said there was no reason why Cheshire's high sheriff should have a 'privilege of immunity' enjoyed by no other. And he commented, 'Surely, any Cheshire high sheriff would infinitely prefer performing official duties usual in other counties, rather than that the horrors that criminals must undergo, at the time of their execution, should be greatly, and needlessly, aggravated.'

The county and city leaders, for once united, achieved the local law change on the back of a fairly mundane piece of legislation entitled 'The Chester Courts Bill', which had been drawn up originally to enable accommodation at the castle to be used for sittings of the city courts, while a new town hall was being built to replace the one destroyed by fire in December 1862. But, with the Cheshire Quarter Sessions petition finding favour with MPs and the public, the bill was hastily withdrawn and redrafted to include a clause making Cheshire's high sheriff responsible for the execution of criminals condemned throughout the county. Unopposed, it became law on 15 July 1867, finally bringing to an end a legal curiosity that, through a mixture of deference and political machination, had survived since Norman times.

Evil Afoot in the Christian Field

For the city authorities – who, in their every previous attempt at reform, had been cleverly outfoxed by the county's ruling justices and their friends in high places – this was a moment to savour. No longer would they have to bear the responsibility, and the cost, of executing criminals, not even their own. After more than 500 years, the city sheriffs could lay down the hangman's burden at last.

* * *

In the old abandoned graveyard of capital punishment Samuel Griffiths's most enduring memorial is that he was the last person to be executed in Cheshire *in public*. Two years later, on 29 May 1868, following an overwhelming vote by MPs, a new law came into force decreeing that, in future, executions would be held in private behind the walls of the county gaols. By order of the management, the open-air National Theatre of Death had been closed; the long-running public execution roadshow was over. Never again would the awful solemnities of capital punishment be demeaned by the kind of uncivilised behaviour so often witnessed in front of the gallows in the past. In the opinion of most right-minded people, it was not before time.

Bibliography
Original Source Documents

Prologue: Cheshire Quarter Sessions documents relating to the abolition of the Palatinate Court of Great Sessions, Cheshire and Chester Archives and Local Studies (CCALS), QCX/1/2, QCX1/3–5. Correspondence relating to the execution of criminals in Cheshire, CCALS, QAB6/25, QAB6/30, QAB6/31.

Chapter 1: Chester Assizes Gaol File, The National Archives (TNA), CHES24/166/5; Chester City Corporation Assembly Book, CCALS, ZAB/4/215. Chester Assembly Files, CCALS, ZAF/54, f.100 and ZAF/54 Part 2, p11. Cheshire Wills, CCALS, WS1762 (Samuel Heald). Registers of the Quarterly Meetings of Cheshire and Staffordshire Society of Friends, CCALS, RG/6/1031. Cheshire (Quaker) Women's Quarterly Meeting Book, CCALS, EFC/1/4/1.

Chapter 2: Chester Assizes Gaol File, TNA, CHES24/173/2. Chester Crown Book, TNA, CHES21/7, p90 (verso), p99 (verso).

Chapter 3: Chester Assizes Gaol File, TNA, CHES24/179/5.

Chapter 4: Chester Assizes Gaol File, TNA, CHES24/176/2.

Chapter 5: Chester City Corporation Treasurer's Account Books, CCALS, ZTAB/9–10. Printed broadside entitled *The Conversion and Death of Samuel Burrows*, CCALS, CR60/4/16.

Chapter 6: Chester Assizes Gaol File, TNA, CHES24/173/3. Chester Crown Book, TNA, CHES21/7, p99. Judge's Report, TNA, HO 47/1, ff 173–177.

Chapter 7: Chester Assizes Gaol File, TNA, CHES24/188/3.

Chapter 8: Chester Assizes Gaol Files, TNA, CHES24/184/1 (W. Proudlove/Glover), CHES24/180/6 (Gibson/Gee), CHES24/180/5 (Clare/Thompson/Morgan). Judge's Report, TNA, HO 47/41.

Chapter 9: Chester Assizes Gaol, TNA, CHES 24/192/3 (J. Proudlove and Leir), CHES24/189/5 (Groom), CHES24/190/1 (Clarke). Judge's Report, TNA, HO 47/64. Transportation registers, TNA, HO 11/5. Chester Castle Gaol transportation records, CCALS, Mf 96/2–4. Broadside entitled *The Trial and Execution of John Leir...and John Proudlove &c*, CCALS, vPR3/CHES/150.

Chapter 10: Chester Assizes Gaol File, TNA, CHES24/190/1. Cheshire wills, CCALS, WS1820 (James Fallows). Broadside entitled *Report of the Trial of Samuel Fallows, charged with the Murder of Betty Shallcross &c*, Stockport Heritage Library, S39 N41.

Chapter 11: Chester Assizes Gaol File, NA, CHES24/190/2. Petitions for mercy, NA, HO 17/30. Broadside entitled *A Full Report of the Trial of Joseph Dale for the Murder of Wm. Wood &c*. Shelf mark 4452.cc.7(6). © British Library Board. All rights reserved.

Chapter 12: Chester Assizes Criminal Depositions, TNA, ASSI 65/1.

Bibliography

Chapter 13: Chester Assizes Criminal Depositions, TNA, ASSI 65/7. Cheshire Quarter Sessions Files, correspondence relating to the execution of criminals in Cheshire, CCALS, QAB6/30, QAB6/31.

Records held by Cheshire and Chester Archives and Local Studies Service are reproduced with the permission of Cheshire County Council and Chester City Council and the owner/depositor to whom copyright is reserved.

Note: All modern equivalents of historic monetary values given in this book are based on formulae contained in *Consumer Price Inflation since 1750* by Jim O'Donoghue and Louise Goulding, Office for National Statistics, and Grahame Allen, House of Commons Library, part of the Economic Trends report No. 604 published in 2004 by the ONS. (Source: National Statistics website: *www.statistics.gov.uk*). Crown copyright material is reproduced with the permission of the Controller of HMSO.

Books And Other Printed Materials

Standard Histories

Hanshall, J.H. *The Stranger in Chester*, 1816.

Hanshall, J.H. *History of the County Palatine of Chester*, 1823.

Harris, Brian E. (Ed.) *Victorian History of Cheshire*, vol. 2, 1979.

Heginbotham, H. *Stockport: Ancient and Modern*, 1892.

Ormerod, George *The History of the County Palatine and City of Chester* (commonly referred to as *The History of Cheshire*), vols 1, 2 and 3, 1819, Revised Edition by G. Helsby, 1882.

Other Titles

Abbott, Geoffrey *Lords of the Scaffold: A History of the Executioner* Robert Hale, 1991.

Arrowsmith, Peter *Stockport: A History* Stockport MBC, 1997.

Bailey, Brian *Hangmen of England: A History of Execution from Jack Ketch to Albert Pierrepoint* W.H. Allen, 1989.

Beattie, J.M. *Crime and the Courts in England 1600–1800* Oxford University Press, 1986.

Briggs, John, Christopher Harrison, Angus McInnes and David Vincent, *Crime and Punishment in England: An Introductory History* UCL Press, 1996.

Burford, E.J. and Sandra Shulman *Of Bridles & Burnings: The Punishment of Women* Robert Hale, 1992.

Calvert, A.F. *Salt in Cheshire* E. & F.N. Spon, 1915.

Cliffe, Steve *Shadows: A Northern Investigation of the Unknown* Sigma Leisure, 1993.

Coutie, Heather (Ed.) *The Diary of Peter Pownall, A Bramhall Farmer 1765–1858* Old Village Publications, 1989.

Davies, Glyn *A History of Money: From Ancient Times to the Present Day* University of Wales Press, 1994.

Dean, Barbara *Bramall Hall: The Story of an Elizabethan Manor House* Stockport MBC, 1977.

Emsley, Clive *The English Police: A Political and Social History* Addison Wesley Longman, 1991.

Emsley, Clive *Crime and Society in England 1750–1900* Longman, 1996.

Fitzgerald, Percy *Chronicles of Bow Street Police-Office* Chapman and Hall, 1888.

Gatrell, V.A.C. *The Hanging Tree: Execution and the English People 1770–1868* Oxford University Press, 1994.

Harris, Brian E. *Cheshire and its Rulers* Cheshire Libraries and Museums, 1984.

Hawkings, David T. *Criminal Ancestors: A Guide to Historical Criminal Records in England and Wales* Sutton Publishing, 1992.

Hughes, Herbert *Chronicle of Chester: The 200 Years 1775–1975* Macdonald and Jane's, 1975.

Hughes, Robert *The Fatal Shore: A History of the Transportation of Convicts to Australia 1787–1868* Guild Publishing edition, 1987.

Lane, Brian *The Encyclopedia of Forensic Science* Headline, 1992.

Latham, Frank A. (Ed.) *Barrow: The History of a Cheshire Village* The Local History Group, 1983.

Lock, Joan *Tales from Bow Street* Robert Hale, 1982.

Marshall, Susan *Disley: The Story of a Village* John Sherratt & Son, 1954.

McLaughlin, E. *Annals of the Poor* Federation of Family History Societies, 1979.

Middleton, Thomas *Annals of Hyde and District* Longden Publications reprint, 1973.

Moss, Fletcher *Folklore – Old Customs and Tales of My Neighbours*, 1898.

Nield, The Honourable Basil *Farewell to the Assizes* Garnstone Press, 1972.

Nield, Maureen *Rope Dance: A Sensational Murder in Regency Cheshire Re-opened* Cheshire Libraries, Arts and Archives, 1993.

Owen, David E. *Cheshire Waterways* The Dalesman Publishing Company Ltd, 1979.

Pettifer, Ernest W. *Punishments of Former Days* EP Publishing reprint, 1974.

Philips, David and Robert D. Storch *Policing Provincial England 1829–1856* Leicester University Press, 1999.

Pringle, Patrick *Hue and Cry: The Birth of the British Police* Museum Press, 1955.

Bibliography

Wilkinson, George Theodore *The Newgate Calendar Improved*, vol. 1 Panther Books abridgement, 1962.

Williams, W.R. *The History of the Great Sessions in Wales 1542–1830* privately printed, 1899.

Yarwood, Derek *Outrages – Fatal & Other: A Chronicle of Cheshire Crime 1612–1912* Didsbury Press, 1991.

Specialist Articles

Brown, R. Stewart *Execution of criminals in Cheshire, Journal of the Chester and North Wales Archaeology and Historic Society*, New Series, vol. 22, 1918. CCALS.

Chaloner, W.H. *Salt in Cheshire 1600–1870, Journal of the Lancashire and Cheshire Archeological Society*, vol. 71, 1961. CCALS.

Hughes, Thomas *The Confession of Mary Heald, The Cheshire Sheaf*, vol. 3, Series 1, 1883. CCALS.

Maddock, George *The Apethorn Lane Murder and its Background, Looking Back at Hyde*, edited by Alice Lock, 1986. Tameside Local Studies and Archives.

Newspapers and Periodicals

Cheshire Observer

Chester Chronicle

Chester Courant

Chester Record

Derbyshire Courier

Knutsford Guardian

Macclesfield Courier

Manchester Chronicle

Manchester Gazette

Manchester Guardian

Manchester Mercury

Stockport Advertiser

Stockport Heritage Magazine

Index

Index